THE FORCE OF THE EXAMPLE

NEW DIRECTIONS IN CRITICAL THEORY

Amy Allen, General Editor

New Directions in Critical Theory
Amy Allen, General Editor

New Directions in Critical Theory presents outstanding classic and contemporary texts in the tradition of crtitical social theory, broadly construed. The series aims to renew and advance the program of critical social theory, with a particular focus on theorizing contemporary struggles around gender, race, sexuality, class, and globalization and their complex interconnections.

Narrating Evil: A Postmetaphysical Theory of Reflective Judgment, María Pía Lara
The Politics of Our Selves: Power, Autonomy, and Gender in Contemporary Critical Theory, Amy Allen
Democracy and the Political Unconscious, Noëlle McAfee

The Force of the Example

EXPLORATIONS IN THE PARADIGM OF JUDGMENT

ALESSANDRO FERRARA

COLUMBIA UNIVERSITY PRESS   NEW YORK

COLUMBIA UNIVERSITY PRESS
Publishers Since 1893
NEW YORK CHICHESTER, WEST SUSSEX

Library of Congress Cataloging-in-Publication Data
Ferrara, Alessandro, 1953–
   The force of the example: explorations in the paradigm of judgment / Alessandro Ferrara.
      p. cm.
   Includes bibliographical references (p.   ) and index.
   ISBN 978-0-231-14072-0 (cloth : alk. paper) — ISBN 978-0-231-51192-6 (e-book)
 1. Justice. 2. Judgment (Ethics) 3. Political science—Philosophy. I. Title.
   JC578. F46 2008
   320.01—dc22

                                                                2007047003

Casebound editions of Columbia University Press
books are printed on permanent and durable acid-free paper.

Printed in the United States of America

C 10 9 8 7 6 5 4 3 2 1

For Donatella

Contents

Preface

Exemplarity and its intrinsic force for some reason have come to share the fate of other "third members" of glorious triads. Just think of *fraternity* in relation to the more fortunate *freedom* and *equality* in the legacy of the French Revolution. Efforts have been made, from time to time, to rescue fraternity as *community*, or as *solidarity*, but by and large the liberal-democratic pantheon only offers pride of place to the "free and equal citizens," and no one feels the need to add the adjective "fraternal." This book is about exploring and vindicating the relevance of another "third term," whose contribution to our understanding of the nature of normativity has thus far as underestimated as the contribution of fraternity to our understanding of the just polity.

The dichotomic view of our world as split between *facts* and *values, facts* and *norms, Sein* and *Sollen, is* and *ought,* descriptive and normative accounts has misled us into overlooking the specific relevance and force of examplars: namely, of entities, material or symbolic, that are as they should be, atoms of reconciliation where *is* and *ought* merge and, in so doing, liberate an energy that sparks our imagination. The "thirdness" of the *force of examples* with respect to the force of facts or things (usually investigated by the empirical sciences) and that of ideas or of the *ought* (which remains the domain of practical philosophy) has combined its peripheralizing effect with the fact that the most articulate account of it has been couched by Kant in terms of an inquiry into the beautiful, thereby suggesting that exemplarity and its force belong in a special domain of our philosophical world: aesthetics.

In my previous work I have addressed exemplarity from the angle of the nexus of authenticity and validity, the relation of justice and judgment, and have reconstructed it from within the Kantian framework of reflective judgment, but with an eye to an enlarged view of exemplarity as a key to that reconciliation of universalism and pluralism that I still consider among the most philosophically urgent tasks of the our time.

In the present book I further pursue the exploration of this philosophical path by spelling out the context to which it is responsive, by discussing alternative understandings of that *sensus communis* which constitutes the universalistic basis for exemplary validity, by trying to prevent unfruitful versions of the exemplary from seducing us into philosophical dead-ends. One of the limitations of the judgment and exemplarity approach to validity has always been the tendency—with very few exceptions—to provide accounts that pivot around judgment as an ability almost exclusively exercised *in foro interno*. One of the aims of the present book is to contribute to a reconstruction of the normativity of judgment and its workings in the public realm. The Rawlsian notion of the reasonable and that of radical evil are both addressed in terms of exemplarity, as a step toward a political theory that gradually gives up grounding its fundamental notions on the transcontextual reach of decontextualized principles and replaces such grounding with one more in tune with our pluralistic intuitions.

Finally, in this book I probe the fruitfulness of the judgment paradigm and its pivotal notion of exemplarity on a number of terrains where political philosophy is called to task today: the justification and enforcing of human rights, the discussion around the European identity, the revisitation of the classical separation of religion and politics in postsecular societies.

More needs to be done, to be sure, in the way of making the metaphor of the "force of the example" an operative model for normative political philosophy and our approach to normativity in general, but hopefully the reflections presented here contribute to corroborate the plausibility of such approach for all those who are skeptical both of the foundationalist accounts of validity that prevailed before the Linguistic Turn and of the neo-naturalist attempts to restore them.

Some preliminary materials, later expanded and edited as chapters of this book, have been presented at various conferences and published in a number of journals. Chapter 1 is based on a paper given at the conference on "Kant's *Critique of Judgment* and Political Thought," Northwestern University, Evanston/Chicago, 2002, and later at the conference "Sovranità, vita, politica," held in Naples and published in Laura Bazzicalupo and Roberto Esposito, eds., *Politica della vita. Sovranità, biopotere, diritti* (Roma-Bari: Laterza, 2003), 88–96; on a lecture given in Vienna at the Institut für die Wissenschaft des Menschen; and, finally, on a paper given at the conference on "Grammatiche del senso comune," held in Forlì in 2004 and later published in *Nuova Civiltà delle Macchine* 23(1): 69–81. For these occasions I wish here to thank Miguel Vatter, Laura Bazzicalupo, Roberto Esposito, Krzysztof Michalski, Cornelia Klinger, Giovanni Matteucci, Tonino Griffero, and Elio Franzini.

Chapter 2 is based on a paper given at the conference "Hannah Arendt: Twenty Years Later" at Harvard University in 1996 and later published with revisions as "Judgment, Identity, and Authenticity. A Reconstruction of Hannah Arendt's Interpretation of Kant," in *Philosophy and Social Criticism* 24(2/3): 113–36. Thanks are due to Seyla Benhabib and David Rasmussen.

Chapter 3 originates from a paper read at the conference "Thirty Years After Rawls's *Theory of Justice*," University of Amsterdam (2001), later discussed at the conference "Philosophy and Social Science" in Prague (2002), at the conference "Globalizzazione, riconoscimento, diritti umani e ragione pubblica" in Gallarate, Italy (2002), at the University of Madrid Carlos III (2003), and published as "Öffentliche Vernunft und die Normativität des Vernünftigen," in *Deutsche Zeitschrift für Philosophie* 50(6): 925–43, and in English as "Public Reason and the Normativity of the Reasonable," in *Philosophy and Social Criticism* 30(5–6): 579–96. I am especially grateful to Beate Rössler, Frank Michelman, Robert Fine, Stefano Petrucciani, Lucio Cortella, and Carlos Thiebaut for their insightful remarks on these occasions.

The core idea for chapter 4 derives from a paper discussed at the conference "Philosophy and Social Science" in Prague in 1999 and published as "The

Evil That Men Do: A Meditation on Radical Evil from a Postmetaphysical Point of View," in María Pía Lara, ed., *Rethinking Evil: Contemporary Perspectives* (Berkeley: University of California Press, 2001), 173–188. I wish to thank María Pía Lara, Maeve Cooke, Peter Dews, and Robert Fine for their comments.

Chapter 5 is based on materials that appeared as "La scoperta del repubblicanesimo 'politico' e le sue implicazioni per il liberalismo," in *Filosofia e Questioni Pubbliche* 5(1): 31–48; on a paper read at the colloquium "Los desafíos de la política del futuro," El Escorial (Madrid, 2003) and at the conference "Republicanismo: persperctivas actuais na filosofia politica," University of Rio de Janeiro (2005). On these occasions I gained new insights from exchanges with Fernando Vallespin, Luiz Bernardo Araujo, Sebastiano Maffettone, Luca Baccelli, Nadia Urbinati, Massimo Rosati, and Maurizio Viroli.

Chaper 6 began to develop as a paper discussed at the Universidad Autonoma Metropolitana in Mexico City in 2000 and at the conference "Menscheit und Menschenrechte," Potsdam (2001). A version of it was published as "Two Notions of Humanity and the Judgment Argument for Human Rights," in *Political Theory* 31(3): 392–420 and further discussed at the conference "Law and Justice in a Global Society," Granada (2005), at the colloquium of the Museo Camón Aznar, Zaragoza (2005), and at the Department of Theory and History of Law of the University of Florence. I am indebted to Christoph Menke, Hans Joas, Hauke Brunkhorst, Stephen K. White, Alyssa Bernstein, Daniel Innerarity, and Emilio Santoro.

Chapter 7 draws on a paper given at the conference on "Democrazia, sicurezza e ordine internazionale," organized by the Italian Association for Political Philosophy in Fano (Italy, 2005) and published in one version as "Fra Westfalia e Cosmopolis. I limiti della sovranità e il dovere di proteggere," in *Parolechiave* (2006): 23–38. I am grateful to Dimitri D'Andrea and Elena Pulcini for their remarks.

Various drafts of chapter 8 were presented at the conference "Identità europea e libertà," Padua (2005), at the workshop "El papel a jugar por Euskadi ena la globalización" organized by the Basque Government in Bilbao (2006), at the conference "Transnational Democracy at the Crossroads? The EU's Constitutional Crisis," University of Indiana, Bloomington (2006), and as a lecture at the Università di Castel Sant'Angelo in Rome. A version was published as "L'Europa come spazio privilegiato della speranza umana," in F. L. Marcolungo, ed., *Identità europea e libertà* (Padua:

Cleup, 2006), 43–61, and in English in *Constellations* 14.3 (2007): 315–31. On these occasions the critical comments provided by Gian Luigi Brena, Alvaro Amann, William Scheuerman, Nadia Urbinati, Dario Castiglione, Glyn Morgan, Jeffrey Isaac, and Claudia Hassan were very helpful.

Chapter 9 is based on various versions of a paper discussed at the *Reset-Dissent* colloquium on "Politics and Religion in Europe and the US," Rome (2005), at the conference "Laicità e società post-secolare," Gallarate (Italy, 2005), at the conference "Philosophy and Social Sciences," Prague (2006), and at the "Journée Mondiale de la Philosophie," UNESCO, Rabat (Morocco, 2006). Those versions appeared as "La religione entro i limiti della ragionevolezza," *Parolechiave* 33 (2005): 125–42, and as "Non c'è voce pubblica senza fatica," *Reset* 90 (2005): 7–9. I am grateful to Giancarlo Bosetti, Elisabetta Galeotti, Giuliano Amato, Klaus Eder, Steven Shiffrin, Virginio Marzocchi, Massimo Rosati, and Simone Chambers for their objections and remarks.

Many of the ideas developed in this book grew out of countless conversations not particularly tied to these specific presentations or events, but occurring in the context of stimulating circles of scholarly discussion—such as the annual conference on "Philosophy and Social Science" in Prague, the critical theory seminar that meets yearly in Gallarate, the colloquium on "Politics, Ethics and Society" at Luiss University, and the reading group on Kant's *Critique of the Power of Judgment,* both in Rome—as well as in the context of informal personal exchanges, often taking place via email. For all the suggestions, objections, encouragements, and new thoughts that have contributed to the making of this book I am grateful to Charles Larmore, Axel Honneth, Jean Cohen, Michael Walzer, Bruce Ackerman, Franco Crespi, Joseph Raz, Rudolph Makkreel, Manuel Cruz, Thomas Pogge, Henry Allison, Christine Korsgaard, Nancy Fraser, Salvatore Veca, Antonella Besussi, Michelangelo Bovero, Furio Cerutti, Adriana Cavarero, Stefano Petrucciani, Walter Privitera, Marina Calloni, Luigi Caranti, Gianfranco Pellegrino, Daniele Santoro, Ingrid Salvatore, Claudio Corradetti, Gianni Dessì, Anselmo Aportone, Marco Santambrogio, and Giacomo Marramao.

Charles Larmore, David Rasmussen, Stephen K. White, Frank Michelman, and Akeel Bilgrami have taken pains to read through the whole of the manuscript and have alternatively offered encouragement, objections, reactions, raised eyebrows, and approving smiles: through their welcome comments they have contributed to improving this text.

Finally, a word of thanks goes to my friends in Capalbio who during the summer of 2006, when I would emerge no earlier than at sunset from my long writing sessions to join them, used to press the issue of what the force of the example is all about and thereby unfailingly caused me to change a few lines the next day, but most of all I wish to thank my family for having graciously endured my hermetic seclusion during this time as well as Giuditta Ferrara for her help and patience in compiling the index.

Rome, May 2007

THE FORCE OF THE EXAMPLE

Introduction

Diverse and far apart though our cultures might be, the world that you and I inhabit is shaped by three great forces. The first and most powerful of them is the force of *what exists,* of what is already there, in place—the force of *things.* We experience this force in two fundamental ways. Sometimes we encounter it as the force of habit and routine, of tradition, of mores and custom, of culture, of convention, of usage, of established practice and received wisdom. Society as we know it would simply be impossible if we were to reinvent the terms of our cooperation each time anew, if we found chaos instead of order upon coming into the world or if the fabric of common meanings and shared expectations that we manage to create, often through laborious negotiations, were to vanish as soon as we disappear from the scene. At other times we experience the force of things in a symbolically less textured but no less objective mode, in the guise of an invisible hand or of a ruse of reason that shapes our destinies through the unintentional consequences of what we do intentionally: just think of the way we experience the oscillations of the market or the tidal tempo of historical efficacy at turning points such as the fall of the Berlin Wall. In either mode the force of *what is* manifests itself most obviously as the resistance met by our efforts to change the world—natural, social, and internal. This is perhaps one of the reasons why—despite the evidence that no social or internal world could exist unless some originary free agency coalesced in persisting patterns, whether intended or unintended—the world would seem to us a prison, inimical to freedom, if the force of what exists or the force of things were the only force that shaped it.

The second force that concurs in turning the environment in which our life unfolds into a human world is the force of what *ought to be the case*—the force of *ideas*. Again, regardless of the culture or historical context in which we are thrown, we experience the world and its manifestations as subject to evaluation and susceptible of being assigned a positive or negative value. Helpless though at times we may feel vis-à-vis the powers of the world, we always retain the capacity to match reality against the normativity of what we think *should* be the case. This normativity may take diverse forms, and, [whenever we are able to identify them,] we experience it as the force of principles: the force of moral commands, of the moral point of view in general, of conscience, of the law, of faith, of cultural values as conceptions of the desirable, the force of the best argument, the force of justice, the appeal of the good life. Nowhere are these normative standards fully satisfied, but we do not consider them inadequate for this reason: it is our world that has to match up to them, ideally, and not the other way around. The picture begins now to convey a familiar scene in familiar nuances of coloring. For us to grasp or to gain an insight into the world shared in common by a group, a people, a religious congregation, a political party, a social movement, a generation or an entire civilization requires that we get a sense of these two things: namely, what the people in question take to exist and what they think should be the case.

If we took this picture to be exhaustive of the dimensions along which the world is constituted for us and conceived of the world as shaped solely by the force of what is and the force of what ought to be the case—the force of things and the force of ideas—the world would now no longer resemble a prison but would be the locus of an unbridgeable gap between these two realms, the locus of a fracture, the locus of a permanent clash between necessity and freedom.

Fortunately, the picture is not yet complete. Alongside the force of what is and of what ought to be, a third force gives shape to our world: the force of *what is as it should be* or the force of the *example*. For a long time unrecognized and misleadingly assigned to the reductive realm of the aesthetic, the force of the example is the force of what exerts appeal on us in all walks of life—in art as in politics, in religious as in moral matters, in economic as in social conduct, in medical practice as in managing large organizations—by virtue of the singular and exceptional *congruence* that what is exemplary realizes and exhibits between the order of its own reality and the order of the normativity to which it responds. *Authenticity, beauty, perfection, integrity, charisma, aura,* and many other names have been attributed to this quality of bringing reality and normativity, facts and norms not just to a passing, occasional, and imperfect intertwining but to an enduring, nearly complete, and rare fusion.

Two distinct kinds of exemplarity appear as well. Sometimes what is exemplary embeds and reflects a normativity of which we are fully aware: we already know of what the example is an example. Examples of virtuous conduct, of best practices in the professions, of statemanship in politics, of courage in combat or of parental care are often of this kind. At other times, however, the exemplariness of the example is so pure and innovative that we first vaguely sense it by drawing on the analogy with past experiences and only subsequently do we succeed in identifying the normative moment so forcefully reflected in the object or action at hand. Fully grasping exemplarity in this case requires that we formulate ad hoc the principle of which it constitutes an instantiation. Political revolutions, the founding of new religions, groundbreaking works of art are often of this kind: with one and the same gesture they disclose new vistas on what exists *and* new dimensions of normativity. The appeal and force with which they inspire everybody to follow their teaching rest on pure exemplarity: neither the necessity of a reality that could be otherwise nor the implications of a norm as yet unrecognized can account for their capacity to shape our world.

While the force of what is accounts for much of the continuity of our shared world over time, and the force of what ought to be accounts for our sense that the world is a place worth living in, the exemplarity of what is as it should be accounts for much of the change undergone by our world over time, for the rise of new patterns and the opening of new paths. Historical change of great magnitude is often spurred by the capacity, possessed by exemplary figures, actions, and events, to illuminate new ways of transcending the limitations of what is and expanding the reach of our normative understandings. Over and beyond providing us with a sense of our possibilities for transformation, the force of the example often provides us with anticipatory prefigurations of reconciliation—in the first place, a reconciliation of the tragic rift of necessity and freedom reverberated by a world shaped only by the force of what exists or the force of things, on one hand, and the force of ideas or of what ought to be, on the other hand.

This book is about making sense of this third force, which, for various reasons, never has, in the history of Western philosophy, received an attention comparable in scope and depth to that dedicated to the other two, with the notable exceptions of Aristotle's notion of *phronesis* and of Kant's concept of *reflective judgment* revisited by Arendt in her *Lectures on Kant's Political Philosophy*. The tools with which we can theorize about exemplarity come basically from these sources, but they will remain in the background, with the exception of Arendt, because my primary intent is not philological, historical, or even primarily reconstructive.[1] Rather, my aim is to explore the uses to which the notion of exemplarity can be put for us in our contemporary philosophical predicament. What is exemplarity? How can something singular possess universal significance? What is the nature of the force exerted by exemplarity? How does it compare with the force of law?[2] How can it bridge the difference between the various contexts that lie within its reach?

I will start with an assessment of our philosophical context that will highlight the special relevance that exemplary normativity—the force of the example—acquires for us. In a nutshell, the force of the example becomes more salient to us as the force of principles becomes more difficult to ground in the light of a philosophical horizon not yet overcome: that of the critique, generated by the Linguistic Turn, of the whole range of versions of modern foundationalism. Unlike twenty-five years ago, when I began to outline this philosophical perspective in terms of the more specific concept of authenticity, now the culturalist and intersubjective bent of philosophical theorizing on normativity and subjectivity inaugurated by the Linguistic Turn has come under attack and new forms of naturalism—spurred by the achievements of the neurosciences, of genetic research, of computer science, of sociobiology—seem to carry more promise as general research programs and to exert more influence as horizon-shaping paradigms. Yet this book builds on a somewhat skeptical appraisal of such promise.

I will not try to develop a defense of the undiminished relevance of the Linguistic Turn in the book—for that argument would require a volume of its own to be properly articulated—but will rather take its relevance for granted. I find it more interesting to explore what can be done in the way of defusing the relativistic implications that have thus far been drawn from its premises and main theses. Yet allow me merely to recall some of the moves that inaugurated the Linguistic Turn in the first half of the twentieth century.

The horizon of modern universalism, wherein the validity of propositions and norms is conceived as resting on their matching the standards of theoretical and practical human reason, already is thrown into question and superseded when Wittgenstein, in proposition 5.6.2 of his *Tractatus,* states that "the world is my world: this is manifest in the fact that the limits of language (of that language which alone I understand) mean the limits of my world." In this passage he is denying that the world can be grasped independently of the mediation of one language. And since a plurality of languages has existed ever since Babel, there is no way of avoiding the conclusion that the diverse limits of the worlds conceivable by you and me are not unrelated to the diversity of the languages through and within which they are conceived.[3]

The modern understanding of universalism is once again questioned in § 217 of *Philosophical Investigations,* where Wittgenstein suggests that after a certain point our attempts to account for what to follow a rule means run against a deep geological bedrock—the pure facticity of a life form—against which the spade of philosophical reflection is inexorably turned and must stop. Again, there is no way of avoiding the consequence that the normativity of a rule and the facticity of the life form wherefrom the rule originates are inextricably linked.[4]

The same modern horizon is radically subverted when Quine, in "Two Dogmas of Empiricism," undermines the fundamental distinction—at the core of both idealist and realist, both rationalist and empiricist philosophy— between what is true by virtue of the facts of the matter (e.g., that it is raining today in Rome) and what is true "a priori" or "analytically," without any need to check how things are in the world (e.g., that a bachelor is an unmarried man). The distinction crumbles, according to Quine, when we realize that the supposedly "a priori," "analytical" quality of the relation between "being a bachelor" and "being unmarried" cannot, just as Wittgenstein's notion of "following a rule," be grasped independently of the lexicographic apprehension (usually recorded in dictionaries) of the "linguistic usage" or practice of a concrete community.[5]

Similar results were generated even earlier, within a vocabulary unrelated to a linguistic perspective, by Max Weber in his methodological reflections on the nexus of knowledge and values. We need not commit ourselves to any dubious metaphysical statement about the infinity of the elements constituting the object of our knowledge. We only need to concede that any object, whether natural or cultural, contains many more constitutive elements than the number we can possibly be able to investigate during our finite lives. It is our finitude that enjoins us to adopt a perspective and to select the elements worth knowing more closely from the exorbitant number of knowable aspects, lest we end up knowing nothing. A map of a continent as large as the continent itself, which leaves out nothing, is totally useless. Now the point is that such selection of what is worth knowing and what we need not bother to know is an act that cannot be justified solely along cognitive lines, in terms of an *adaequatio intellectus et rei,* which obviously cannot have taken place yet. On the contrary, only on the basis of the hermeneutic foreunderstanding concerning the "worth-knowingness" of the object of knowledge—a foreunderstanding of which we need not be aware—can we speak of truth in a nonsubjectivistic sense.[6]

Thus to those of you who wonder whether the moment may have finally come to dismiss the Linguistic Turn and its postmodernist, deconstructionist, poststructuralist, culturalist, hermeneutic aftershocks as something *passé,* I would address the following questions: do you have a convincing argument, against Wittgenstein, for the claim that we can gain differentiated and not just immediate sensory knowledge of the world independently of any language? Do you know of such a way of ascertaining whether a rule has been followed that, against Wittgenstein, is independent of any practice typical of a life form? Do you know how to draw once again, against Quine, the line that separates what is true by virtue of a state of affairs and what is true by virtue of the meaning of the terms with which we describe it? Are you in a position to deny, against Weber, that all forms of cognition embed a moment in which we single out what is worth knowing of our object and that such attribution of salience is linked with the pursuit of distinct and often rival values not reducible to a neat and uncontestable hierarchy? Are you not in a position to provide conclusive answers to these questions? Then the postmodern horizon opened up by the Linguistic Turn is still entirely before you, unsuperseded, and so will remain until you are able to meet these challenges.

Nevertheless, I find it worthwhile to address the kernel of truth embedded in the exhortation, so appealing since the last decade of the last century, to distance ourselves from the hermeneutic, postmodernist, postcolonial, cultural studies sirens. For much as the hermeneutic, culturalist, and postmodernist philosophies maintain an undiminished critical bite with respect to modern foundationalist universalism, their unabated shortcoming consists in a persistent failure to ever move beyond this critique. Of all the philosophical streams issuing from the common source of the Linguistic Turn, postmodernism in particular seems doomed to bore us with its litany of difference constantly repeated and never followed by a positive proposal of a new, truly postfoundationalist way of conceiving true and false, just and unjust.

On this philosophical context, which forms the backdrop of the present book, more will be said in chapter 1. What I will add here is that instead of seeking to rescue a universalist perspective via the return to some kind of neonaturalism predicated on that philosophical chimera, second only to the "thing in itself," constituted by the appeal to uninterpreted "facts"—the "facts" of the mind, the "facts" of neurobiology, the "facts" of social complexity—a more promising path seems to me connected to a thorough revisiting of the very concept of universalism. Although occasionally contemporary authors have suggested nonfoundationalist forms of universalism, such as "reiterative universalism" and "universalisme de parcours,"[7] they have never gone beyond suggestive remarks and have never investigated the philosophical underpinnings and structure of a possible nonfoundationalist universalism. In fact, the most articulate, reflective, and fine-grained thematization of a nonfoundationalist universalism has rather taken a *proceduralist* direction, captured in Jürgen Habermas's "postmetaphysical" program of a discursive foundation of validity, on whose problems I will not expand here.[8]

A different and still underexplored path consists in revisiting the modern notion of universalism—taken for granted wholesale both by its postmodern, poststructuralist, and deconstructionist critics and by its fervent neonaturalist and even proceduralist defenders—from the perspective of the paradigm of judgment and its core notion of *exemplary* validity. In the philosophical context in which we are immersed, more options are open to us than the alternative of returning to forms of naturalism or of embracing discursive proceduralism in the hope of avoiding a hermeneutically informed relativism. One of these additional options consists in drawing from the exemplarity of the work of art or of the well-lived life a notion of universalism that presupposes no antecedent principles and yet does not lend itself to a reduction to the reflection of locally shared and unquestionable preferences.

The aim of exporting this model of normativity beyond the realm of aesthetics in order to establish a nonfoundationalist view of validity, true to the premises of the Linguistic Turn, requires that the context to which this proposal represents a response be spelled out in greater detail, that the central notion of reflective judgment be reconstructed, and that the philosophical basis of a universalism without principles be articulated. If not transcontextual principles, what is it in judgment-based approaches to validity that can account for the reach of normativity beyond its original context? What is it that explains and justifies our confidence that our judgment, despite its being indemonstrable, will be shared by others?

In chapter 1 these questions will be addressed. If it is not our deriving examples and judgments from principles that can explain why we expect them to be accepted by or exert an appeal on others, then one possible alternative is to have this expectation rest on the sharedness of a *sensus communis* different from the locally variable commonsense or received wisdom. In chapter 1 this option is investigated more closely in relation to two competing and variously problematic ways of understanding the commonality of *sensus communis:* the hermeneutic idea of a "horizon" and the phenomenological notion of a lifeworld, on one hand, and the Kantian minimalist, naturalized concept of *sensus communis* on the other. A third alternative is outlined. Finally, in the same chapter the relevance of the judgment perspective for political philosophy is addressed, for the field of politics is prima facie one of those where the exportation of the originally aesthetic model of exemplary validity seems most urgent, useful, and promising at the same time.

In chapter 2 the judgment approach to nonfoundationalist universalism is further expanded with reference to Hannah Arendt's work. More specifically, the discussion of *sensus communis* is pursued further by highlighting the problems inherent in Arendt's account of the relation of examples to what Kant called schemata. In the concluding section an alternative reconstruction of the notion of exemplarity is offered that draws on the conception of *sensus communis* articulated in the previous chapter and aims at avoiding the reductionist implications of assimilating examples to schemata for the decoding of actions and virtues.

The judgment paradigm, however, should not be understood solely or even primarily as an assessment of the course of the world in the private forum of our conscience. Rather, the challenge with respect to which its potential must be tested consists in making sense of how shared normative evaluations and political justification are possible in the public realm of our pluralistic societies. How can the force of the example succeed where the force of principles is often contested, especially if the significance of examples has to meet the challenge posed by the diverse cultural orientations from which examples are appraised?

These questions are addressed in the next two chapters. chapter 3 pivots around the idea that the Rawlsian notion of "public reason" and its attendant standard of the "reasonable," as distinct from principle-based "practical reason," are but a tiny area of the largely unexplored continent of deliberative reason, a form of reason for which reflective judgment represents the fundamental organon. The different meanings of the term *reasonable* and the entwinement of judgment, exemplarity, and of the reasonable (at least in one of the most important of its meanings) are reconstructed. The normative force of the reasonable is argued to be best understood as one manifestation of the force of exemplarity if public reason is to be prevented from collapsing into principle-guided practical reason.

Examples, however, are not always positive, and their force is often pernicious. Reflection about the significance of exemplarity in public life cannot dispense with facing the challenge posed by radical evil. Radical evil, evil on the scale of the Holocaust, threatens to burst the neat philosophical symmetries underlying the account of the force of the reasonable provided in the previous chapter. Radical, as opposed to ordinary, evil cannot be even remotely equated with the "merely unreasonable," and yet how can we make its unconditional rejection independent of the foundationalist embracing of a comprehensive conception of the good? Things are complicated further by the fact that never does radical evil ostensibly present itself as such. We encounter it always in disguise, under the cover of a conception of the good that in the end turns out to be perverse. But how can a conception of the good—often shared by millions of people and for a certain period of time regarded by them as a source of inspiration and guidance for their lives—be called evil by an external observer, evil in the eyes of everyone and not just in our own, consistently with the postfoundationalist assumptions on which we want to build a liberal and democratic polity?

In chapter 4 some steps are taken toward solving this paradox by pointing to the internal inconsistency of any modern conception of the good (including the Nazi vision of the good, as reconstructed by James Bernauer) that failed to embed equal respect for all human beings and at the same time purported to present itself as a conception of what ought to be. No conception of the good can be acceptable that enjoins its proponents to embrace an inconsistent project. At the same time, radical evil is distinguished from ordinary evil once again in terms of its embedding a *negative exemplarity* that is missing in ordinary evil: only radical evil exemplifies us "at our worst."

More specifically, in our effort to rethink radical evil in postmetaphysical terms we can draw on Durkheim's understanding of the sacred. Just as the production of the sacred is part and parcel of social life and cannot be eradicated from it—secularization may be said to affect the religious sedimentation of collective experiences of the sacred and the role of religion in social life, but not the production of the sacred as such—so radical evil is best understood as the polar opposite of the sacred. Whereas the sacred is a projection of us *at our best* (and the world of the profane is a representation of us *as we actually are*), radical evil can be conceptualized as a projection of us *at our worst,* the worst that we can be while still maintaining those characteristics that distinguish us as a community, society, or humanity.

Evidence for this view comes from the fact that the horror we experience when facing the same evil deeds increases with the proximity of their perpetrators to our moral life. This suggests that perhaps the criterion for the radicality of radical evil ought to be internal to us rather than external. Radical evil then is perhaps best conceived as a *horizon* that moves with us, rather than as something that stands over against us. One of the interesting consequences then is that evil, even radical evil, cannot be overcome. Concrete manifestations of it can, of course, be overcome, but if evil is a horizon that moves with us there will always be collectively shared representations of what we, as a single moral community or we as humans, can be at our worst. The idea of a good society where evil has been eradicated is, from a postmetaphysical standpoint, as meaningless as the idea of a pacified moral world where conflicts of value no longer exist.

The discussion of radical evil completes the general outline of the paradigm of judgment—including the backdrop to which such paradigm is designed to respond, the peculiar kind of normativity it presupposes, the nature of the force of the example, its positive and negative manifestation in the public realm. In the remaining chapters the potential of this paradigm in a number of areas, all related to politics, is explored.

In chapter 5 I discuss the persisting relevance of republicanism as the one strand of political theory that exhibits the most pronounced elective affinity with the fundamentals of the judgment paradigm, including the priority of examples over principles. The "republican challenge" to liberalism is not to be found in a thicker and more robust notion of freedom, as contemporary proponents of republicanism have often contended, but rather in its greater constitutive propensity to ground its fundamental tenets in a hermeneutic appraisal of the significance of historical examples than in abstract principles of political legitimacy. Republican theory is constructed from the ground up on the basis of reflection on historical cases; it is a sort of "political criticism" parallel to art criticism in that it purports to bring to light the exemplarity of certain institutions, political arrangements, regimes, and norms: they are envisioned as demanding our consent, no less than works of art, by virtue of their capacity to set the imagination—*political* imagination in this case—in motion by virtue of their exceptional self-congruence.

In chapters 6 and 7 the judgment paradigm is put to the test on the issue of justifying human rights and limiting state sovereignty in a global yet culturally diversified world. The wager is that when we break free from the strictures of "methodological nationalism" and begin to rethink the major categories of politics, justice, freedom, equality, power, legitimation, and so on—assuming the globalized world and no longer a single national society as the default unit of analysis—the judgment approach affords resources that enable us to better meet the challenge of justifying binding norms and a cosmopolitan rule of law in the face of more pronounced cultural divergence. Why is this so?

On the one hand we are faced with the trends of a globalizing world: the new stage entered by the formation of an economic world system, the formation of a global financial system, where the fluctuations of currencies and equity values outdo the steering capacities of any economic actor, including the most powerful central banks, the rise of ecological risks that transcend national boundaries, the formation of migratory currents whose pressure no state is fully able to withstand, the global reach of certain media of communication that contribute to the rise of a global public sphere, which at times comes to expression in emotional, compassionate or indignant terms, the growth of a culture industry that markets its products worldwide and contributes to the growth of global pop culture.

On the other hand, these trends could be compatible with different ways of responding to the challenges they pose for the nation-state. The judgment approach starts from the idea that the best philosophical response to globalization is a thorough rethinking of politics, not just of international relations, but of politics as such in a way that reflects this new predicament. Freedom secured in one single country could lose its meaning unless freedom is guaranteed in relations between the countries of the world. Justice could easily become a travesty unless a measure of distributive justice across the various countries of the world is secured. The equality of the citizens of a single country makes little sense vis-à-vis massive inequalities in the world. Peace in one region of the world is not unaffected by the wars that ravage another part. What is considered legitimate in one country may very well fail to stand the scrutiny of a broader form of consciousness, no longer bound to a parochial locality. In a way this has always been the case, but what is new is the coming into being of the societal infrastructure of a global form of conscience and a cosmopolitan understanding of the fundamental political notions.

More specifically, the justification of human rights as fundamental limits to state sovereignty and their enforcement cannot follow the familiar liberal path of appealing to the consent of free and equal citizens of a global society, for the simple reason that, as Rawls pointed out in *The Law of Peoples,* we cannot project our liberal understanding of legitimation to worldwide law making and law enforcing without thereby implicitly imposing a Western modern scheme—the notion of free and equal individual citizens—onto nonmodern and non-Western political cultures that proceed from different understandings of legitimacy. The liberal idea of legitimacy cannot legitimately be projected at the global level unless we assume (quite implausibly) or we anticipate (in a quite utopian vein) that all of the 193 existing states actually are, or will soon be, based on a Western-style liberal-democratic political culture.

The judgment approach is obviously not the only one to urge these considerations on us: over and beyond, John Rawls, Michael Ignatieff, and Frank Michelman have in different terms insisted that the legitimacy of *cosmopolitan* governance be independent from the narrative of free and equal individuals coming to a consensus on constitutional essentials,[9] lest our embracing of human rights should turn into yet another of those comprehensive doctrines that are universal only in the eyes of their believers.

The question then is, if we cannot rely on forms of political justification that rest on less than universal assumptions and if presumably we cannot just wait for them to become universally shared, what could the yardstick of cosmopolitan, worldwide legitimacy rest on?

The suggestion that a judgment-based approach can contribute toward answering such a question draws on the idea of public reason but disentangles public reason and the standard of reasonableness from the presumption of free and equal *individuals,* urging us to rely on the converging will of existing states—some of which are associations of free and equal citizens and some not—as the legitimating source for human rights and to posit humanity as the possessor of the one identity, reconstructible via public reason, whose fulfilment requires that we, among other things, establish and enforce respect for human rights.

In chapter 6 this argument is articulated in more detail. The difficulties incurred by Rawls's and Habermas's approaches to the justification of human rights are illustrated, then the basics of a judgment-based approach to human rights are outlined and the distinction between a moral and a political notion of humanity is drawn. At this point a judgment-based, as opposed to principle-based, argument for the universality of human rights can be vindicated and, in the final section, this perspective can be related to an appraisal of globalization trends along the lines of a revisited Hegelian analysis of the implications of modern civil society.

In chapter 7 the problems associated with the *enforcement* of human rights are discussed from the angle of the judgment paradigm. Assuming that the justification aspect is adequately solved, the threshold, criteria, and procedures for overriding state sovereignty when violations of human rights occur are examined in light of the "Responsibility to Protect" Report of the International Commission on Intervention and State Sovereignty. The transition from a normative framework centered around the "right to intervene" to a new one centered around the "responsibility to protect" is argued to constitute the main contribution of the Commission's Report and to enhance the reasonableness of the ensuing guidelines due to the exceptional inclusiveness (measured in terms of public reason) of their normative premises.

Resuming one aspect of the previous discussion, the adequate "political" justification of human rights as endowed with priority over state sovereignty is best understood not in the guise of a philosophical, least of all "comprehensive," argument but rather as the enacting, via some process of political will formation *not* premised on the image of free and equal individuals, of a new authoritative legal source that identifies, from within the undifferentiated wealth of human rights mentioned by the existing documents, the few *fundamental human rights* that all peoples of the world are prepared to consider as ranking above state sovereignty. In chapter 7 the nature and substance of this suggested new Charter of Fundamental Human Rights is contrasted with the resolution of the General Assembly of the United Nations advocated by the commission as the proper instrument for publicizing the new limits of state sovereignty entailed by the "responsibility to protect."

In chapters 8 and 9 the judgment paradigm is put to the test in two further areas: the articulation of European identity and the fine-tuning of separation of religion and politics in light of a new form of "postsecular" consciousness.

In recent years philosophers have often used the expression "the idea of Europe." Taking issue with the project of deriving identity from comprehensive philosophical argument, I argue that the "Treaty Establishing a Constitution for Europe," whose substantive core is incorporated in the subsequent Treaty of Lisbon, contains enough substantive pronouncements to ground what might be called a European identity in a "political" sense. In chapter 8 the reconstruction of the main components of this European "political" identity is carried out in some detail and, second, some reflections are offered about the reasons why the European Union may reasonably hope to realize the main aspects of such identity if it ever overcomes its current constitutional crisis. The political influence that a more integrated EU may exert on the global scene is finally argued to rest, more than with anything else, on the force of its constituting an example of how human dignity can be optimally protected and how diversity can be reconciled into unity without dissolving itself into homogeneity.

In the last chapter the relation of politics and religion is addressed from the angle of a judgment-based approach. During the last decades many events have forced us to rethink not the basics of the separation between politics and religion, but certain aspects of its institutionalization. The role of religion within the public space and, consequently, the meaning of the ideal of religious neutrality in what Habermas has called a postsecular society appear in need of closer examination. The nature and extent of this reconsideration of the relation between religion and politics is the subject under discussion in this chapter. The general point defended is that the demand emerging, within as well as outside Western democratic societies, for a more public role for religious faith, or at least for its deprivatization, is worth considering and obliges us to address three issues: the achievement of full equality between citizens who are believers and nonbelievers, the different evolutionary pace of religious and secular conscience, the anthro-pological difference between the various forms of religiosity in their adapt-ing to the separation of church and state. In the last section of the chapter the role of historical and cultural context in the implementation of the principle of the religious neutrality of democratic institutions is examined, and again on this terrain the judgment perspective proves capable of best reconciling the reasons of universalism and our sensibility for the unique-ness of contexts.

Finally, one word of caution on what you should not expect to find in this book. True to the second clause in the title, this book is more about exploring what the paradigm of judgment can do for us in a number of areas of contemporary political theory than about laying out a philosophical jus-tification for it. Although it provides an outline of what exemplary validity means—how it can operate in the public realm and how it can exert a force beyond the context wherein it originates—the first group of four chapters should not be expected to offer a demonstration of alternative principles of validity whose application is then illustrated with reference to cases. That way of proceeding would expose the whole paradigm of judgment to the charge of containing a performative contradiction. Consistently with its own premises, then, the case for an exemplary notion of validity is rather made in exemplary terms, by attempting to have the force of inspiring in-stances of application reflect back onto the general philosophical appeal of the paradigm of judgment as such, more or less as the worth of a new style is established less by its poetic manifesto than by the appeal of the works couched in it.

1 *Judgment as a Paradigm*

The conversation of philosophers unfolds over the ages with a continuity of themes and paradigms that only at infrequent junctures undergoes a significant reconfiguring. One of the most interesting among these turning points is constituted by the publication of Kant's *Critique of the Power of Judgment*. Kant's work of 1790 inaugurates a new paradigm for thinking of validity and normativity—the *judgment paradigm*—that further modifies a philosophical horizon already reshaped in depth by the more often celebrated *Critique of Pure Reason* and *Critique of Practical Reason* and whose full promise begins to be recognized, for reasons that I will try to clarify, only two centuries thereafter.

I deliberately use the ambitious term *paradigm* because I think that the idea of normative validity presupposed by Kant's concept of reflective judgment extends its significance well beyond the realm of aesthetics, to which it has traditionally been confined, and does provide a coherent and inspiring model for a large range of disciplines, including political theory.[1] The reasons for such significance and for the delay with which it has come to be appreciated, however, cannot be fully grasped unless we understand our own contemporary philosophical predicament along lines that make such relevance perceivable.

The Philosophical World That We Inhabit

We live in a philosophical predicament, which, in at least one respect, resembles the one inhabited by Kant. Kant was fascinated by Newtonian physics because physics promised to bring together two things that in the philosophical world he had inherited from the past had always been separated by an abyss, namely, *certainty* and *experience*. In classical and medieval thought, certainty was associated with logic, mathematics, and other formal disciplines, whereas the realm of human experience was the realm of *doxa,* opinion, and *un*certainty. Newtonian physics, instead, had the potential for enabling us to know things related to experience with the same degree of certainty afforded by the formal disciplines—*a priori synthetic judgment* is the technical name that Kant gave to this philosophical treasure embedded in modern physics.

More than two centuries thereafter, we live in a structurally similar predicament, characterized by another abyss that seems equally unbridgeable. Ever since Wittgenstein's and Heidegger's different but converging versions of the Linguistic Turn, many of us have become convinced that it is impossibile to grasp any segment of reality independently of the filter of some interpretive framework (be it a language game, a tradition, a paradigm, a conceptual scheme, a vocabulary) and that the plurality of existing interpretive frameworks cannot be reduced to unity without some significant loss of meaning. This way of summing up our experience of plurality does not amount to the dubious postulation of a sort of radical incommensurability between the various interpretive frameworks used by different human communities in negotiating their way in the world. Rather, the philosophical horizon to which the judgment paradigm represents a response embeds a much more modest claim: namely, the claim that *perfect commensurability* is a myth—especially in view of the positional character of meaning, combined with the morphological, syntactic, lexical, semantic, and pragmatic diversity of concrete historical languages—and that *im*perfect translatability inevitably affects the transcontextual grip of general principles by way of limiting their potential for subsuming local meanings without failing to include semantic residues whose crucial relevance cannot be ruled out a priori.

If we assume that, in a philosophical context where the human subject is supposed to be intersubjectively constituted by web of relations that necessarily have to have a culturally local anchoring, principles and laws cannot do the old trick of allowing the residueless subsumption of all particulars, as if culture and social relations of recognition were just a colorful addition to a subject whose making is best accounted for in naturalistic or transcendental terms, then we come to the realization that we live in a philosophical world where our longing for universalism, theoretical and normative, cannot be easily reconciled with a genuine acceptance of the pluralism of interpretive frameworks.

We currently have on offer theories and conceptions—such as the theory of rational choice, game theory, computer science, analytical Marxism, utilitarianism, systems theory in social science, and several others—that embed universalistic claims but poorly match our pluralistic intuitions. And on the other hand we are confronted with theories and conceptions that start from pluralistic assumptions—think of cultural anthropology, cultural studies, the sociology of culture, Rorty's ironic philosophy, the Gadamerian rehabilitation of prejudice, the communitarian emphasis on tradition, postcolonial studies—but fail to vindicate our urge for universalism, even if by "universalism" just the simple requirement is meant that theories and norms exert some kind of cogency not just *within*, but somehow also *beyond* their context and time of origin.

It might not be too implausible, then, to say that for us aesthetics, and within it *reflective judgment* in particular, play the role that physics played for Kant, namely, that of constituting not so much a specific doctrine but rather a *model* of validity, which, through the notion of *exemplary validity*—exemplary validity as predicated originally, but certainly not exclusively, of the work of art—is capable of bringing together what no contemporary philosophical doctrine seems able to fully reconcile: *universalism* and *pluralism*. Why should we expect reflective judgment and its inherent notion of exemplariness to succeed where illustrious predecessors—monological neotranscendentalism, discursive proceduralism, poststructuralism, deconstructionism—have failed?

Reflective judgment, let us recall, as all other kinds of judgment, consists in thinking the particular as "the particular as contained under the universal"—indeed that is the object of reflection as such. In certain limited cases—for example, solving an equation, assessing the correctness of a move on the chessboard, or the eligibility for a certain office—our power of reflection has no trouble in identifying a principle or rule and then subsuming the single concrete case as an instance to which the general principle or rule applies. Then the closure that is the natural outcome of such process of reflection—yes, this is indeed a case of *x*—leaves us with a kind of judgment called *determinant* by Kant.

The tremendous appeal that this special form of judgment has exerted and continues to exert not only in natural science but also in the social sciences and in moral theory, in legal thought and in political philosophy lies in its appearance of objectivity, reliability, and transmissibility. The *objectivity* of the universal, its validity independent of your or my perspective, angle, situation, context, tradition, culture, or historical time is something believed to impose itself on us, and to enjoin our recognition, with inescapable cogency. Its *reliability* means that "anyone" will reach the same conclusion if given the same initial information, and if not impeded in her reasoning by affects or interests, and that one, if she fails to reach the same conclusion, can legitimately be labeled "irrational." *Transmissibility* means we can connect this form of judgment to a set of rules or principles that can be stated and taught prior to, and independently of, all applications of them.

Powerful and fascinating as this model of judgment might be, it is vitiated by a weakness that has remained invisible, for comprehensible reasons, up until the Linguistic Turn of the first half of the twentieth century exposed the dependency of subjectivity, perception, and meaning upon holistic frameworks that are situated and do always come in the plural. For the operation of determinant judgment or of reflection with a built-in determinative closure presupposes that translation flows effortlessly and without loss of essential meaning back and forth between the locally prevailing frameworks of meaning and the rules or principle, of whatever nature, that need to be "applied to them" or are used as a benchmark for assessing their soundness. Only then can the context-transcending capacity of "the universal" be fully displayed.

Reflective judgment, instead, is a kind of judgment in which "only the particular is given, for which the universal has to be found." In this process of "ascending from the particular in nature to the universal" we are in need of a guiding principle, argues Kant, but this principle cannot be borrowed from experience nor from "anywhere else," including conceptual analysis.

For in that case our judgment "would then be a determinant judgment."[2] Thus reflective judgment is the model of choice for thinking of validity when the nature of the question raised, the cultural plurality of ways of framing it, the historical distance in time, or whatever other reason puts us in a predicament where no clear-cut, generally accepted or otherwise established "universal" can be invoked for answering it or testing available answers. Provided that the question at hand is one about which we do assume the sensibleness of speaking of better and worse answers, we are then typically left with the "particular" in our hands while our eyes scan the horizon in search of an adequate principle in light of which to assess it and under which to bring it. With a token in our hands, we look for a type that we have never separately experienced. Indeed, we may have to create an ad hoc type in order to make full sense of the token at hand. Thus the difference between the models of validity underlying the *Critique of Pure Reason* and the *Critique of the Power of Judgment* should not be understood as the difference between a paradigm that excludes reflective judgment or reflection as such and a subsequent one that revolves around it.[3] For determinant judgment indeed starts with the process of reflection and also needs reflection when it comes to its applications. The difference lies rather in the fact that, while for a first model of validity no universalism is achieved unless the process of cognition ends with the successful identification of a concept that then paves the way for determinant judgment, the model inaugurated by *Critique of the Power of Judgment* offers us a broader way of conceiving of universalism, according to which even "merely reflective judgments" (or judgments that cannot amount to the identification of a univocal *concept* that subsequently allows for determinant subsumption) can legitimately claim to be universally valid beyond their context of origin.

As with all paradigms, the basic idea underlying the paradigm of judgment is simple. The traditional modern answer to the question "How can a theory or conception born in a 'here and now' project a cogency 'there and then'?" used to be: "By virtue of a law or principle that originates from no local context—being ingrained in a cosmic order, in a disenchanted nature, in God's will, in the transcendental constitution of the subject—and under which therefore all local contexts can be subsumed." The new answer that can be gleaned from the *Critique of the Power of Judgment* replaces the normativity of a *law* or *principle* with the normativity of the *example*. What emerges from within a historical and cultural context—be it a theory, a constellation of cultural values, a political institution—can exert a cogency outside its original context by virtue of entering a relation of exceptional congruency with the subjectivity, individual or collective, that has brought it into being, an exceptional congruency, for the designation of which in the past I have found the term *authenticity* particularly congenial.

There are a number of performances that no longer can be expected of the model of exemplary validity, and this accounts for the relative marginality the paradigm has suffered up until the Linguistic Turn failed to reveal the mortal weakness of the more fortunate and mainstream approach to validity in terms of principles and laws. If we harness the capacity to free us from the particularity of context to the inspiringness of the example rather than to the compellingness of a law, we instantly lose the "objectivity," reliability, and transmissibility of the older way of conceiving of normative validity. There simply won't be any way of labeling irrational those who fail to accept the hypothesized "type" as the right type under which to bring the given token. Therefore there won't be any guarantee, rather only a weaker "expectation," that everyone will agree to the labeling of a certain type as the best one for that purpose and there won't be any way of extrapolating from our fortunate reflection a "method" susceptible of being stated independently of the given case, let alone taught separately from the example and applied to all future instances of the same token.

But these obvious dimensions of philosophical loss pale by comparison with the tremendous advantage that this approach to validity affords in the new horizon opened up by the Linguistic Turn. The problem of translating across contexts and back and forth between what is particular and what is (supposedly) universal simply fades away—and we all know how intractable that operation of transcontextual translation is. The promise of the new model, which in and of itself makes it worth exploring further, is that of freeing us from the twin dangers—the Scylla and Charybdis of today's philosophy—of either trivializing difference, by postulating perfect commensuration and translatability in a neutral language, or of jeopardizing universalism by failing to reunify the plurality of local contexts and ultimately remain hostage to it.

Why does this problem of translation fade away if we move from a universalism of principles or laws to exemplary universalism? Because the cogency of the example, differently than the cogency of a law or principle, is entirely self-referential, immanent to the subject matter, typically immanent to the work of art, the cultural form, the human identity. Thus in its being apprehended *juxta propria principia*, the normativity of an example requires no translation. And yet for Kant the reflective judgment as to the exemplarity of the example, no less than the judgment as to the beauty (to stay with Kant's perhaps dated terminology) of the work of art, cannot be reduced to a mere report of idiosyncratic and unquestionable preferences (like the judgment on the pleasurable), but raises a claim to the effect that everybody else *ought to* agree.

Therefore normativity and universalism are present in reflective judgment, in the form of an anticipation of the general consensus of those who possess the necessary expertise for assessing the matter, no matter where they are situated. Their consensus cannot be enjoined on penalty of irrationality, as in determinant judgment, but can only be wooed.

The *Critique of the Power of Judgment* is a treatise in aesthetics, and that is in a way unfortunate, because it has contributed to sectorialize its insights to the domain of art and of natural beauty. Instead, the methodological *paradigm* that it has inaugurated extends its relevance well beyond the territory of art and natural beauty. The idea that normativity proceeds from the suggestive force of the example just as much as from the subsumptive power of the law can be applied to virtually every domain beyond aesthetics. So can its understanding of the nature of exemplarity as the ability to set the imagination in motion and to further or enhance our life.

Drawing on the vocabulary of the third critique, we can say that the exemplarity of a political institution, a constitutional essential, a social movement consists, no less than the exemplarity of a work of art, of its ability to set the *political* imagination in motion by virtue of an exceptional self-congruency. Differently than suggested by Arendt in her interpretation of Kant, which will be the object of critical scrutiny in the next chapter, in politics no less than in art the exemplary provides guidance and exerts cogency beyond its immediate context of origin *not* as *schemata* do, by providing prior cases to which we can assimilate the present one, but as works of art do, namely, by providing outstanding instances of authentic congruency that are capable of educating our discernment by way of exposing us to selective instances of that special pleasure called by Kant the feeling of "the promotion of life" (*Befördeung des Lebens*). This kind of exemplary universalism needs no transcontextual, umbrellalike "covering-laws" or transcendental principles, not even discursive or procedural principles. It functions—as Paul Ricoeur has nicely put it—as "a *trail of fire* issuing from itself," that sets an entire forest on fire yet always by catching one tree after another, in a singular way.

The notion of reflective judgment allows us to export this form of exemplary universalism without principles beyond the realm of aesthetics, into the realm of moral judgment, political judgment, legal judgment, and even theoretical judgment of a cognitive nature—into all the realms of inquiry where we painfully feel the tension between our persistently universalistic understanding of validity and our awareness of the impossibility of speaking from a privileged location beyond all language games, all traditions, all paradigms.

If the current interest in a notion of validity bound up with what can be called reflective authenticity or "reflective endorsement," to use Christine Korsgaard's phrase,[4] is arguably related to the perception that the concept of exemplary validity can free us from the difficulty of reconciling universalism and the pluralism of cultures, then justice and, more generally, political theory are among the most important terrains on which to put this potential to test. For what we demand of any conception of justice—be it Rawls's "justice as fairness," Habermas's discursive theory of justice, or any other approach to justice—is that it be able to settle conflicts of interest and of value in ways that are recognized valid across the cultural divides that traverse contemporary complex societies. Similarly, what we demand of a conception of political justification, or of freedom, or of rights, is that it be able to equally speak to members of diverse and not fully reconcilable political cultures. And what we demand of a justification of fundamental human rights, understood as rights that have primacy over and impose limits to state sovereignty, or of the justification of a redistributive scheme for global justice, is once again that it be able to bridge the differences among the diverse conceptions of the person, of human life, of value embedded in the main cultures of the planet.

The Core of the Paradigm: Exemplary Universalism and *Sensus Communis*

Yet if we assume that exemplarity, as grasped through reflective judgment, is the key to the articulation of an approach to validity sensitive to the plurality of contexts but not hostage to it and not vulnerable to the critique of foundationalism, we are still faced with the need to answer—albeit in a profoundly changed philosophical context—the same question that troubled Kant in the initial forty paragraphs of the *Critique of the Power of Judgment*: "What must we assume that all human beings share, if we wish to conceive of the transcontextual validity of a judgment about exemplarity as resting neither on a factual consensus nor on the application of a principle?" Such question is answered by claiming that we all share "a *sensus communis*," but as soon as we try to spell out what it is exactly we share when we share a sensus communis, we find ourselves cornered between two alternative philosophical strategies that are both deeply problematic, albeit for quite different reasons. On the one hand we have a strategy that I will describe as a hermeneutic and phenomenological thickening of the concept of sensus communis. On the other hand we have the opposite strategy, which I will call Kantian quasi-naturalistic minimalism. I will briefly reconstruct them and then will outline an alternative approach to sensus communis that still remains compatible with the gist of the Kantian approach.

I consider the first strategy more part of the problem than of its solution. Gadamer's rehabilitation of *Vorurteil* as an ineliminable component of a process of understanding reinterpreted in an ontological vein, as the constitutive condition of a human subjectivity always already immersed in interpretive processes, ends up paving the way to a banalization of sensus communis as common sense. Common sense, as understood by that humanistic tradition that Gadamer accuses Kant of ignoring, acquires substance—it becomes a collection of handed-down judgments as to right and wrong, the appropriate and the out of place—but this substantiality, enshrined in the notion of "horizon," takes us back to square one. For, if a successful interpretation amounts to a fusion of horizons, and we cannot but assume the existence of a plurality of horizons, the validity of any interpretation is hostage to the "host-horizon" within which it takes place.[5] It is no accident that Gadamer's antimethodical stance leaves his hermeneutics by and large silent on the question of what validity in interpretation is.

An equivalent trajectory is followed by the phenomenological investigations of Edmund Husserl and Alfred Schutz, where a common-sense-like sensus communis reappears under the heading of the *Lebenswelt*. According to the author of *The Phenomenology of the Social World*, in order to understand how social action and even cognition is possible we must take on an intersubjective perspective from the outset: we must presuppose the existence of a plurality of human actors who interact in a common space. And in order for this interaction to be possible, we must also assume the existence of a world shared in common, a world inhabited together with others.[6] Sensus communis is thus understood by Schutz as a shared world, a

Lebenswelt, and in turn such a *Lebenswelt* is understood as a shared stock of tacit knowledge—a kind of knowledge whose validity is taken for granted by all the members of a society when they operate within the "natural attitude." These implicit cognitions, assumptions, and judgments, taken all together, constitute a "relatively natural view of the world." The lifeworld is the totality not simply of what everybody knows—for in that case it could be exhaustively reconstructed by an external observer—but the totality of "what everybody knows that everybody knows." It is a kind of knowledge that constitutes a public domain not only factually available to everybody but also *known* to be available to everybody.

This hermeneutic and phenomenological approach to the conceptualization of sensus communis is haunted by two obvious limitations.[7] First, sensus communis so understood becomes a kind of "body of knowledge," more specifically an inconsistent and only partially clear body of knowledge. It is a partially clear body of knowledge because the social actor who acts in the lifeworld is interested more in the practical efficacy of her action than in cognition as such. As social actors we are interested in buying particular merchandise and paying for it, not in knowing all the intricacies of production and of the circulation of money. Thus the kind of knowledge stored in the lifeworld is often just superficial knowledge, knowledge by word of mouth, little more than reinforced rumors. Furthermore, it is a knowledge that encompasses an infinite variety of domains and, given the absence of any self-conscious effort to integrate these diverse domains, we often barely notice the inconsistencies between what we believe in one area (say, religion) and what we take for granted in another (say, the economy).

Second, sensus communis so understood is inherently incapable of transcending its own context of origin. Bound up as it is with our beliefs, values, concrete experiences, it is untranscendible. As any horizon, it moves with us. Paraphrasing what two disciples of Schutz's, Peter Berger and Thomas Luckmann, have aptly stated of the project of submitting the lifeworld to a thorough critical examination, we could say that trying to critically assess sensus communis is like trying to push the bus on which one is riding. In the end, to conceive of sensus communis in terms of this philosophical strategy imprisons us in a bus whose doors may never open.[8]

The second strategy, traceable back to Kant, starts from the opposite intuition. Namely, it starts from the intuition that injecting any kind of substance (historical, ethical, cultural) into our notion of sensus communis is bound to inevitably detract something from the universalism of sensus communis. Consequently, sensus communis is best understood as a *natural* faculty of the human being. The deliberate distancing of this version of sensus communis from the concept of common sense is signaled by the dual lexical choice adopted by Kant: he uses the term *sensus communis* (*Gemeinsinn*) in opposition to *gemeine Verstand,* common sense as understood by the British tradition of commonsense philosophers. In § 19 Kant points out why in matters of taste we cannot rely on the consent of all those who will examine the matter, but at most can "solicit" such consent. We cannot rely on such consent, continues Kant in § 20, because we do not possess, as is the case when we deal with logical reasoning, a principle we cannot but assume to be shared universally. And yet, should these judgments be completely independent of *any* principle—as the judgments concerning the pleasurable are—the issue of their universal validity could not even be raised. Thus the judgments concerning the beautiful and those concerning exemplarity must be located somewhere in between the entirely subjective judgments about the pleasurable and those cognitive or moral judgments that instead proceed from principles specifiable via concepts.

To be "located somewhere in between" means that such judgments proceed from a *subjective* principle, which determines not a concept but a feeling—the feeling of pleasure or aversion linked with the perception of certain objects—yet determines such feeling *in a universal way,* namely, in a way that allows us to expect the convergence of everybody's consent. This "principle" is really a sensus communis distinct from sound understanding or common sense. We may perhaps call it a communal feeling or a communal sensibility, unrelated to concepts. Nonetheless such communal feeling or sensibility must have some kind of content.[9] Whence does this sense or feeling or *koiné aisthesis* come, and how can we make sense of the assumption that it must be present in all human beings?

We are told by Kant that such sense is connected with the "free play of our cognitive powers,"[10] namely, the imagination and the understanding. But, again, why should we assume that such sense, feeling, or capacity is present in all human beings as such? The answer can be found in § 21. If we did not presuppose its presence in all human beings, Kant argues, we would thereby lose the possibility of envisaging a connection between the world of objects and our own representations: our cognitions and judgments about the external world would then just be a "subjective" play of our mental faculties. As all skeptics in all times have maintained, cognition would then just be a rhetorical exercise. The assumption of a universal communicability is what protects the idea of a correspondence of our representations to the object and with that also a nonskeptical view of validity, including aesthetic validity. Kant then proceeds to analyze further this universal communicability but, as we will see, there arises a difficulty with which we shall be concerned.

The operation of aesthetic judgment is reconstructed in the following way: when we make contact with an object, our senses set the imagination in motion, and the imagination transforms the sense product of our entering contact with the *Mannigfaltig*, the concrete manifold, into a *representation*. This creation of a representation, on the part of the imagination, in turn activates the understanding, which begins to supply concepts for the synthesis of the manifold. These concepts, however, instead of subsuming the entire object as a particular case of any of the reinstantiated concepts, bounce the mental materials back to the imagination. The imagination, in turn, uses these incomplete or unsuccessful "attempts at synthesis" as materials for further refining its own representation. A virtuous mutual feedback is thus set under way between these two faculties—a mutual feedback that, instead of being brought to closure by the intellect through the production of a definitive concept, remains unamenable to closure and indefinitely active.

Furthermore Kant mentions a "proportion" or relation between the imagination and the understanding—a proportion that characterizes in different ways the diverse kinds of mental processes. For example, we will have different "proportions" between the imagination and the understanding depending on whether we are dealing with an object of cognition, an object of moral appraisal, or an object to be assessed in terms of taste. The crucial point is that among all these different "proportions"—understood as the prevailing of either the imagination or the understanding or, as a third possibility, their equal influence—there should be one of them that is most adequate for the production of knowledge, and this "proportion" should be universally communicable, otherwise we would not have knowledge but mere rhetorical convergence concerning the objects in the world. But then, Kant continues, also the "feeling" of such proportion must be universally communicable. And the "universal communicability of a feeling presupposes a common sense," a shared sensibility.[11]

Here we touch on the limitations of Kant's strategy of "naturalizing" sensus communis. First, Kant wishes to establish the universal communicability of a feeling on the basis of what still remains to be demonstrated— namely, the indefensibility of skepticism and its unappealingness—rather than to rest his case for the indefensibility of skepticism on a demonstration of the full communicability of our cognitions and judgments. Furthermore, he tries to show that sensus communis, understood as a shared feeling, is presupposed by the very idea of the communicability of pleasure—a communicability that in turn can be seen as connected with the structure and interrelation of the imagination and the understanding, arguably shared by all human beings. Consequently, the universality of aesthetic judgment becomes conceptually dependent on the universality of the cognitive apparatus that forms the object of the *Critique of Pure Reason*. Even if we share the antihermeneutic Kantian intuition that by understanding this feeling "in the plural," as rooted in the sensibility of the various epochs and traditions, we condemn ourselves to fail to account for its universality, a solution to the converse problem should nonetheless be provided: how can the common feeling or sensibility presupposed by aesthetic judgment be understood as a natural endowment of the human being, directly connected to the human perceptive apparatus? Should we embrace a conceptual strategy that gives to us the universality of aesthetic judgment, and thus frees us from the prison of the traditions inhabited by the substantively thickened sensus communis, at the price of naturalizing the basis on which such universality rests? In the end, does this naturalization of the communicability of the feeling of pleasure not fall prey to that dream of Sancho Panza's on which Hume has written memorable pages, recently revisited by Stanley Cavell?[12]

In his essay "Of the Standard of Taste" Hume reports the anecdote narrated by Sancho to Don Quijote: two relatives of his, famous wine connoisseurs, had been summoned to give their opinion on the supposedly excellent wine from a big barrel to be offered on an important occasion. They both tasted the wine with gravity several times and then pronounced their verdict: yes, indeed it was an excellent wine, said the first, yet a slight leathery aftertaste could be detected. The second connoisseur agreed on the outstanding quality of the wine, but added that he could still detect an iron-type aftertaste. The attendants to the tasting were happy with the response, but mocked them for what they perceived as a conceited and exaggerated sophistication of their judgment and, last but not least, for their disagreement despite all their affectedly refined tasting ability. Those who mocked them, however, in turn felt ridiculous and grossly incompetent when, much to their surprise, at the end of the party, an iron key with a leather string attached to it was found at the bottom of the barrel.

Sancho's dream is all too transparent. It expresses the aspiration that—without reaching the extreme of reducing aesthetic judgment to the application of concepts and principles—in the end there should be "something in the real world" on which the validity of aesthetic judgment too, no less than that of cognitive judgment, might rest. It would be unfair to Kant to accuse him of falling prey to Sancho's dream. Nevertheless, a trace of this "something in the real world," a philosophical equivalent of the iron key with the leather string, continues to affect Kant's theorizing on the universality of aesthetic judgment: this philosophical equivalent of the key is the idea of a spontaneous match between the perceptual apparatus, supposedly identical in all human beings, and the features of the beautiful object represented by our imagination[13]—a spontaneous match detected by sensus communis and on whose existence sensus communis grounds its anticipation of a universal agreement.

Cavell points out that the anecdote fails to report to us whether the by and large favorable judgment of the two connoisseurs in the end was indeed crowned by that famous universal consensus, which should set it apart from the pseudo-appraisal of any two incompetent people who merely pose as wine connoisseurs. We are however left with the disquieting realization that, not unlike Kant, we too yearn for two philosophical things in profound tension with one another—a tension that constitutes the most important limitation of the second strategy for conceiving of sensus communis. For, on the one hand, we wish that the aesthetic critic *not* be in a position, like the logician, to *force us* to agree with his conclusion under penalty of being legitimately accusable of irrationality, but, on the other hand, we also wish that critics not be *hostage* of the history of taste qua ultimate validator of their judgment. We rather want the critic to be someone who *makes* the history of taste through the exceptional perspicuity of his judgments. The Kantian strategy of naturalizing sensus communis leaves us with the unfinished task of reconciling this tension.

At this juncture a third alternative can be introduced, which remains compatible with the Kantian overall perspective, but that enables us to articulate a notion of sensus communis less naturalistic yet not reducible to the Gadamerian concept of a tradition or to the phenomenological notion of *Lebenswelt* and that still gives us a plausible shared bedrock on which to rest the exemplary universalism of aesthetic judgment. If we interrogate the *Critique of the Power of Judgment* on the subject of the true nature of aesthetic pleasure—which after all *is* the crucial notion, given that the universality of aesthetic judgment depends on a shared way of feeling pleasure and aversion—we can find passages wherefrom an entirely different tonality emerges than the naturalization of aesthetic pleasure suggested by paragraphs 20 and 21. One of the most interesting formulations in this sense is provided in § 23, where Kant compares the pleasure connected with exposure to the beautiful and the pleasure connected with the feeling of the sublime.

Both kinds of pleasure presuppose a certain disinterestedness, both are connected with reflective and not with determinant judgment, and, furthermore, both in the case of the beautiful and in the case of the sublime concepts do somehow enter the scene without being able, however, of bringing judgment to "closure." Finally, both the judgment about the beautiful and that about the sublime operate in close connection with the faculty of the imagination and are singular judgments that aspire to universality, albeit to a universality resting on a feeling rather than a concept. Several differences set them apart, however, one of which is of particular interest for us in that it concerns the feeling of pleasure bound up with our coming into contact with the object of our judgment. While the pleasure linked with the sublime derives from the sudden release of a tension related to the bridling or reining in of vital forces, the pleasure linked with the beautiful always affords us a sense, as Kant puts it, of the promotion, affirmation, or enhancement of life (*Beförderung des Lebens*).[14]

Here we reach a philosophical bifurcation whence a different strategy departs, according to which the pleasure connected with, and induced by, every aesthetic experience does not solely consist of the gratification derivable from the reciprocal interplay of the imagination and the understanding, cannot be reduced to a by-product of a sort of preestablished harmony between nature and the physiology of the human perceptive apparatus, but unfolds on the different plane of a reflection on "the human"—the "peculiarly human" as that level which can neither be reduced to the plasticity of culture nor anchored in a naturalistically understood facticity.

Every human being is mortal, has a body, lives in a context that provides her with the symbolic means for articulating her own intentionality, rich or limited, traditional or innovative as it might be, depending on the constraints of the context and the human actor's own creative capacities. One's own life is for each human being a temporal lapse within which he may make use, at least in the "embodied" mode, of the capacity to create meaning with which we enter the world. In her shaping, to a greater or lesser extent, the circumstances of her life and infusing meaning into her actions, each human being cannot but experience directly—no matter the historical and cultural coordinates within which she lives—what it means for her own life as a whole, with the whole web of projects and meanings that constitute it, to be promoted, affirmed, or enhanced or, on the contrary, to be mortified or frustrated: in one word what it means for her life to flourish or to stagnate.

Moving further along the line of this third strategy for reconstructing sensus communis, what Kant used to call the feeling of the "promotion of life" can be understood in terms of *self-realization* or *progress in self-realization* or progress toward an *authentic* relation with oneself, where the expression "authentic relation of the self with itself" designates an optimal congruence of an identity with itself. Considered from this vantage point, the well-formed work of art arouses a pleasure of which we can expect that it be universally shareable insofar as it evokes the flourishing of a human life: the beauty of the work of art is experienced and "understood" on the basis of our shared intuitive feeling, irreducible to a checklist of concepts or features, that a human life is flourishing.

Let us return now to sensus communis. The sought-for notion of sensus communis, alternative to both the Kantian official "naturalistic" version of sensus communis and the hermeneutic thickening of sensus communis as a common sense equated to tradition and lifeworld, consists of this universal capacity to sense the flourishing of human life and what favors it. Such a notion is then consistent with other twentieth-century accounts of the nexus of pleasure and aesthetic experience—for example, Heidegger's idea of world disclosure, Dewey's concept of experience, Danto's notion of the "transfiguration of the commonplace."

Sensus communis revisited is then this wisdom concerning the flourishing of human life, a wisdom that can be further spelled out in terms of a series of dimensions of the realization or flourishing of an identity that draws on a vocabulary located somehow "before" or "underneath" the differentiation of cultures. My project is not to reconstruct an ontological doctrine with an anthropological coloring; it is rather the effort to reconstruct intuitions located in a space equi-accessible from the plurality of existing cultures, a space whose existence cannot be taken for granted but, on the contrary, must be proven by exploring tentatively, as though probing around with a cane.

An example of the kind of the precultural, yet non-natural, intuitions that I have in mind comes from a mental experiment devised by Nozick.[15] Imagine two life courses A and B, hypothetically characterized by an equal amount of happiness, whatever our definition of happiness might be. Let the only relevant difference be the temporal distribution of this equal amount of happiness. Within life course A the amount of happiness we are destined to enjoy is concentrated by and large within the first quarter of our life, then a small amount is located in the following quarter, and the tiny fractions left are distributed across the rest of life, with a long final segment lived in total absence of happiness. Within life course B, instead, the same amount of happiness is evenly distributed across the whole life cycle, with a modest increase toward the end. Which of these two life courses would we rather choose? If we have few doubts in choosing the second alternative, this indicates that we possess intuitions concerning what is good for a human life and the nature of human flourishing that are independent of the culture within which we are immersed, even though we could not even begin to *articulate* these intuitions without drawing on some linguistically and historically situated cultural heritage. Elsewhere I have tried to reconstruct, on the basis of an extensive revisitation of psychoanalytic theory, the dimensions that play a constitutive role for our notion of a fulfilled identity.[16]

Although the psychoanalytic vocabulary is but one of many vocabularies available for the purpose of spelling out what it might mean for an individual human being to flourish or attain authenticity, it is certainly one of the richest and differentiated ones. It suggests the salience of four fundamental dimensions of the authenticity, well-being, or fulfillment of an individual identity: *coherence, vitality, depth,* and *maturity.* On these dimensions a significant convergence can be found on the part of many authors who for the rest openly and deeply disagree on many essential aspects of their approaches.

Coherence includes moments of cohesion, continuity, and demarcation. No human life, in any culture, can be understood as flourishing if it does not have a modicum of cohesion around a theme, a recognizable project, even if it were the postmodern project of pure nomadism, if it does not have a minimal continuity, understood as narratability of its constitutive episodes, and without a however minimal demarcation from what is other.

Vitality includes more specific aspects, such as the perception of one's own self as *worthy of love and esteem,* the *capacity to enjoy life* and to develop an *emotional interest* in it, at the opposite of which we find attitudes of apathy and detachment. Vitality includes also an immediate sense of *self-presence,* whose opposite is constituted by a sense of futility and of being "out of place," and finally includes a perception of one's own self as spontaneous and real, as opposed to conceited or false. There is no human life that we can perceive as flourishing if our self-representation is accompanied by a sense of *indignity or shame* and we perceive our self as *phony* and *empty.*

In its most general sense the dimension of *depth* designates a person's capacity to have access to her own psychic dynamisms and to reflect such awareness in the construction of her identity. We can conceive of it in cognitive terms as *self-knowledge* or *self-reflection* or, in a practical vein, as *autonomy.* The intuition captured by this dimension is that no human life can be considered to be flourishing if the person fails to show a modicum of self-awareness or if the commitments he enters are not autonomously posited.[17]

Finally, a person who lives a fulfilled life possesses to some extent a quality of *maturity* understood, in general, as the ability and willingness to come to terms with the facticity of the natural and social world, as well as of the internal world, without thereby compromising one's coherence and vitality—without becoming another. More specifically, maturity can be understood as the capacity to distinguish between one's own representations, projections, or wishes and reality "as it is" or, better said, as it appears to those who interact with us and to unconcerned third parties; as the capacity to tame one's own fantasies of omnipotence, to tolerate the inevitable ambivalence of human motives, to exert flexibility in carrying out one's projects in the world, and to come to terms emotionally with the fact of one's finiteness. Also in this case, the basic intuition, located at a topographical point where culture has not yet set in but we have left immediate naturality, is that no fulfilled human life is possible unless we develop a solid sense of the distinction between the external world and one's own fantasies, wishes, and volitions.

To the extent that we consider plausible that these intuitions may not be inconsistent with cultures other than our own, we can make sense of how a judgment that does not rely on principles or concepts, and communicates something about the conduciveness of an object, an action, a symbolic whole to enhance and further our life, could possibly claim universality.

It may legitimately claim universality by appealing to a layer of intuitions that we have reason to consider accessible from a plurality of perspectives insofar as these intuitions are linked with the universal human experience, along with mortality and embodiment, of the flourishing or stagnating of one's own life. It is the task of a philosophical theory of sensus communis to reconstruct these intuitions as completely as possible.

This reformulation, denaturalized but not culturally thickened, of the notion of sensus communis is perfectly compatible with the framework underlying the *Critique of the Power of Judgment* and finds indirect confirmation in several *loci* inside it. For example, in § 49 Kant contrasts the truly beautiful works of art, animated by genius and capable of arousing an aesthetic experience in us, and those other artworks that he calls *without spirit* or *geistlos,* which neither engage nor enthuse us even though "one finds nothing in them to criticize as far as taste is concerned."[18] It is hard to understand how, from the standpoint of his "explicit theory" of sensus communis, developed in paragraphs 20, 21 and 40, an object could exist—in this case a work of art—whose representation does satisfy the requirement of spontaneously matching with our cognitive faculties ("one finds nothing in them to criticize" from an aesthetic angle) and yet fails to arouse that feeling of the *Beförderung des Lebens* with which aesthetic pleasure is by definition equated. In order to make sense of this phenomenon we need to move to a more complex and differentiated picture than the one constituted by a naturalization of sensus communis qua anticipation of a match between perception and world. We need to understand sensus communis as the capacity to mentally anticipate the potential, inherent in an object, to enrich, enhance, or otherwise make the life of human beings flourish, in order for us to make sense of how "works of *art* without spirit" could possibly exist.

This is one of the directions in which a reconstruction of the Kantian notion of sensus communis in the light of a philosophical agenda rooted in our own time could go.

The Judgment Paradigm and Political Philosophy

All that has been said thus far could be taken as an abstract claim to the effect that philosophers, and political philosophers in particular, if and to the extent that they wish to truly reconcile pluralism and universalism, had better reconfigure their understanding of central normative notions such as truth, justice, obligation, freedom, political justification and the like in terms of a model of exemplary normativity that draws on Kant's concept of reflective judgment. I think that more than that can be said concerning the relevance of Kant's *Critique of the Power of Judgment* for the contemporary political philosopher and theorist. For the gist of this model of normativity can be found to *already be somehow at work* in the conceptions of justice and political justification propounded by several leading figures of political philosophy of liberal orientation. I would not be surprised if a similar relevance of the judgment paradigm—and its key notion of reflective judgment—would emerge from a reconstruction of the notions of freedom, legitimation, obligation, and representation.

Consider the history of political philosophy during the last third of the past century. Underlying the contributions of authors such as Rawls, Habermas, Dworkin, Ackerman we can discern a decline—slow, hesitant, and intermittently fraught with relapses to older schemes—of the once prevailing paradigm of justice, centered on principles and the normativity of determinant judgment, and the beginning of a reorganization of their conceptions of justice and, more generally, of normative validity around the judgment paradigm of *exemplary* universalism.

In the case of Rawls such transition manifested itself in the distance that separates *A Theory of Justice* from *Political Liberalism*. While deliberation in the original position is thought of as taking place in terms of rational choice—and thus within the framework of the traditional universalism of determinant judgment—within *Political Liberalism* the justification of a fair scheme of constitutional essentials, capable of ensuring the fair and stable cooperation of free and equal citizens who embrace rival conceptions of the good, rests on the claim to being "reasonable," as distinct from "rational." The transition from rational choice to public reason as the organon for justifying normativity in the political realm signals a deeper seated shift toward the judgment paradigm, which becomes apparent as soon as we address the question "What kind of normativity is involved in the operation of public reason?" or "What is the normativity of the reasonable?" But I will leave this development aside, for the moment, because it will be investigated more in detail in chapter 3. There it will be argued that in the end we cannot make sense of the being "more reasonable" of a view of justice, of a policy proposal, of a certain constitutional essential with respect to another competing view, proposal, or constitutional essential without at some point invoking the notion that what is "most reasonable" exerts influence on us by virtue of who we are, of our self-conception, namely, through the force of the exemplary.

And in order to unpack the peculiar normativity of the reasonable—which cannot be the normativity of consequences drawn from principles, on penalty of reducing public reason to a pale replica of practical reason—the most useful paradigm is, once again, not the one associated with the application of principles to facts of the matter but rather the notion of normativity associated with the operation of reflective judgment in the service of the flourishing of an identity.

For all its realist emphasis on the tracking of "the one right answer," one model of normativity, within contemporary legal and political philosophy, that is *explicitly* based on this methodological analogy with aesthetic judgment is Dworkin's legal hermeneutics. When Dworkin speaks of the process of adjudication in constitutional law as a process in which the judge, operating like a novelist of serial installments, tries to "make the most" of the work of his predecessors and to find the solution that "makes the most" of the legal, jurisprudential, and more broadly political heritage of his legal community, there he is making use of a notion of normative validity that projects a universalistic cogency without relying on subsumption—a notion in the light of which the *exemplary,* the element that fits best and *makes the most* of a preexisting symbolic structure, becomes synonymous with *the most appropriate.*[19] The normative force of the best interpretation is not a force originating in a single principle—which would make judicial interpretation superfluous relative to the practical reason that captures and applies such principle—but rather a force that exerts influence on us by virtue of how we understand ourselves, namely, the force of the exemplary.

Other major examples of authors who have been slowly moving in the direction of rethinking normative validity in ways that are more receptive to the judgment paradigm are Bruce Ackerman and Jürgen Habermas. Ackerman started out with a notion of political justification and normative validity based on an abstract scheme of distributive justice—a conversation over the distribution of initial endowments constrained by the principles of rationality, consistency, and neutrality as presented in *Social Justice in the Liberal State*—but in the two volumes of *We the People* thus far published we can observe an interesting shift of perspective.[20] While the normative acceptability of ordinary law can be justified in terms of its consistency with the more encompassing higher law, the acceptability of the framing and subsequent transformation of a constitution is entirely a matter of a situated judgment, which cannot but be reflective.[21] The object of this judgment is ultimately whether and to what extent the framing, the conservation, or the modification of the constitution is congruent with the fullest realization of a specific political identity, that of "we the People." In *Transformations* Ackerman develops an entirely identity- and judgment-based justification of his own proposal for a *Popular Sovereignty Initiative*, aimed at supplementing the traditional avenues for constitutional reform provided by article 5 with a new process initiated by the presidency and completed by popular approval at two consecutive presidential elections. The rationale is entirely couched in judgment terms, as the bringing to fruition of a process of affirmation of a federal identity, where each citizen has equal influence on the ratification of higher law regardle ss of the state in which she lives and the last residues of state-bound processes of will formation (still preserved in the equal number of senators allotted to each state) are eventually eliminated.

Furthermore, in Ackerman's reconstruction of the three fundamental junctures of constitutional change in the history of the United States—Founding, Reconstruction, and New Deal—we observe time and again the occurrence of a kind of "normative bootstrapping," namely, the establishing of the normative validity of a constitutional provision on the basis of a "rule of recognition" created simultaneously with the provision to be enacted.

This kind of radically reflexive self-grounding—indeed a Münchausen-like normative bootstrapping—really constitutes the backbone of Ackerman's book and, though Ackerman never addresses the analogy between constitutional innovation and artistic innovation, lies within the space of judgment. Innovators, whether artistic or constitutional, move precisely in that space. In fact, while innovators cannot be understood to be under a normative obligation to transform the inherited framework, political or artistic, no one can claim that their innovations are the mere products of arbitrary stylistic or political preference either. Innovations of consequence are regarded not as the expression of idiosyncratic preferences but rather as providing for an enlarging and deepening of our understanding of the world and of ourselves or, in a different terminology, as being *world disclosing*. The New Deal, according to this reading, was neither an implication of the original constitutional text nor the political whim of a transient majority: it was a political world-disclosing innovation made possible by the Constitution.

The transition toward the judgment paradigm is more complicated in Habermas's conception of deliberative democracy, due to the simultaneous presence of two motifs not easily reconcilable. According to the cooriginality thesis articulated in *Between Facts and Norms,* normativity—the normativity of rights or the normativity of a constitution—is the product of a democratic will formed in accordance with certain self-imposed limits. The normativity embedded in the rule of law then, for example, should not be construed as something that *constrains* the democratic will of citizens but rather as an *explication* of what *democratic self-legislation* is all about, namely, deliberation in the light of rights accorded one another by free and equal citizens.[22] But then, when it comes to the problem of justifying how this normativity, articulated in the form of positive higher law, can be binding also on *subsequent* generations of citizens who by no means partook of the initial discursive and reciprocal granting of rights, the two divergent strands of thought present in Habermas's work become visible. *Discourse,* as we know, and its principle "D," are the shorthand terms for a whole set of idealized conditions that provide the sought-for justification. But then, on the one hand, certain parts of Habermas's work suggest that "D" be understood as a quasi-transcendental principle, anchored in universal-pragmatic structures of language that bypass the parochialism of life forms[23]—a principle that peoples in the process of designing or transforming their constitutions ignore at their own peril. On the other hand, elsewhere Habermas seems to suggest that the principle of discourse and the discursive view of normativity are best understood as ways of capturing the normative core of the communal identity of peoples living within the modern life form, namely, as the most authentic philosophical rendition of that modern ethos of equal respect that each modern people, by virtue of its own unique attempt to fulfill its own version of the modern identity, tries to institutionalize in a code of "laws of lawmaking." One could build two competing interpretations of Habermas's political philosophy (a more traditional, almost foundationalist one and a radically identity-based, but still "discursive," one) depending on the source to which one traces the cogency of principle "D" as a test of discursive generalization.[24] I find the second interpretation more consonant with the postmetaphysical intentions of Habermas's conception of validity. Yet, if the authority of the constitution cannot be anchored in anything transcending the political identity of the people; if the normative finds its ultimate source in a certain self-interpretation of the modern Western identity, then by virtue of what should that normativity exert a cogency beyond its context of origin? Why should we expect that normative ideas, rights, the very notion of constitutionalism should bear any significance for political communities differently situated? If we want to avoid the quasi-foundationalist anchoring of rights and the rule of law in the principle of discourse, and of the principle of discourse in the universal pragmatic structures of language, and if we want at the same time to salvage a sense in which constitutional democracy, rights, and the rule of law might have an inherent normative valence, and not be just a mere redescription of "the way we do things here," this valence should be understood, once again, as resting on the *force of authentic exemplarity*—i.e., on something similar, though by no means identical, to the capacity possessed by the exemplary work of art to induce an aesthetic experience beyond the bounds of its context of origin without relying on external principles or laws.[25]

This silent yet highly consequential reorganization of major conceptions of normative validity, justice, and political justification around a new paradigm of judgment, however, is fraught with tensions and relapses into the old model of modern universalism that I have discussed elsewhere.[26] It is possible, however, to already discern the contours of a new view of justice entirely based on judgment. I have tried to speculate on what such a conception of justice could look like and I'll conclude with a few remarks on this point. The guiding idea is that whenever two parties come to a conflict, the adjudicating function that in traditional, principle-based views of justice was played by context-transcendent and thus now problematic standards can be played by the requirements of the flourishing of the new communal identity formed at the intersection of the conflicting ones. We know from Davidson, Gadamer, Putnam, and Williams that the notion of total incommensurability makes no sense: for two cultures, identities, or traditions to perceive themselves as being in conflict they have to have some point in common. The key idea of a judgment view of justice is to identify that locus of intersection in order to have it play the role of a vantage point from which we can counterfactually envisage an identity encompassing the conflicting ones. Then this counterfactual identity can be treated like an identity in its own right whose own exemplary fulfillment—which in the case of *moral* judgment comes to coincide with a counterfactual anticipation of the realization of humankind—does all the work that traditional views of justice are supposed to do. It orders the conflicting claims on a scale of justifiability, for one thing, and helps us set legitimate limits to the pursuit of certain conceptions of the good. And it does so by relying not on general principles, which we would no longer know how to vindicate across cultural difference, but on the kind of self-contained, reflective, exemplary authenticity of a larger identity topographically located before the bifurcation of the conflicting parties.

This view allows us to conceive of the universalism of justice as originating in an *oriented reflective judgment* on the requisites of the fulfillment of a superordinate identity—a reflective judgment oriented in this case not simply by the dimensions of the fulfillment of identities in general but also by the modern ideal of *equal respect*—and to conceive of the moral point of view as the vantage point of the fulfillment of humanity, taken as the most inclusive imaginable identity, which includes all other human identities, contending or not. The fulfillment of humanity is not a formula, an abstract principle of reciprocity or consistency, but a kind of "concrete universal" bound up with substantive presuppositions that change over time, and that is why the judgment as to which solution to a practical conflict best serves its fulfillment is a *situated* yet universalistic reflective judgment.

Finally, the judgment paradigm allows for a reflexive validation of itself. We can draw on an insight embedded in Rawls's essay on Kantian constructivism, where he states that what ultimately justifies justice as fairness or any other political conception of justice "is not its being true to an order antecedent to and given to us, but its congruence with our deeper understanding of ourselves and our aspirations, and our realization that, given our history and the traditions embedded in our public life, it is the most reasonable doctrine for us."[27] Borrowing from this already judgment-based understanding of the justness of justice as fairness, we can develop an argument, based on a reconstruction of the normative core of our modern identity, to the effect that the notion of normativity inherent in the judgment paradigm is the most congruent with what, given our own history—a history conceived as the history of the different views of normativity embraced by us—we have become from a philosophical point of view. In this grounding the appeal of the judgment paradigm on nothing other than its exemplary congruence with our own philosophical identity, and on its potential for bringing this identity more in line with itself, lies a vindication of the insight into the self-contained, self-referential, ultimately exemplary nature of normativity that underlies Kant's *Critique of the Power of Judgment.*

That *tertium datur*—that a third, and not merely procedural, option between the universalism of principle and the mere reconstruction of subjectivity-shaping local frameworks into which validity remains imprisoned is available: this is the enduring lesson that philosophers and political theorists of the twenty-first century can still draw from the *Critique of the Power of Judgment.*

2 *Making Sense of the Exemplary*

One of the most interesting contributions to an understanding of the legacy and import of the *Critique of the Power of Judgment* is Hannah Arendt's doctrine of judgment. For the purpose of further exploring the potential of the paradigm of judgment, it is essential to come to terms with her version of the notion of *exemplary* validity. In this chapter I begin with a brief reconstruction of the role of judgment in Arendt's thought and of the main points of her theory of judgment, then will discuss that which in my opinion remains a problematic area, and will conclude with some tentative considerations on a possible way of solving the difficulties raised by Arendt's account.

"The Most Political of Man's Mental Abilities"

For Hannah Arendt, judgment, "the most political of man's mental abilities,"[1] is the most elusive and yet the most crucial of the human faculties.

Action would be impossible without judgment, but so would reflection in general. Yet judgment—understood by her in a broader sense as the "ability to tell right from wrong, beautiful from ugly"[2]—is elusive in that it lacks the strict criteria of validity that apply to other human abilities. While thinking "can be assessed in terms of consistency, logic, soundness, and coherence" and willing can be appraised "by its resoluteness or the capacity to determine our actions," judgment shares some of these features but is not exhausted by any of them: "in judgment we look not only for soundness or consistency, but also for discrimination, discernment, imagination, sympathy, detachment, impartiality and integrity."[3] Arendt, as we know, never had the possibility of fully developing her theory of judgment and the excerpts available to us do not add up to a unified and coherent statement but rather seem to proceed from two different and, as some commentators underscore, incompatible perspectives. While in "Freedom and Politics," "The Crisis in Culture," and "Truth and Politics"[4] Arendt explores the relation between judgment and *action*—that is, judgment as guidance for the action of human beings who "can act as political beings because they can enter into the potential standpoints of others" and "can share the world with others through judging what is held in common"[5]—in *The Life of the Mind* and in "Thinking and Moral Considerations"[6] she focuses on the inner workings of judgment as a mental faculty related to *thinking* and to *willing,* on judgment as bound up primarily with the standpoint of a spectator who tries to understand the meaning of events of the past.[7] Some commentators have pointed out that for Arendt judgment appears to have a direct relevance for human action only at exceptional times of crisis, when the current standards and mainstream morality provide no guidance.[8] Others maintain that in the end the two models of judgment, underlying which one can detect the tension between the Aristotelian view of *phronesis* and the Kantian theory of aesthetic judgment, come together in Arendt's view of the actor as capable somehow of taking the standpoint of the spectator or the critic as well. Writes Arendt:

the public realm is constituted by the critics and the spectators, not by the actors or the makers. And this critic and spectator sits in every actor and fabricator; without this critical, judging faculty the doer or maker would be so isolated from the spectator that he would not even be perceived. . . . He [the spectator] does not share the faculty of genius, originality, with the maker or the faculty of novelty with the actor; the faculty they have in common is the faculty of judgment.[9]

There seem thus to exist two different relations of judgment to the *vita activa*. On the first interpretation, judgment is relevant at times of crisis, "when the chips are down." On the second, judgment is relevant all the time, through the capacity of actors to have access to an "enlarged mentality."

Much has been written also on the tension that Arendt imports into her view of judgment by subscribing first to the Aristotelian approach to judgment in terms of *phronesis* (where judgment is the ability of the few *phronimoi* and is bound to the horizon of the substantive ethical life of the polis) and subsequently to the Kantian doctrine of judgment (according to which *everyone* is endowed more or less with judgment, and judgment appeals to a sensus communis quite distinct from the common sense typical of a concrete community).[10] The two perspectives, however, appear to be less far apart than one may suppose and are certainly not mutually inconsistent.

Consider the following. Nowhere does Aristotle set limits on the number of those who can share phronesis, and, on the other hand, the capacity for aesthetic judgment is certainly not possessed by all human beings to the same extent. It needs a cultivation that not everybody can be willing or able to pursue. A number of similarities also exist between phronesis and judgment, which suggests that Aristotle and Kant were focusing on the same faculty from different angles and vocabularies. First, in contrast with *techne,* which remains external to the personality of the expert, *phronesis,* just as taste, can neither be learned through a method nor forgotten. Phronesis and taste can only be cultivated through exposure to *exemplary* cases of good judgment or to someone already endowed with superior ability in this respect. Second, differently than with *episteme,* and again in analogy to taste, the conclusions suggested by phronesis cannot be demonstrated but only shown and made plausible. As in the case of judgment, in the case of phronesis as well we cannot compel but only "woo" the consensus of others. Third, contrary to *sophia,* which is concerned with universal truths, phronesis focuses on particular courses of action, just as taste focuses on particular works of art.

Another issue that has elicited interest among the interpreters of Arendt's theory of judgment is the relation of judgment to knowledge, rationality, and argumentation. Habermas has argued that "an antiquated concept of theoretical knowledge that is based on ultimate insights and certainties keeps Arendt from comprehending the process of reaching agreement about practical questions as *rational discourse.*"[11] Wellmer has accused

Arendt of failing to see the connection between judgment and argumentation, thereby creating a "mythology of judgment" whose main article of faith is the existence of a *self-standing* faculty of judgment. According to Wellmer, to the contrary, the faculty of judgment "is not an addition to, but rather an expression of what we might call the faculty of discursive rationality" and is "inexplicable without some internal relationship to an ability to argue and deliberate well." [12] In this case I think that Arendt's view needs to be defended. Indeed, it is her view of judgment as a faculty in its own right that provides insight into the way in which argumentation functions and produces results that we regard as valid. While in fact one can agree with Wellmer that there must be some connection between judgment and the ability to argue and deliberate well, this connection becomes relevant only if we evaluate judgments from a third-person standpoint. On the other hand, when we are immersed in the deliberative context from the standpoint of the participant, we certainly cannot invoke, as a justification for our choice, the rationality of a consensus not yet formed. We have to choose one among the alternatives at hand on some basis other than an as yet nonexistent consensus—a consensus that indeed we will contribute to generating through our act of choice. The strength of Arendt's position, in my opinion, lies precisely in understanding the correctness or validity of such choice as being based on *judgment* and thus on postulating the *autonomy* of judgment. Good arguments and good reasons are recognized as such in unconstrained dialogue because they rest on sound judgment, not the other way around. This last remark leads me to the relation of judgment to its own specific form of validity.

Judgment, Imagination, and the Enlarged Mentality

To understand Arendt's view of the workings of judgment requires that we understand the special role played by *communication* and *imagination* within it. While unbiased, impartial determinant judgment requires no communication but merely insight into principles, in reflective judgment the terms *impartiality* and *enlargement of the mind* are strictly interwoven. *Impartiality*—broadly understood as the *not-merely-subjective* quality of our judgments—"is obtained by taking the viewpoints of others into account." [13] Rather than being "the result of some higher standpoint that would actually settle the dispute by being altogether above the melée" (42),

impartiality in reflective judgment is linked, according to Arendt's interpretation of Kant, with one's ability "to 'enlarge' one's own thought so
as to take into account the thoughts of others" (42–43). In her *Lecture
Seven* Arendt reminds us that such ability is not to be understood as a kind
of empathy writ large by means of which one is able to find out "what actually goes on in the minds of all others." Instead, the ability to enlarge
one's thought is to be understood as the result of a. the capacity to abstract "from the limitations that contingently attach to our own judgment"
(among which chiefly features self-interest) and b. the capacity to assume
the standpoint of more than one, and as many as possible, significantly situated others. In a move reminiscent of Rousseau's indictment of *amour
propre* and extolling of authenticity, the impartiality or validity of judgment
is understood as a function of the actor's ability to extricate herself from
her concern for her good standing before the other actors' eyes and, at the
same time, as a function of the actor's ability to take into account a larger
number of significantly situated others. There is no tension between these
two requirements. For one can be *disinterested* about the others' opinion of
her and yet not *uninterested* in their standpoint.

On Arendt's view, then, the validity or impartiality of our purely reflective judgments does not depend on hitting on the right principle or on
"getting it right." For there is no such thing as an overarching principle or
a universal under which to subsume both one's own and the other's competing standpoints. Valid, then, are those judgments that are *as inclusive as
possible* of all competing standpoints and are thus as "general" as possible
while remaining "closely connected with particulars"—i.e., while remaining linked with "the particular conditions of the standpoints one has to go
through in order to arrive at one's own 'general standpoint'" (44). Here is
the juncture at which *communication* enters the picture of judgment. As
Arendt puts it, "the condition *sine qua non* for the existence of beautiful
objects [as opposed to mere pleasure-inducing objects—about which *non
est disputandum*] is *communicability;* the judgment of the spectator creates
the space without which no such object could appear at all" (63).

The nonsubjective or impartial element in judgment about beauty, in
other words, lies in its "intersubjectivity"—a quality inherent in Arendt's
view of *thinking,* also called by her "the two-in-one of the soundless dialogue."[14] *Communicability,* as distinct from intersubjectivity, rests on the
peculiar relation of the object of judgment to community and sensus communis. In paragraph 40 of Kant's *Critique of the Power of Judgment,* sensus

communis is said to include "the idea of a *communal* sense, i.e., a faculty for judging that in its reflection takes account (*a priori*) of everyone else's way of representing in thought, in order *as it were* to hold its judgment up to human reason as a whole."[15] The idea of an enlarged mentality or broad-minded way of thinking is part and parcel of this sensus communis, along with the other two maxims—"Think for oneself" and "Think consistently."

Another facet of the idea, presented in chapter 1, according to which sensus communis cannot be understood as synonymous with what happens to be believed in the community to which the actor belongs is here highlighted. The agreement of others, courted or "wooed" in rendering one's judgment, is not the agreement of those who belong in a given community, but the agreement of all those who are capable of taking the enlarged standpoint. As Beiner has noted, "the predominant concern here is with a world, or a community of world citizens, to whom we appeal even more urgently than we do to those immediately around us."[16] Arendt underscores the role that this normative notion of humanity as a larger object of loyalty—an idea whose consequences for political philosophy and for the justification of human rights will be explored in chapter 6—has for Kant's understanding of the validity of judgment:

> It is by virtue of this idea of mankind, present in every single man, that men are human, and they can be called civilized or humane to the extent that this idea becomes the principle not only of their judgments but of their actions. It is at this point that actor and spectator become united. (75)

We have thus far discussed the role of communication in the workings of judgment. *Imagination* is relevant when it comes to understanding the solution given by Arendt to one of the problems she inherits from Kant. The problem is that judgment is, to use Kant's words, "the faculty of *thinking* the particular," but—adds Arendt—"to *think* means to generalize," hence judgment is "the faculty of mysteriously combining the particular and the general." How is this possible? Arendt's answer to this question draws on her reconstruction of Kant's own implicit answer. A judgment that unites a focus on particulars and yet a universal scope in its claim to validity is possible insofar as it appeals to *exemplary validity*. Exemplary validity represents an alternative way of understanding how it is that we are able to identify single objects as instances of a certain type of object, for instance, to identify the chairs in this room as specific instances of what we call a chair. One could account for the possibility of this act of judgment by invoking the equivalent of a Platonic idea or a Kantian schema. One could either postulate that each of us carries a kind of archetype of chairness in his mind and then identifies concrete instances of chairs by comparing them with the idea of a chair or, the other way around, one could postulate that we form an abstract notion of chair by way of stripping our concrete experiences of chairs of all the singular factors. The *exemplary* form of valid judgment is reached, continues Arendt, in a third way: namely, we identify a given chair as such by matching the chair that we perceive with our image of some chair encountered in the past and judged to be the best possible one—the *exemplary* chair. Now, the point is that this exemplary chair "remains a particular that in its very particularity reveals the generality that otherwise could not be defined" (77). The exemplary enshrines the *typical* but remains distinct from the *normal,* if by that term we mean the statistically most frequent. In fact, it is more closely related to the exceptional and the extraordinary than the ordinary.

Now, a central role in validity so conceived is played by the *imagination.* For it is imagination—"the faculty of making present what is absent"—that evokes in our mind examples that might apply to our case. Imagination allows us to join together, under the different modalities of determinant and reflective judgment, particulars with general notions. It does so by means of providing schemata for cognition and *examples* for judgment (79–80). A schema, in the case of cognition, is "an image for a concept," a tangible instantiation of the concept. As far as *cognition* is concerned, points out Arendt,

> without a "schema" one can never recognize anything. When one says: "this table," the general "image" of table is present in one's mind, and one recognizes that "this" is a table, something that shares its qualities with many other such things though it is itself an individual, particular thing. If I recognize a house, this perceived house also includes how a house in general looks. (81)

But schemata are important not only for *perception* and *cognition.* They are crucial to *communication* as well. What "makes particulars *communicable* is a. that in perceiving a particular we have in the back of our minds a 'schema' whose 'shape' is characteristic of many such particulars *and* b. that this schematic shape is in the back of the minds of many different people" (83). In a different vocabulary, Arendt here shifts to the first of the two alternative strategies distinguished in chapter 1. She appears to follow Husserl's and Schutz's understanding of the dependency of communication on the constitutive role played by some kind of background or lifeworld shared by all participants.

To understand the role of imagination in cognition is important in order to highlight the problems raised by a certain analogy that Arendt wants to establish. In the *Critique of the Power of Judgment*, maintains Arendt, we find an analogy to the "schema": Kant accords examples *the same role* in judgments that the intuitions called schemata have for experience and cognition (84). This formulation, however, appears quite problematic. How can the role of examples be the same as that of schemata, given that in reflective judgment we find no relation of subsumption of a particular under a concept? Yet Arendt is quite explicit on this point, reiterated shortly thereafter when she states that "the example helps one *in the same way* in which the schema helped one to recognize the table as a table" (84). Knowing about Saint Francis and Achilles, in other words, allows me to identify the particular instances of human conduct that I am exposed to as good and courageous actions:

> When judging, one says spontaneously, without any derivation from general rules, "This man has courage." If one were a Greek, one would have "in the depths of one's mind" the example of Achilles. Imagination is again necessary: one must have Achilles present even though he certainly is absent. If we say of somebody that he is good, we have in the back of our minds the examples of Saint Francis or Jesus of Nazareth. (84)

Schemata and Examples: A Problematic Analogy

The analogy between schemata and examples somehow obscures what it should clarify. For the way in which my knowing about Achilles and Saint Francis—usually, as Arendt concedes, by having read or heard something about them, not by having experienced their deeds personally, and thus through a culturally sedimented, perhaps even stereotyped, image of both—allows me to say about a given action "This is a courageous action" cannot, strictly speaking, be *the same* as the way in which the schema of a table allows me to recognize this table as a table. The schema of a table helps me to recognize this table as a table because I recognize in this particular table all the distinctive traits of "tableness" contained in the schema. In other words, the schema helps me to bridge the diversity of the single concrete tables that I encounter by averting my attention from their idiosyncratic features and directing it to those features, invariable across contexts, that qualify them as tables.

None of this applies to the case of action. For actions are *interpretations* of doings. And while doings can be brought under the subsumption model, *actions* strictly speaking cannot. Like in the example of seeing a table, I can identify what somebody is *doing* as "running" via the application of some schema. Running, however, can amount to an act of courage as well as cowardice, and in order to determine whether it counts as the former or the latter examples do not guide us in the same way as schemes guide our judgment concerning doings or tables. My knowing about Achilles cannot help me to identify his "running" as an act of courage in the same way as my mental image of a running person—perhaps once again Achilles, this time considered under the aspect of his equally proverbial ability to run—can help me to identify the bodily movements of the actor as an instance of running.

To be more specific, two difficulties are raised by Arendt's account of judgment, and we shall consider them in turn. The first difficulty is that examples are usually open to questions in a way that schemata only at times of crisis are. Does Achilles really embody courage or a self-absorbed desire for aggrandizement in the context of a warrior society? Does Gauguin's sailing off to Polinesia count as an example of tragic dedication to one's self-chosen mission or of plain selfishness? People still debate what Madame Bovary is really supposed to exemplify. The point is that those attributions, and consequently what the example is an example of, depend on evaluations that are themselves of problematic validity and can by no means be taken for granted.[17]

This point can be illustrated most clearly if we consider how a reincarnated Eichmann, knowledgeable about Arendt's thesis of the banality of evil, might defend himself against the charge of thoughtlessness. Eichmann reincarnated could challenge the charge of thoughtlessness leveled against him precisely by invoking Arendt's account of judgment as it is formulated in the *Lectures on Kant's Political Philosophy*. Avoiding any reference to a morality of duty understood as the rigid application of inflexible rules, Eichmann would protest that in his conduct, in his unflinching carrying out of orders, we should see a supreme instance of *obedience*. "Obedience," Eichmann would contend, "is the virtue that, to the best of my judgment, I pursued and the standard by which my conduct should be judged. And obedience is a virtue with its place in our tradition. It also has its glorious and revered examples." The Achilles of obedience, the Jesus of Nazareth and the Saint Francis of obedience—to whose example Eichmann reincarnated could appeal—is Abraham. And Abraham is no Nazi, but an honorable man. "Abraham," would continue Eichmann, "was ordered by God to slay his only son Isaac, to sacrifice him. Abraham was prepared to do so, took his son to the place indicated by God, lied to his son, asked his son to carry the wood on which he would be burnt, and then, as *Genesis* tells us, "laid the wood in order, and bound Isaac his son, and laid him on the altar upon the wood" and then "stretched forth his hand, and took the knife to slay his son." [18] Only at that point the Lord stopped him and blessed him for having obeyed his voice. "Now my only fault," would conclude our reincarnated Eichmann, "is that no angel was sent to stop *me,* and that the contingencies of history have given those against whom I fought the power to pass a verdict on me. But really I am being nailed today for the same thing that Abraham is revered for: being prepared to do *anything* at the request of the highest authority that I recognize."

Against this line of defense Arendt would have to contend that what Abraham did was really *different* from what Eichmann did, but the burden of proof would be on her to show where the difference lies. Regardless of whether enough differences could be pointed out and the counterobjections of reincarnated Eichmann conclusively met—and I do believe that eventually this would be possible—the tenor of the dispute supports my point. Examples are by no means as fixed as schemata with respect to what they symbolize or to what they help us recognize or identify. To treat them as *the same* as schemata means to betray their *exemplary* nature, to turn the process of a "merely" reflective judgment into one that eventually leads to the closure of determinant judgment. For when people take Achilles as the epitome of courage, Saint Francis as the epitome of goodness, and Socrates as the epitome of a person living "the examined life" they address themselves not to their direct experience but to received images that work no differently from the stereotyped image of a table as a piece of furniture with four legs on which you eat your meals.

That, however, is the opposite of what reflective judgment is all about. Judgment begins where the analogy between examples and schemata breaks off. Judgment begins when the examples that we resort to are examples interpreted in an *autonomous* way. Hannah Arendt was not unaware of this aspect of judgment, as it is testified by the famous passage in which she mentions "the wind of thought." Here judgment, also called "the by-product of the liberating effect of thinking,"[19] is said to set in when the wind of thought has blown away the untenable crystallizations of received words and images.

The second difficulty incurred by Arendt's theory of judgment is that even when we have no reason to doubt that certain actions performed by Saint Francis exemplify goodness, our example by no means contains a number of necessary and sufficient traits that can be applied in the guise of a checklist to *another* doing in order establish whether it amunts to a good action. Examples rather provide us with *holistic images* that remains concrete. Our ability to judge thus cannot be equated with the ability to compare lists of discrete and isolated traits, but must be understood as the ability to identify a certain *unity of purpose,* a certain "point" underlying a temporally extended sequence of doings, as well as to grasp as many similarities as possible between the two contexts within which the exemplary and the given action took place.

The question whether two actions are the same is similar in some respects to the question whether two texts are the same. Both actions and texts have a *surface* structure (constituted respectively by the series of the sentences that make up the text and by the series of bodily movements of which the observable aspect of the action consists) and a *deep* structure, constituted by the meanings carried by the elements of the surface structure and by the relation that such meanings entertain with relevant features of the context. Thus the answer to the question "Under which conditions are two texts or two actions the same?" cannot be that two texts or two actions are the same when all the surface sentences or the bodily movements are the same. Changing one sentence obviously does not give me the right to publish under my name the entire text of *Remembrance of Things Past.* Nor would the omission of a chapter do, perhaps not even a skillful paraphrase of the whole text. On the other hand, in the text of the draft of a statute, even the change of one word within one sentence, let alone the omission of an entire clause, would be a legitimate basis for denying that the old and the new text are the same.

The same holds in the case of action. The bodily movements involved in my taking part in a funeral, while remaining exactly the same, may amount to an act of courage if it is the funeral of a political opponent of a totalitarian regime or to an act of coward acquiescence if it is the funeral of a mafia boss ruling over a territory in which I serve as a public official. In sum, the impossibility of providing a priori and external criteria for the self-sameness of texts and actions supports the idea that we understand texts and actions as symbolic wholes with an identity of their own.

Translations provide another analogy on the basis of which it is possible to account for how we judge actions. Good judgment in translation depends on knowing as much as possible of the original and the target language. In evaluating action, good judgment depends on knowing as much as possible about the two contexts within which the exemplary and the given actions acquire their meaning. Poor judgment is based on applying received stereotypes to stereotyped reading of doings. Also, as it happens with translations, sometimes we find instances of actions for which no exemplary archetypes can be readily brought to mind. Good judgment then amounts to the ability to recognize the *originality* of action, the element of newness that makes of the action of Saint Francis a truly exemplary one. In such a case *exemplary* validity is best understood in terms of *creating* an example rather than *applying* an example—a difference that is captured by Kant's distinction, recalled by Arendt, between "subsuming under a concept" and "bringing to a concept." Identifying an action as exemplary in the latter sense means to "bring to a concept" the uniqueness or particularity of it.

For instance, Freud offers a new interpretation of the meaning of Michelangelo's Moses by reinterpreting the action represented by the sculpture. While traditional interpreters had understood Moses to be calming himself down after an outburst of rage against the corruption of his people, Freud suggests that the originality of the sculpture consists in representing a *different* action: for Freud, Moses is about to spring up in rage but actually forces himself to remain seated and calm. Thus Moses' action exemplifies repression in a positive sense, the kind of repression of impulse without which no culture could exist.

In sum, both these difficulties indicate that judgment is bound up with the *interpretation* of action, and consequently good judgment is linked with the question concerning which interpretation is better.

Exemplarity Reconstructed

As the preceding discussion suggests, exemplary validity, in the context of Arendt's theory of judgment, is the name for a problem, not for a solution. The problem of accounting for the specific form of validity of pure reflective judgment—a form of validity that carries the promise of delivering us from the curse of limited commensurability—is twofold: 1. how is the validity of our interpretations of action to be understood? 2. how can judgments that are not demonstrable exert an influence beyond their context of origin, how can they be compelling? In the remaining section of this chapter some considerations will be offered on a possible strategy for answering these questions, a strategy that—just as my reconstruction of sensus communis was not literally the same as Kant's but still largely compatible with his intent—remains within the conceptual orbit of Arendt's account of judgment, though not necessarily faithful to all its details.

The question concerning the validity of our interpretation of action has a Janus face, whose two sides correspond to the two difficulties incurred by Arendt's view of exemplary validity. On the one hand, to account for the validity of an interpretation requires that we account for the appropriateness of our understanding of (always contestable) examples of courage, nobility, baseness, or pusillanimousness. On the other hand, we need to account for the appropriateness of our interpretation of the single actions that we happen to be exposed to.

As far as the interpretation of our models is concerned, we should dispel the impression that the interpretation of *action* is at stake. None of us contemporaries ever witnessed the actions of Achilles, Jesus of Nazareth, or Saint Francis and no one at all ever witnessed the conduct of Madame Bovary. We are exposed to *texts,* written or oral, that tell us about these examples. Thus the question of what our examples really exemplify is closely related to the question of which interpretation of the relevant texts is to be considered the best. This is no easy question.[20]

The first and traditionally most renowned answer understands the better quality of an interpretation with respect to another as the quality of capturing more faithfully the intention of the author of the text, where the contingencies of time, distance, decay of the supporting media, deliberate correction, or contextual opacity have obscured it. Another answer is constituted by Gadamer's view of interpretation in terms of what he calls *fusion of horizons.* The outcome of a successful interpretation, from this perspective, is the constitution of a single horizon that contains the unsolvable differences of perspective—what Lyotard calls the *différends*—between us and the text. Another powerful alternative to the "author's intention" approach to interpretation is developed by Ronald Dworkin in his hermeneutic theory of law. In *Taking Rights Seriously* and *Law's Empire* Dworkin rejects both the legal positivist view, popular among conservative jurists, according to which the just sentence is the one that keeps closer to what the existing statutes and past court decisions prescribe and the pragmatic view, popular with the critical legal studies movement, that the right sentence is the one that promotes more progressive policy objectives. Even more problematic is for Dworkin, for reasons that cannot be reviewed here, the view according to which the normative content or meaning of a statute is equated with the legislator's intention in conceiving the statute.[21]

I can neither reconstruct here the convergence of these views of textual interpretation nor the identity approach to it that I have tried to develop elsewhere. Suffice it to recall that the alternative suggested by Dworkin, who believes in the existence of *one right answer* to hard cases, relies on reflective judgment and amounts to a view of adjudication as guided by *integrity*. In legal matters the best sentence when conflicting interpretation of the law exist is the one, according to Dworkin, that *makes the most* of the existing legal tradition, understood not only as a collection of statutes but also as a tradition of academic jurisprudence, as a series of relevant court decisions, all interpreted against the background of the history of the community of which the legal tradition is an expression. Thus in every just sentence a judgment is implicit regarding the best identity for the community in whose name the sentence is pronounced. This judgment obviously includes a reconstructive moment in which one takes into account the past history, legal and political, of the community, but it includes also a projectual moment oriented toward the future.

And suffice it to recall that the notions of identity and authenticity become relevant when we try to address the two questions left unanswered by Gadamer and Dworkin: What does it mean to "make the most of a text"? What does it mean to best bring horizons to a fusion? The main idea suggested in my previous work is that a text can be considered as a symbolic whole with a kind of identity, abstract and purely formal, yet an identity sui generis. And just as in the case of persons we can speak of identities that have different degrees of *cohesion*, of *continuity*, of *demarcation*, of *vitality*, of *self-reflectiveness*, of *maturity* and so on, also texts and other symbolic complexes—for example, disciplines—can be metaphorically said to have identities too, more or less well constituted on a number of dimensions and whose overall pattern our interpretations can grasp or miss to a greater or lesser extent.

To sum up a more detailed analysis, the dimensions of a fulfilled individual identity can be shown to be applicable, mutatis mutandis, also to the reconstruction of our intuitions about what constitutes a well-formed text and thus of what it means for an interpretation to give us a superior rendition of the textuality of a text. Also in the case of a text it makes sense to speak of the sequence of its sentences as being organized around a *coherent* focus, being consistent, exhibiting a thematic continuity, as expressing with *vividness* the overarching meaning that unifies the whole sequence, and of the text as possessing a modicum of *depth,* in the sense of embedding references to the way the parts-whole relation is constituted, and finally it makes sense to speak of the structured sequence of its component speech acts as *commensurate* with the pragmatic goal underlying the text.

Conceptions of validity in textual interpretation can then be understood in reflective terms: while interpretations can be understood as reflective judgments that enable us to identify the well-formedness or *textuality of a text*—where "textuality" is understood in terms of the above dimensions—judgments concerning the validity of specific interpretations of a text are second-order reflective judgments about the adequacy of those first-order judgments, and theories of interpretive validity—for example, the judgment and authenticity approach suggested here—are reconstructions of what we generally do when we perform these second-order reflective judgments on the adequacy of single interpretations.

At this juncture we can appreciate the usefulness of the dimensions of textuality mentioned above. They are of help when we need to differentiate the very notion of the going wrong of an interpretation. Has the interpretation done justice to the coherence of the text and, more specifically, to the internal consistency of its local structures of meaning and to the development of its thematic progression? Has the interpretation grasped the vividness of the central meaning of the text? Has the interpretation done justice to the self-referential depth of the text, to its self-questioning, distancing from, and hedging of its own presuppositions? Has the interpretation brought to light the congruency of the argumentative, narrative, or stylistic means deployed by the text with the overall pragmatic goal that inheres in it?

The reflective judgment nature of interpretation becomes then self-evident. We simply cannot answer the question "What do we mean when we say that an interpretation of a text is better than another?" with a list of criteria that identify the best interpretation apart from the concrete case. The dimensions of coherence, vividness, depth, and commensurateness lack the determinacy of criteria and cannot be ranked. We cannot say whether *in general* the interpretation of a text is improved by modifications that, for example, bring about a gain on the dimension of capturing the vividness of the text but entail a loss on the dimension of grasping its coherence. In other words the judgment as to the textuality of a given text does not proceed from criteria and does not allow subsumption of the particular under a predefined universal concept. It is a kind of judgment facilitated by those dimensions that are used as guidelines that *orient* both our first-order reflective judgments concerning the textuality of texts and our second-order reflective judgments concerning the adequacy of interpretations.

The interpretation of *action* follows a similar model. Based on our participation in a lifeworld, we construct expectations and foreunderstandings about the meaning of an observable doing and then test these holistic expectations against the piecemeal appraisal of details of the observed doing and of the relevant contextual features as soon as we become aware of them. As in the case of texts, good judgment concerning the meaning of an action is a matter of managing to include as many particulars as possible within a unitary framework, of grasping as much as possible of the coherence underlying details, of the spark of innovation underneath the customary and the routine, of the traces of reflectiveness and of the effort to make commensurate the ends to the available means as well as the means to the possible aims. As in the case of texts, we can undergo the experience of the coming to nothing of our expectations, of their leaving out too much uninterpreted material or their being contradicted by too many details. The difference is in the role played by the actor's intention. Unless we make action coextensive with intentional action by definition—an extreme move that raises more problems than it solves—the actor's intention plays no different role from the one it plays in the construction of textual meaning. That is, action may *acquire* certain meanings due to contextual features of which the actor is only vaguely aware.

Good judgment also allows us to recognize instances of real innovation, namely, the actions that acquire exemplary significance. They are the action correlate of the work of art, in that they are the product of *genius*.

Innovative action—for example, the action of Weber's responsible politician who can say "Here I stand. I can do no other"—like *aesthetic ideas*[22] embedded in works of art has the ability of setting "the mental powers into a motion, i.e., into a play which is self-maintaining and even strengthens the powers to that end."[23] The ability of exemplary action to set the imagination in motion is one of the junctures at which the relation of judgment to authenticity becomes clear. Furthermore, through their capacity for stimulating a never-ending play of all our mental faculties, aesthetic ideas and innovative actions alike provide a tangible instance of the universalism sui generis inherent in our experiencing exemplarity and authenticity.

In order to grasp the implications of this statement and to give a solution to the problems raised by Arendt's account, we have to return to, and expand further, what we have said in chapter 1 about how it is that something exemplary can exert some kind of influence beyond the context from which it arose.

If judgment in general—which, again, consists of "thinking the particular as contained under the universal"—is about the appropriateness of some element to an identity, about whether something, be it an action, a norm, or whatever, fits or not with the whole of a relevant identity, then the authenticity or integrity of an identity, what is best for its flourishing, is the regulative idea that makes judgment function. This is an aspect of Kant's theory of judgment that Arendt, had she the opportunity to expand and reelaborate her notes, would have certainly noticed and emphasized. In a number of passages concerning the nature of the special pleasure afforded by the aesthetic experience of things beautiful, Kant uses the term *feeling of life* in a way close to what is here designated by authenticity and implicitly comes close to this point.

In paragraph 1 of his *Critique of the Power of Judgment* Kant denies the presence of any cognitive content in aesthetic judgments. Rather, aesthetic judgments involve the awareness that the representation of a certain object is accompanied by a "sensation of delight." Such representation, continues Kant, "is related entirely to the subject, indeed to its feeling of life—under the name of the feeling of pleasure or displeasure—which grounds an entirely special faculty for discriminating and judging that contributes nothing to cognition."[24] In a subsequent passage of the text Kant specifies what he means by "delight": the beautiful "brings with it a feeling of the *promotion of life*."[25] As we have seen in chapter 1, this formulation gives us the possibility of a different, less naturalistic understanding of the basis for the universal claims raised by aesthetic judgments.

Now, if by pleasure we understand the ability, on the part of a representation, to arouse in ourselves the feeling of the furtherance of our life, the question arises: How can I anticipate that the experience of an object that I judge beautiful will translate—not just in the "promotion" or furtherance of my life, in the advancement of my own life project, in the flourishing of my identity or the enhancement of my authenticity—will translate into an equal feeling of the promotion or furtherance of *anyone*'s life?

We can make better sense of how this is possible if, alongside the neither naturalist nor hermeneutic understanding of sensus communis discussed in chapter 1, we introduce a distinction between *pure* reflective judgment and *oriented* reflective judgments—a distinction that constitutes one of Makkreel's contributions to the interpretation of Kant's theory of judgment. As Makkreel points out, Kant presents his own notion of "orientation" in the 1786 essay "What is Orientation in Thinking?" and cursorily or implicitly refers to this notion in the *Critique of Pure Reason* and in the *Critique of the Power of Judgment*. In its most elementary sense, *orientation* refers to the ability, on the part of the actor, "to proceed from one quadrant of her field of vision to the other three which make up her horizon."[26] My ability to bring what I see in front of me into a relation with the other quadrants originates in the imagination—the ability to instantiate what is not present to the senses—and rests on the immediate bodily feeling bound up with the left and right distinction. At a more mediated level, Kant mentions the possibility of a "mental orientation of the thinking self to the transcendent realm,"[27] and in the *Critique of the Power of Judgment* mentions the principle of "finality" as a concept potentially capable of "orienting" reflective judgment. In the latter case, we relate to the manifold phenomena of nature *as if* the laws that regulate them would add up to a unity, not because such is required by a principle of nature or by a principle of freedom, but because this "transcendental concept of a purposiveness of nature . . . represents the unique way in which we must proceed in the reflection on the objects of nature" *if* we want to get a "thoroughly interconnected experience."[28]

Makkreel suggests that we further distinguish a notion of "aesthetic purposiveness" (namely, "an aesthetic orientation that evaluates the world on the basis of the feeling of life") and a notion of "teleological purposiveness" (understood as a "teleological orientation that interprets culture on the basis of common sense or the *sensus communis*").[29]

These considerations cast light on the intrinsic connection that binds together the notion of the *enhancement, promotion,* or *furtherance of life* or *authenticity,* the notion of orientation and the universality sui generis of reflective judgment. Our question concerning the nature of the universalism of judgment can then receive a new answer, which still remains in line with Kant's own view of judgment and compatible with Arendt's own reading of it. The universalism of judgment rests neither on the biological setup of the sense apparatus nor on an improbable sharedness of the examples that are brought to bear on our evaluations—a sharedness that would presuppose a common culture encompassing the whole human species. It rests on that sensus communis which in the previous chapter has been characterized as neither reducible to the biological nor merely cultural and at whose core the notion is found—independently of the culture we inhabit and just by virtue of simply existing, in the way human beings exist, with a body, a mind, a consciousness of the self and its finiteness—that we all have an intuitive sense of what it means to enhance and further, or to constrain and stifle, our life. Though we express it differently, we all have a sense of what it means for our identities to flourish or to stagnate. Cultures articulate this basic feeling of well-being or flourishing and stagnation in different vocabularies, to be sure, and there exist local variations that emphasize one aspect over another. Neither Kant nor Arendt are in a position to tell us anything more specific about this feeling.

If we elaborate further on this point, in a direction that Arendt *could* have taken, we might say that under our present conditions the feeling of the "promotion or furtherance of life" must be understood in terms of *self-realization* or the attainment of an *authentic* relation to the self. The expression *authentic relation to the self,* in turn, designates an optimal congruency of an identity with itself—an interpretation corroborated, among other things, by Arendt's approving quote of Socrates's saying "It would be better for me that multitudes of men should disagree with me rather than that I, *being one,* should be out of harmony with myself and contradict me."[30]

Congruency, however, cannot be reduced to mere consistency. Rather, we should understand it as including those more specific dimensions explored in *Reflective Authenticity* and mentioned in chapter 1: *coherence* (i.e., the possibility of summing up the modifications undergone by an identity during its lifetime in the form of a narrative), *vitality* (i.e., the experience of *joyful empowerment* resulting from the fulfillment of one's central needs), *depth* (i.e., a person's capacity for self-reflection and moral autonomy), and *maturity* (i.e., the ability and willingness to negotiate the facticity of the natural and social world, as well as of the internal world, without thereby becoming another).

Though the vocabulary with which we reconstruct our intuitions concerning what it means for a human identity to flourish or attain authenticity may be culture bound, our belief that these dimensions capture intuitions somehow relevant for all individuals living in the human condition enables us to make sense of how a judgment that invokes no principles or concepts and addresses the potential, inherent in a given object of interpretation, for enhancing or furthering our life, can claim universality after all.

From this vantage point we can now go back to the Arendtian question of exemplary validity. Our examples—Achilles, Saint Francis, Jesus of Nazareth—become *exemplary,* i.e., capable of exerting an influence on us, who are not within their context of origin, by virtue of their ability to realize, within the horizon of an action or of a life course, an optimal congruity between the deed and a certain inspiring motive underlying it—a congruity that in turn resonates with us by tapping the same intuitions that works of art, for all the diversity of styles and intentions underlying them, are capable of tapping. Examples orient us in our appraisal of the meaning of action not as schemata, but as well-formed works of art do: namely, as outstanding instances of congruency capable of educating our discernment by way of exposing us to selective instances of the feeling of the furtherance of our life. And the force of examples transcends local boundaries more easily than the force of laws or principles because they tap intuitions that run deeper, in the constitution of our subjectivity, than the level that requires translations.

3

The Exemplary and the Public Realm

Reconstructing the Normativity of the Reasonable

The notion of exemplarity can be of only limited use to our reflections about politics unless we develop an understanding of what exemplarity could mean in the public realm and how its inherent normativity could play a role at that level. One way of contributing to such an understanding consists in reconstructing the kind of normativity underlying Rawls's notions of public reason and of the reasonable. According to a somewhat popular but deeply misguided view, the transition from the framework of *A Theory of Justice* to that of *Political Liberalism* would entail a loss of normativity, so to speak, and therefore a diminished relevance of the Rawlsian framework for articulating social criticism. On the contrary, the framework of *Political Liberalism,* including the related ideas of public reason and the reasonable, presuppose a notion of normativity sui generis far more consistent, relative to the framework of *A Theory of Justice,* with the premise of the fact of pluralism and thus ultimately more defensible. Consequently, also from the standpoint of social criticism, Rawls's work of the nineties is to be understood not as a demise of the critical potential of normative political philosophy but, with special reference to the ideas of public reason and of the reasonable, as a further enhancement of that potential.

I will not spend much time reviewing the different iterations of this allegation raised against Rawls, except to recall that in one of its most articulate and authoritative versions—spelled out by Habermas[1]—it is contended that Rawls would fail to draw an adequate distinction between the "justified acceptability" and the "actual acceptance" of a political conception of justice and would fail to account for the relation of the reasonable to the "morally valid" as determined by practical reason. I will not spend time on the exegesis of this criticism, but will rather proceed from the outset to unpack the basic notion of normativity underlying public reason and the reasonable and in the closing section I will discuss the critical potential of that notion of normativity.

The Limits of Public Reason

The idea of public reason is perhaps the most important contribution to be found in the work of John Rawls after *A Theory of Justice*. In *A Theory of Justice* public reason was not explicitly discussed, but the fundamental insight underlying this notion was already present, under the headings of "justification" and of the "principle of publicity." While "proof" aims at showing logical relations between certain (not necessarily shared) premises and certain conclusions, "justification" is understood by Rawls as the practice of trying to convince others of the reasonableness of our claims concerning issues of justice and of constitutional essentials. This is why "justification proceeds from what all parties to the discussion hold in common," from premises that are accepted by everyone.[2] "Publicity" is described by Rawls as a condition that "arises naturally from a contractarian standpoint" and intimates that the parties in the original position assume that they are "choosing principles for a public conception of justice."[3] But publicity, in a Kantian vein, is understood also as a fundamental ingredient of a well-ordered society.

In the writings of the transitional stage between *A Theory of Justice* and *Political Liberalism*, Rawls further develops these two concepts. The ideal of publicity becomes a three-layered "publicity condition,"[4] and the notion of justification evolves into the idea of the "reasonable," as distinct from the rational. The notion of the "overlapping consensus" begins to be used in order to designate a new way of determining the basic structure of society: the representatives of citizens no longer simply report their unanimous conclusion reached in the original position, but try to adjudicate disagreement by way of argumentatively identifying a common set of political values.

I will not discuss the details of this transitional stage, and will take as my starting point the systematic conception of public reason expounded by Rawls in chapter 6 of *Political Liberalism* and in his 1997 essay "The Idea of Public Reason Revisited."

In *Political Liberalism* public reason is conceptually linked with a certain ideal of democratic citizenship. It is "the reason of citizens as such, it is the reason of the public; its subject is the good of the public and matters of fundamental justice; and its nature and content is public."[5]

Public reason is best understood by way of understanding five *limitations* that bind its operation. First, it is reasoning from premises that are shared by all the participants, as opposed to reasoning from what each party sees as the "whole truth" on the basis of its comprehensive conception of the good.[6]

Second, public reason can concern itself only with matters related to "basic justice" and to the "constitutional essentials" of a democratic society.[7]

Third, public reason is not to be understood as the only standard of correct reasoning in the public discourse of democratic societies. There are other forms of public discourse that should not be confused with the exercise of public reason: namely, "declaration" (when we explain to others our own comprehensive doctrine without expecting them to share it, but only for the purpose of showing them how we can derive from it reasons to endorse the political conception of justice that is shared), "conjecture" (when we argue from the comprehensive doctrine that we attribute to other people in order to show them that they do have reasons for endorsing the political conception under discussion), and "witnessing" (when we believe in the good faith with which all the citizens have deliberated, following public reason, on a certain matter and recognize the legal cogency of the ensuing decision, while questioning its substance from the standpoint of our comprehensive doctrine).[8]

Fourth, even if proceeding from shared premises, taking matters of fundamental justice as its object, and not falling in the cases of declaring, conjecturing, or witnessing, a political argument counts as one in which public reason is operative only if it occurs in the context of what Rawls calls the "public forum," as opposed to the "background culture." A public forum is a context of argumentation in which a decision eventually must be made. This distinction is not the same as the distinction between the sphere of political decision making and the public sphere in Habermas. For the public forum includes not only the arguments taking place among office holders in legislative, executive, and judicial institutions when deliberation about the relevant matters is at stake but also deliberation in the larger citizenry when voting "in elections when constitutional essentials and matters of basic justice are at stake," arguments offered by "members of political parties" and candidates in their campaigns.[9] In the "background culture," instead, we find arguments exchanged on the basis of nonpublic reasons in churches and universities, scientific societies and professional groups.[10]

Fifth, Rawls draws a distinction between the "exclusive" and the "wide" view of public reason. According to the former, "on fundamental political matters, reasons given explicitly in terms of comprehensive doctrines are never to be introduced into public reason."[11] On this account, the abolitionists did overstep the boundaries of public reason. The "wide" view, instead, allows citizens "in certain situations, to present what they regard as the basis of political values rooted in their comprehensive doctrine, *provided they do this in ways that strengthen the ideal of public reason itself.*"[12] Rawls considers the latter the correct view. In "The Idea of Public Reason Revisited" he further relaxes the stringency of this wide view of public reason. In the famous proviso, the "in certain situations" qualification is replaced by the phrase "at any time." Operating within the framework of public reason now is said to allow us "to introduce into political discussion *at any time* our comprehensive doctrine, religious or nonreligious, provided that, in due course, we give properly public reasons to support the principles and policies our comprehensive doctrine is said to support."[13]

Finally, Rawls warns us against placing excessive expectations on what public reason can deliver us. The fact is that the common point of view from which public reason proceeds is not exhaustively captured by a single philosophical conception of justice, not even by justice as fairness.[14] In other words, aside from and in addition to the pluralism of reasonable conceptions of the good, the standpoint of reciprocity and fairness among free and equal citizens who wish to live under a rule of law can be captured by a plurality of philosophical conceptions of justice, which all meet the criterion of being "political." This is up until today the most extraordinary effort to incorporate the acknowledgment of pluralism at the heart of a liberal conception of justice. Rawls is certainly still convinced that justice as fairness occupies a special place within this plurality, but that special place amounts to no more than a "coherence bonus," consisting of the fact that the two principles of justice, understood as a freestanding doctrine, provide for more continuity (relative to any other existing doctrine) with the central notion of fairness and reciprocity[15] public reason sets as a standard for *any* conception of justice that embeds the aspiration to be considered "political." The exercise of public reason is thus not only never supposed to overcome the reasonable pluralism of conceptions of the good but is also supposed not to lead to one privileged political conception of justice.

In the end, public reason can help us understand the coexistence of rival conceptions of the good as being not incompatible with the pursuit and stabilization of fair terms of cooperation among free and equal citizens; it can perhaps help us defuse conflicts rooted in the various interests connected with differences in status, class, occupation, ethnicity and gender, but is not expected to put an end to "conflicts arising from the burdens of judgment."[16]

With this reconstruction in mind, we can now address the question "What kind of normativity is involved in the operation of public reason?" Identifying correctly the concept of normativity presupposed is a key to reassessing whether the transition from the model of *A Theory of Justice* to the model of *Political Liberalism* (and later to the model of *The Law of Peoples*) entails a loss in the potential of Rawls's approach to function as a standard for social criticism.[17]

In order to address this question let me start from a definition of public *reasons,* in the plural, as those reasons that are authoritative for us insofar as we are citizens and as such partake of the same overlapping consensus.[18] The authoritativeness of public reasons for us qua citizens, in turn, can be accounted for if we see these reasons as all partaking of the cogency of public reason in the singular. And of public reason in the singular we are told, by Rawls, that it is normative argument that proceeds from the truth we share, as opposed to the whole truth as we see it. The crux of the matter, it seems to me, lies in that verb *to proceed.* How are we to understand the relation between the shared truths from which we start and the conclusions of which we want to convince our fellow citizens? In order to grasp the nature of that relation, crucial for the purpose of unpacking the normativity involved in the reasonable, two problems need to be addressed: namely, the problem of determining *when* allegedly shared truths, the building blocks of public reason, are really such and, second, the problem of what it means for one reason to *follow* or *proceed* from a shared basis.

When Are Premises Shared?

Concerning the first problem, contentious claims about whether the requirements of public reason have been met often revolve around the exact identification of the shared quality of reasons that are shared only "in the eyes of the beholder." I believe that Rawls's own discussion of abortion is quite instructive in this respect.[19] In a footnote to the first edition of *Political Liberalism* Rawls starts from the assumption that the "troubled question of abortion" should be addressed, by anyone willing to move within the space of public reason, as the question of properly balancing, among others, the three following political values: "the due respect for human life, the ordered reproduction of political society over time . . . and finally the equality of women as equal citizens."[20] Furthermore, he contends that "any reasonable balance of these three values will give a woman a duly qualified right to decide whether or not to end her pregnancy during the first trimester"[21] and, furthermore, that any doctrine amounting to the exclusion of that "duly qualified right" in the first trimester would be "unreasonable." It is hard to see how that conclusion can be counted as falling within the scope of public reason, given the deep disagreement over the exact meaning of the term *human life* as it occurs in the phrase "due respect for human life": for some human life proper begins at birth, for others at conception. There simply doesn't seem to be a shared truth from which to let a common conclusion proceed, though Rawls seems to assume its existence.

Subsequently, in "The Idea of Public Reason Revisited," Rawls restates his position in different terms. He denies that the footnote cited above should be read as an argument for the right to abortion in the first trimester and concedes a. that a discussion within public reason need not generate a "unanimity of views," b. that a set of reasonable political conceptions of justice need not "always lead to the same conclusion," and c. that even citizens holding the same conception don't necessarily always agree on particular issues,[22] presumably on account of the burdens of judgment. Furthermore, Rawls concedes that, at least in some form, the Catholic argument against the right to abortion, when based, as in the case of Cardinal Bernadin, on the three political values of "public peace, essential protection of human rights, and the commonly accepted standards of moral behavior in a community of law," "is clearly cast in some form of public reason," though a judgment on its justified, fallacious, or mistaken character may still be pending.[23]

This discussion is instructive in that it shows at least two things. First, it shows that the shared quality of shared truths may be a contentious issue, in that clearly in the position expressed in *Political Liberalism* Rawls's premise that the permissibility of terminating pregnancy within the first three months does not violate the value of "due respect for human life" is not shared by the Catholic position. *Human life* appears then to be an ambiguous expression that some believe to be using in terms shareable by all, whereas others deny that.

Second, this discussion shows that for Rawls arguments legitimately articulated within the bounds of public reason may be wrong from a substantive point of view. Such is the case with Cardinal Bernadin's view of abortion: certainly within the bounds of public reason, but possibly wrong. I'll return to this issue below, because it touches on the problem of what it means for a reason to follow from a shared premise.

Concerning the problem of contested sharedness, one could envisage the actual sharedness of the shared starting point as susceptible of being ascertained from a third-person perspective, i.e., from the standpoint of an observer. This move is problematic and, ultimately, unavailable to Rawls because it leads *beyond* the framework of public reason. In fact, if we could authoritatively *describe* what the contending parties share, regardless of their own way of construing it, we would be in possession of a neutral yardstick for the adjudication of normative questions, and public reason would just be superfluous. An enlightened philosopher-king could solve all normative controversies.

The alternative route is to consider reasons as indeed shared when the participants mutually recognize them as shared. Yet things are more complicated than they appear at first sight. For one can no more be the arbiter of whether one is following a rule in Wittgenstein's sense than one can be the arbiter of whether one is following public reason. If we didn't insert a conceptual wedge between "following a rule" and "presuming to be following a rule," between "operating within public reason" and "presuming to be operating within public reason," the *normativity* (as opposed to the pure factuality) of rules and of public reason alike would instantly collapse.

If the normativity of public reason were bound immediately with what the participants to public debates explicitly profess to embrace, then for example the Southern slaveowners' refusal to recognize the equality of all human beings regardless of race would definitively sink Lincoln's and the abolitionists's effort to end slavery to the level of a comprehensive, nonpolitical, nonpublic, ultimately "metaphysical" conception. Rawls appears to be unwilling to follow this route either. He goes to great lengths in *Political Liberalism* to argue that the abolitionists "did not go against the ideal of public reason," despite their opponents' claim that acts of government such as the 1862 Proclamation, which in any event emancipated African American slaves only "where the Union writ did not run," amounted to a violation of the liberal neutrality of the State. As Rawls puts it, even though Lincoln and the others often appealed to religious beliefs, they were still within the bounds of public reason to the extent that they thought "that the comprehensive reasons they appealed to were required to give sufficient strength to the political conception to be subsequently realized."[24] Thus Rawls must be taking something other than the participants' own explicit self-understanding as the criterion for the public quality of the premises of public reason, without going all the way to the opposite extreme of making the sharedness of shared premises ascertainable from a third-person perspective.

One possibility that is left open in order to reconstruct this specific aspect of Rawls's account of public reason is to understand the sharedness of the premises from which public reason proceeds not just as a *de facto* convergence, but as a *reasonably imputable* convergence or a convergence that *ought* to take place, given the ideas publicly professed by the parties. We can gather no hint from Rawls's texts as to what "reasonable imputability" might mean, but reasonable imputability could be understood as a kind of attribution that could not, if made the object of a specific public discourse, eventually be rejected by those who were imputed those contents.

Three Meanings of the Reasonable

Moving on to the second problem, namely, "What does it mean for one reason to *follow* or *proceed from* a shared basis?" we should recall the second teaching gleaned from Rawls's discussion of abortion, that arguments can be within the bounds of public reason yet fallacious, mistaken, or unreasonable. How are we then to understand the normativity of the reasonable? How should the term *reasonable* be reconstructed?

While Rawls tends to explicate the meaning of the reasonable by way of exemplifying the kinds of entities that may be called reasonable (such as "reasonable citizens," namely, those "who are willing to accept the burdens of judgment,"[25] "reasonable comprehensive doctrines," "reasonable principles," "reasonable institutions,"[26] etc.) in the context of a discussion about the normativity of public reason perhaps it could be more useful to reconstruct the meaning of this fundamental term along different lines. Holding constant the kind of entity to which it applies—we are basically dealing with *the reasonableness of arguments in the political forum*—we should rather distinguish three senses in which the predicate *reasonable* can apply to arguments. These three senses are ordered on a scale of increasing normative force.

In the first of these senses, for an argument to be "reasonable" simply means that it falls within the bounds of public reason in a somewhat loose sense: its subject falls within the scope of what belongs to public reason and it incorporates reasons and premises that its author can defensibly consider shared by all the citizens. This is the least normatively demanding version of the reasonable. As we have seen in the case of Cardinal Bernadin's argument against abortion, knowing that an argument is reasonable in the sense of falling within the scope of public reason for Rawls doesn't necessarily mean that the argument is binding on anyone—in fact the argument may even be flawed from a logical or empirical point of view.

In the second of the three senses of the term *reasonable,* for an argument to be "reasonable" means to fall within the scope of public reason *and* at the same time to be sound. Here a conceptual space opens up within which a *stronger* and a *weaker* version of the reasonable-in-our-second sense can be distinguished. Recall that all we know from Rawls is that in a reasonable argument the conclusion we reach "follows" or "proceeds" from premises that are shared by all citizens. Is the term *proceed* to be interpreted in a *strong* sense, as a relation of *logical implication*? Or should we rather interpret it in a *weaker* sense as a relation of *consistency,* in which case the requirement of public reason is that the new reasons not necessarily follow from the shared truth but be "nonincompatible" with it? Rawls does not say much on this issue, but there does not seem to be much ground for justifying the strong view. Were we to understand the relation between the shared truths that we start from and the conclusions that we reach as of the form $p > q$, public reason arguments would be severely limited in the possibility of introducing new substantive ideas in the public political forum. Furthermore, public reason would be thereby deprived of its essentially intersubjective nature: the decrees of public reason would be tantamount to logical inferences that a computer could draw.

We must then see the relation between the conclusions and the shared premises of public reason in other terms. But as we move on to explore the *weaker* option—conceiving of that relation in terms of consistency rather than material implication—we realize that also the ideas of *consistency*, of *coherence*, and of *compatibility* with shared truths can be understood in a variety of ways. First, each of these ideas could be seen in *propositional* terms—namely, as the idea that at no point in the public forum must reasons be offered including propositions that contradict, run against, or are incompatible with any of the propositions contained in the set of shared truths. Once again, this would be a somewhat reductive approach. The reasonable so understood would not place public reason within the circle of the tautological, leaving space for substantive innovation and breakthrough, but still reasonableness would *not* have the intersubjective quality that Rawls intends to assign to it. Again, computer-assisted "reasonableness assessment"—by comparing the two propositional lists of the shared truths and the suggested implications—could not be ruled out.

Thus it seems that a fully intersubjective understanding of public reason enjoins us to take a broader view of "compatibility" with shared truths: namely, to understand "compatibility" as meaning that all the citizens who by hypothesis share the initial truths are also *willing* to endorse, based on their diverse comprehensive conceptions, the conclusions—where such "willingness" cannot be known a priori.

Furthermore, for any public controversy there might be a number of competing arguments on the floor, all reasonable in the first two senses of the term. This leads us to suspect that if we want to make sense of public reason as exerting a normative force, then a third notion of the reasonable must—like an invisible planet—be present in and somehow influence Rawls's thoughts on the matter. This third, normatively more demanding, sense of the reasonable can be reconstructed by addressing the question What does it mean for an argument to be comparatively "more reasonable" than another, as, for example, in the statement, quoted in chapter 1, where Rawls grounds the justifiedness of a certain conception of justice not on "its being true to an order antecedent to and given to us," but on the realization that "given our history and the traditions embedded in our public life, it is *the most reasonable* doctrine for us?"[27] Or the one conception of justice "most reasonable for us."[28] The question concerning the meaning of that phrase—"the most reasonable doctrine for us"—is the one that, in my opinion, best highlights the peculiar sort of normativity presupposed by the reasonable.

The Space of Reasons, the Space of Judgment

Whether drawing on Hegel's critique of Kant's neglect of the "institutional" moment of moral reasoning, and of the entwinement of law-testing moral reason with a whole normative world of substantive assumptions that forms the background of its seemingly only procedural operation, or drawing on Wittgenstein's view that, given the impossibility of deciding alone on a solipsistic basis whether a rule has been followed, to follow a rule means to engage in an inherently social practice, or, finally, drawing on Sellars's understanding of reasons giving as occurring within an intrinsically public "space of reasons," in recent years authors like Christine Korsgaard, Robert Brandom, Jürgen Habermas, Hilary Putnam, and many others have defended a view of reasoning as reasons giving that, though couched in a plurality of vocabularies, pivots around the notion that one can no more formulate, give, and accept reasons in private than one can develop a private language. Reasons exist in an intrinsically *public* space, though derivatively one can certainly deliberate *in foro interno*. Speaking of moral, individual reasons for action, Korsgaard goes so far as stating that our private reasons are "never more than incidentally private in the first place."[29] A fortiori the relation of new reasons to the truth already shared is itself something that is not up to the individual to determine. The space of (public) reasons is really the space of judgment, and public reason is reasoning from the standpoint of everyone else.

Yet here's the rub. If the normative hold that the most reasonable argument in a public reason controversy exerts on us can neither be accounted for merely in terms of the *logical* quality of the relation between conclusions and shared premises, nor be accounted for in terms of its superior potential for attracting an *actual* consensus on the part of the free and equal citizens (not even in terms of an idealized dialogical consensus, which by definition has not yet coalesced), then what is it that can account for that normative force?

I will begin by characterizing that normative hold exerted by the most reasonable argument as a peculiar sort of *practical obligation*—the obligation *to recognize the superior reasonableness of that argument*. Given our shared commitment to *p*, we are shown by the most reasonable argument that we can't but commit ourselves to *q* as well. The task is to highlight what that phrase "can't but" might possibly mean. As anticipated above, the nature of this new commitment is best highlighted not by normativity associated with the application of principles to facts of the matter, but rather the normativity of reflective judgment, understood as judgment in the service of the fulfillment of an identity—a kind of judgment paradigmatically enshrined in Luther's saying "Here I stand, I can do no other." To be convinced by a reasonable argument means to come to Luther's position, where Luther's position amounts to the most famous vindication of the idea that, as Korsgaard has aptly put it, "normativity derives from our self-conception" (249), ultimately from a reflective endorsement of that self-conception.

In *The Sources of Normativity* Christine Korsgaard develops a philosophical program in which a person's capacity "to act for a reason" (which for our purposes I will take as equivalent of "acting on the basis of an obligation") requires not just that the person have a capacity for "reflectively endorsing" her own first-order desires—for "taking them up," as it were, on the basis of a certain representation of her own self or, in her words, on the basis of a "description under which you value yourself" (101), but requires also a capacity to *act under universal laws* or to *universalize* our act of will (232). The interesting point is that Korsgaard wants identity to function not only as an *empirical* source of selectivity with regard to first-order desires but also as a *normative* one, so that the obligation-dimension of "I can do no other" remains dependent on at least some reasons that are not solely peculiarly mine but are somehow "agent neutral." It is this neutrality that renders the "I can do no other" stance ultimately irreducible to the arbitrariness of an "I don't *want* to do any other" stance. Agent neutrality, in turn, is construed by Korsgaard in terms of two gradients of universality, so to speak, corresponding to two layers of the actor's identity: namely, the individuated "practical identity" of the particular actor and the "moral identity" that constitutes a motivational core shared by all moral actors. The normative dimension of "practical identity" (an equivalent of

Habermas's *ethical* identity) consists in the fact that to take up a certain reason to act means to raise the claim that anyone would have to do the same *if analogously situated*. Under this reading of normativity, the normative dimension of Luther's "I can do no other" lies in the fact that a certain line of action is posited as obligatory for anyone in the same position as Luther. But the normative dimension of identity in the second and *stronger* sense consists of the fact that a certain line of action is posited as obligatory for anyone qua moral actor, regardless of the particular contents, and thus of the situatedness, of her practical identity.

It is not necessary here to assess the merits of Korsgaard's Wittgensteinian argument in defense of her stronger version of identity-based normativity. What is relevant for our purposes is that, by her own admission, such stronger and more universal moral identity is quite thin: its function of bringing integrity and therefore unity "and therefore, really, existence" to the acting self (229) does not depend on its ability to *dictate* solutions to the problems of justice that arise in the public forum. In this sense the normative picture sketched out by Korsgaard does contain principles, but these principles play a different role than in the Kantian picture. They have lost the power to *subsume* specific courses of action within the categories of morally admissible or forbidden action. We move here within the circle of reflective judgment from the outset.

Going back to public reason, we can think of the reasonableness of the most reasonable argument as a normativity that proceeds—via *reflective judgment*—from a certain description under which "we value ourselves"— the "we" being the political community to which the contending parties admittedly belong. The practical obligation to accept q given that we share a certain premise p doesn't stem therefore from logical principles or moral principles antecedent to the situation at hand, but stems from what the inner integrity or authenticity of the political identity shared by us and our opponents qua citizens demands for its flourishing. If we wish to talk of general principles such as the principle of equal respect or the right to demand justification or the discourse principle, or other such principles as normative elements whose reach spans beyond our own particular identity, we can certainly do so. The point is, however, that the role played by them is best understood as that of *orienting* our reflective judgment in the assessment of what best proceeds from our shared truths.[30] The real normative weight is carried, as in aesthetic judgment, by our judgment as to what can or cannot fit the already established singular normativity of a symbolic whole. The reasonable is then the equivalent, in the realm of political argument, of what the exemplary is in the aesthetic realm. We call most reasonable what fits best the shared truths that form our starting point, just as we call exemplary the artistic element, device, representation, or solution that best fits certain aesthetic intentions that form the recognizable starting point of a given creative process.

The force of the reasonable is not the force of a moral law—which would make public reason superfluous relative to the practical reason that captures and applies such law—but rather the force of that which exerts influence on us by virtue of who we are, of our self-conception, namely, the force of the exemplary.

Reflective endorsement of what is reasonable, however, only starts from our parochial self-conception, but by no means remains hostage to it. The enlightening contribution that comes from others within the common exercise of public reason may change that self-conception by pointing to new and as yet unexplored alternatives.

I cannot go any further into this view of the normativity of the reasonable. It is now time to briefly address the significance of this view of normativity for social criticism.

The Reasonable and the Exemplary

I have begun my reconstruction of the model of normativity underlying Rawls's ideal of public reason and his notion of the reasonable by questioning the idea that it is premised on a weaker form of normativity and as such constitutes a less apposite basis for articulating social criticism with respect to *A Theory of Justice*. One obvious reason for questioning this idea is that the ideal of public reason sets a standard for criticizing all those instances of actual political practice—ranging from the functioning of institutions to discussions in the public forum, from the conduct of public officials to deliberation on matters of enough consequence, from the adjudication of constitutional cases to the designing of policy in State institutions, and so on—in which controversial comprehensive conceptions are imposed on recalcitrant citizens through external threats or pressure or outright coercion or any other means that in any way contradict the assumption of free and equal citizens jointly seeking fair terms of cooperation across their ideological divides. From this vantage point it is hard to make sense of the claim that the transition to the framework of *Political Liberalism* is marked by a loss of critical potential relative to the one embedded in the original position argument that was central in *A Theory of Justice*.

There is also another reason why such claim appears questionable. Its explication requires that we briefly recall the gist of Habermas's reservations against Rawls's transition to the model of *Political Liberalism*. Habermas has accused Rawls of failing to adequately distinguish between the "justified acceptability" and the "actual acceptance" of a political conception of justice and of overlooking the fact that in order to avoid "a merely functionalist" interpretation of justice as fairness, some sort of "*epistemic* relation" must be postulated "between the validity of his theory and the prospect of its neutrality toward competing worldviews being confirmed in public discourses."[31] Rawls instead—Habermas continues—ends up obscuring the conceptual connection between the "reasonable" and the "morally valid," thereby missing the possibility of identifying a moral point of view independent of the formative power of the comprehensive conceptions of the good. One is left wondering, according to Habermas, what meaning could then be attributed to the term *reasonable* if it is not to be taken as connected with the *morally true*.

Habermas's initial point is certainly to be shared. For a political conception of justice, as well as for any of the conclusions reached within public reason, to possess a normative valence, they must appeal to something beyond their mere acceptance, something *by virtue of which* they demand acceptance. Should this standpoint on the basis of which they demand acceptance be conceived as a moral point of view independent of the formative power of our broader conceptual schemes, however, Habermas's contention would constitute more of a problem than a needed solution. For such view of the source of the normativity of public reason would conflict with the idea of the unavailability of descriptions of reality unmediated by one among several competing interpretive frameworks—an idea that has defined our philosophical horizon ever since the first half of the twentieth century. Such a tension would arise regardless of our reconstructing the moral point of view as the Kantian categorical imperative or as the Habermasian discourse principle or as a utilitarian principle, insofar as a moral point of view so understood would inevitably purport to constitute a true description of a normativity inscribed in the moral subject qua member of the kingdom of ends or qua human being reproducing her life in the midst of communicative action or qua utility maximizer. My point is that from the necessity to postulate *a* standpoint, on whose basis the claims of public reason demand our allegiance, does not follow a necessity to postulate it in those terms. The legitimately requested distinction between acceptability and acceptance can be drawn *without* referring to an external normative standpoint if, drawing on Kant's view of reflective judgment as articulated in the *Critique of the Power of Judgment,* we conceive it in terms that are entirely *internal* to the horizon of the competing arguments developed within public reason.

As we have been reminded a number of times, reflective judgment about the beautiful (as opposed to judgment about the pleasurable, which is just an unquestionable report of our preferences) raises a normative claim: everybody *ought to* agree with its conclusions,[32] whether or not such consensus materializes in practice. Nonetheless, this normative claim is not anchored in anything external to the matter being judged, does not rest on an antecedently established principle being applied in our judgment. Rather, it rests on the aesthetic exemplarity of the object of judgment—where exemplarity can be understood as the ability to set the imagination and all our mental powers into a peculiar "self-maintaining motion" and where the pleasure provided by this never-ending play of all our mental faculties consists in giving us the sense that our life is being "promoted or furthered." Of course exemplarity could be construed from other perspectives, for example, along the lines of an experience that comes to fulfillment (as in Dewey) or in terms of the ability to disclose a whole new world for us (as in Heidegger), but in these cases as well exemplarity remains a major source of normativity.

In a similar way, mutatis mutandis, the conclusions suggested by arguments that move within the circle of public reason exert a normative force that cannot rest just on the eventual de facto convergence of the people subscribing to different competing alternatives. After all, the materializing of that convergence (in this Habermas is right) cannot be taken as a fact, but is to be understood as the effect, always subject to adverse contingencies, of the normative force of the most reasonable conclusion. That normative force—and with it a *nonfoundationalist* distinction between acceptability and acceptance—rests on the exemplary quality of the relation established by the conclusion with the shared initial premises from which "it follows."

The reasonable—when we understand it in the sense of "the most reasonable among the conclusions urged on us by competing arguments all moving within the circle of public reason"—then is inherently a critical force. In order for it to exert normative force, and to demand our acceptance more convincingly than the competing conclusions and arguments, it must embed a claim to fit more exemplarily than the alternatives with our shared premises and, since we can't view its relation to the premises in merely logical terms, it must embed a claim to fit more exemplarily with our shared sense of who we could be at our best. Within that claim is lodged a standard for criticizing the "actual acceptance" of norms, institutions, policies, and so on—a standard that does not locate acceptability in some principle that transcends who we are qua political community but, on the contrary, understands acceptability ultimately as exemplary congruence with a concrete modern identity premised on the notion of fairness and equal respect among free and equal citizens. In this sense, *if* we want to draw the distinction between acceptability and acceptance along nonfoundationalist lines, then *the reasonable* (in the sense of the "most reasonable" among reasonable public reason arguments) is best understood as *the exemplary*.[33]

The question about the nature of the exemplary, obviously raised by this way of understanding the reasonable, cannot be addressed in this context. In a cursory way it can only be stated that for something—in our case, an institution, a policy, a constitution or a constitutional amendment, a statute, a verdict, a Supreme Court opinion, etc.—to possess exemplarity does not mean "to be an example of" anything else. For, were it so, reasonability would be again connected with a foundationalist moral claim concerning the a priori cogency of the normative notion of which the matter being judged reasonable would be an example.[34] For something to possess exemplarity, rather, means to be a law unto itself, to possess that exceptional self-congruency for which the term *authenticity*—born within a specific moral tradition but not confined to it—seems particularly apposite. But this quality should not be understood, in turn, along merely coherentistic lines. If we conceive of exemplarity as the ability to set the imagination in motion and all our mental powers into a self-maintaining motion, thereby producing an aesthetic experience linked with the feeling of the promotion, affirmation, or furtherance of life, we need not confine the relevance of this nonfoundationalist kind of normativity to the realm of aesthetics, as it appeared sensible to Kant at a time when stronger views of normativity, including his transcendental reconstruction of the nature of the human subject, were considered unproblematic.

Indeed, the Rawlsian notion of the "reasonable" represents one of several possible ways of exporting such view of normativity into the realm of politics. For the purpose of extending the relevance of exemplary validity to the realm of political life, however, we need to provide an adequate reconstruction of what it means for a *political,* as opposed to an aesthetic, idea—again: for an institution, a policy, a constitution or a constitutional amendment, a statute, a verdict, or a Supreme Court opinion, and so on—to set the *political* imagination in motion and to produce the feeling of an expansion, enhancing, or furthering of the range of possibilities of our *political* life or, to draw on an entirely different vocabulary, what it means for such an idea to be *politically world disclosing.* This task falls beyond the bounds of a reconstructive discussion of Rawls's view of the reasonable but opens up a new direction of theorizing that moves from Rawls's pioneering distinction of the reasonable and the rational.

4 Exemplifying the Worst
Facing up to Radical Evil

Unfortunately, exemplarity in the public realm is not just about the force of the reasonable. Just as crucial, for buttressing the viability of the paradigm of judgment, is the task of making sense of the repulsive force exerted by radical evil when it is identified as such. The flip side of reasonability is *negative exemplarity,* that from which we recoil in utter horror—as the hero of *Heart of Darkness* at the end of his life—or, in other words, evil as the exemplification of the worst we could possibly be. In this chapter the relation of radical evil, judgment, and exemplarity will be explored.

The transformation of our philosophical horizon induced by the Linguistic Turn has made it increasingly difficult to conceive of *radical evil* without resorting to "prepostmetaphysical" ways of thinking. Has the death of God as a publicly and nonritually invokable figure—the fading away of Jahwe mentioned once by Jaspers—led to the disappearance of a notion of radical evil? Can evil on the scale of Auschwitz, the Gulag, ethnic cleansing, the massacre of the Tutsi or the Cambodian "killing fields" be conceived at all within a postmetaphysical horizon? Or does evil of this magnitude call for some transcendent, even religious, notion of an absolute normativity against which it could then be defined as transgression?

Two problems seem to stand in the way of understanding radical evil along thoroughly postmetaphysical or nonfoundationalist lines. First, most of us are pluralists when thinking of the good. Very few of us would envisage conclusive arguments on the superiority of one conception of the good life (say, *bios theoretikos*) over another (say, *vita activa*). Yet, when it comes to radical evil, we feel very uneasy with the idea that what appears to us as an instance of radical evil—Auschwitz or the Gulag—may become more acceptable or less of an evil when considered from a different perspective. Are we contradicting ourselves? How to we reconcile these two seemingly contrasting intuitions?

Second, the intuitive gap between "ordinary" evil and radical evil also creates unsettling consequences for a postmetaphysical sensibility. Ordinary evil can enter a relation of "definition by opposition" with the good. Lying is the negative counterpart of "telling the truth," being disloyal is the negative counterpart of loyalty. Evil on the scale of Auschwitz, instead, cannot be brought into any such relation: there is no good that can be defined as "not doing what was done at Auschwitz." Simply, we feel that evil of such magnitude ought to be eradicated from the world—this sort of evil is too evil even to function as "the opposite of the good." Thus the ensuing difficulty is that radical evil seems to resist being brought into any meaningful relation with the shared basis of human action.

Despite these two problematic aspects, I would like to defend the idea that a nonfoundationalist notion of radical evil can be conceived, and in the rest of this chapter some of the basic ideas underlying it will be outlined.

Radical Evil and the Human Will

I will start from the assumption that radical evil—provisionally defined as that which is repugnant to our conscience to bring into any kind of relation to the good, *even into an opposition to the good*—is never pursued *directly* by human beings. As Plato reminds us in *Protagoras*, no one commits evil actions while thinking that they are evil. People commit evil actions while carried away by their misconceived views of the good. A similar point is made by Kant. In the section "Man Is Evil by Nature" of book 1 of *Religion Within the Limits of Reason Alone,* Kant points out that "man (even the most wicked one) does not, under any maxim whatsoever, repudiate the moral law in the manner of a rebel (renouncing obedience to it)." [1] In fact, according to Kant a "reason exempt from the moral law" or a "*malignant reason*" or a "thoroughly evil will" cannot be a *human* form of reason. It can only be the form of reason of a *devilish* being (30). The evil person, instead, differs from the morally good one neither because the moral law is absent from her heart (for Kant, the moral law is innate to our inner constitution qua moral subjects) nor simply because of her receptiveness to incentives of a sensuous nature (for that receptiveness is equally part of every human subject), but rather is set apart from the good person on the basis of the priority she accords to sensuous incentives, over the moral law, in shaping the maxims of her conduct: "man is evil only in that he reverses the moral order of the incentives when he adopts them into his maxim" (31). Thus, concludes Kant, we cannot locate the source of evil in a "*corruption* of the morally legislative reason—as if reason could destroy the authority of the very law which is its own, or deny the obligation arising therefrom" (30).

If we try to apply Kant's line of reasoning to our own philosophical context, as described in chapter 1, we immediately run up against a major obstacle. [2] We live in a philosophical world where even fervent advocates of moral universalism like Habermas and Rawls do find the notion of "one transcendentally anchored moral law" problematic in various ways. For instance, we would not understand the distinction, drawn by Rawls, between classical liberalism and *political* liberalism if we didn't understand how deeply problematic the notion of one moral law objectively directing the conduct of the moral subjects has become. This predicament in a way raises new challenges, but also opens up new philosophical possibilities. For instance, where Kant could not think of an evil will as devoted to the deliberate subversion of the moral law because he conceived of the law in objectivist terms, we, on the contrary, are in a position to make sense of a moral will that orients itself to a reconstruction of the moral point of view, which happens to be misguided or flawed *in its own terms*.

The Nazi Conception of the Good

In the twentieth century people of my generation, born after World War II and already grown into adulthood when the Berlin Wall fell, experienced with dismay the rapid evaporation of the hope that the post–cold war world would be marked by a peaceful march toward global democratization; events such as those occurring in former Yugoslavia, in Rwanda, in Darfur have given rise to moral sentiments of horror at the radically evil practices of ethnic cleansing, mass ethnic rape, forced deportation. I will not address these events, however, but will rather discuss the one paradigmatic example of radical evil in the twentieth century: the Holocaust.

If we can reconstruct our intuitions concerning radical evil with respect to Nazism and bring them into one coherent postmetaphysical picture, we will acquire a compass that can orient us in the moral intricacies of the new tribal, ethnic, regional wars of the post–cold war era. The first point to understand, in this respect, is that a demonic view of what happened at Auschwitz as the embodiment of Evil would amount to a posthumous vindication of a Hitlerian understanding of the moral world as the theater of a deadly confrontation between Good and Evil. Instead, it adds to the tragedy of it that what was done at Auschwitz was done in the name of the good—of a certain conception of the good for a certain community. It was not done as a deliberate denial of the moral law, but as an intended affirmation of it. As Hitler put it "only the German people has turned the moral law into a reigning principle of action." [3] We should never overlook this fact, but should rather concentrate on grasping where the mistake was made. And our starting point will be James Bernauer's reconstruction of Nazi ethics.

At the core of the Nazi moral vision was a biological understanding of the good as the furthering of the racial purity of a people. Racial purity, in turn, was deemed valuable as a way of increasing the chances of survival in a Darwinistically conceived process of evolution in which the human species, and the peoples or races that compose it, are always immersed. The life of humanity was conceived as an evolutionary process of an eminently biological, as opposed to cultural, nature. Culture mattered insofar as its processes impinged on biology. For example, the cultural anomie, individualization, differentiation, and rapid cultural change associated with the processes of modernization—symbolized in turn by the independent, secularized, and kaleidoscopic spiritedness of Jewish high culture, together with the lightness of the *civilization* typical of French culture—were understood as the vehicles of an enfeebling of the temper of the German people. The chances for a people's success or failure within this larger evolutionary process were thought to be primarily affected by that people's capacity to prevent contamination by foreign genes—interracial promiscuity being obviously the chief vehicle of the infiltration of exogenous diseases. Hitler and the other Nazi leaders presented themselves not simply under the semblance of military leaders but also under the semblance of "collective physicians" who would take adequate measures for eradicating what they had discovered—namely, the ominous consequences of a racial virus called *internationale Judentum,* which had begun to spread its effects everywhere, but with particular virulence in Germany. World history was recast as a biology lab—where *Rassenhygiene* became the main imperative.

This bioevolutionary, consequentialist morality generated its own *Tugendlehre* or catalogue of virtues. As Goebbels summed it up, this catalogue included "generosity" (*Grossartigkeit*), "heroism" (*Heldentum*), "masculine courage" (*Männlichkeit*), "readiness to sacrifice" (*Bereitschaft zum Opfer*), and "discipline" (*Zucht*).[4] It was a kind of disciplinary asceticism in which the individual was required to adhere to a regimen of strict bodily and moral training in order to eradicate the seeds of depravity within himself and was asked to subordinate his own private interests to the advancement of the common good. Himmler summed up these virtues in the SS ideal of "severity" or "hard-heartedness" (*Härte*) understood as a combination of personal honesty, the capacity to overcome feelings of compassion, and the capacity to feel permanently at war.[5] That "life" and "death," evolutionary triumph or defeat, were the leading moral metaphors is also signaled, among other things, by Hitler's understanding of politics as "the art of leading the struggle of a people for its earthly survival."[6] Within this naturalized moral world there was no place for the modern notions of *equal respect* and *human dignity.* Again, in *Mein Kampf,* Hitler connects the right to life to the factual capacity for self-defence, thereby emptying it of all normative substance: "When a people no longer possesses enough strength to fight for its own health, then its right to survive in this world of struggle comes to cease" (54).

Bernauer highlights the elements of continuity that connect the Nazi moral vocabulary with a number of respectable vocabularies. On the one hand, Hitler and the Nazi failed to grasp the extent to which the moral conception expounded in those books by Sigmund Freud that they publicly burnt in the squares shared with their own ideology the central idea of an eternal struggle between Life and Death, Eros and Thanatos. The biological was at the center of Freud's moral world, and he too understood life as a primarily *natural* force, a natural force that naturally opposes death (54). On the other hand, the use of Christian symbols alongside the more well-known neo-pagan ones, as well as the existence of pro-Nazi Christian movements, testify to the possibility of tracing continuities between the traditional paleo-Christian anti-Judaism and the new post-Christian Nazi antisemitism. More than external symbols, however, Nazi ethics seems to have appropriated and radicalized a certain Christian ideal of *purity*—not so much the "purity of blood" that became the object of attention during the Counterreformation in sixteenth-century Spain as a kind of "spiritual purity," which under the heading of "simpleness of spirit" stood in opposition to the classical Greek ideal of *megalopsyché* or the Roman ideal of *magnanimitas* and provided the ground for a kind of anti-intellectual populism tinged with authoritarian propensities. But through its ideal of purity Nazism also appropriated another cultural source—the *Catholic ethics of sexual purity*—and gave it a peculiarly racist twist. Purity became an ideal not just of private conduct but an ideal binding for entire races. Purity of race came to constitute a projection of sexual purity on a collective plane (57–58).

Thus, underneath the Holocaust was not just a misguided reconstruction of the good for a single historical community (the German *Volk* as construed by the Nazi leaders) but also a misguided reconstruction of the moral point of view. Misguided in what sense? Not in the sense that *formally* one could not generalize the maxim of practicing *Rassenhygiene* into the imperative of maximizing racial purity within each nation—an idea that, couched in cultural and religious rather than biological terms, has dramatically come back to center stage during the 1990s under the heading of "ethnic cleansing." Rather, the Nazi conception of the moral point of view was misguided in the sense that the background assumptions against which a "generalization" of *Rassenhygiene* was supposed to make sense were untenable. Among these assumptions were the following three propositions: a. the moral life is a struggle of nations for survival, b. racial purity is the best means to assure survival and evolutionary success to a nation understood as a race, c. human races incapable of raising themselves up to purity or who live to corrupt other races do not have a right to survive.

It is very important to distinguish between, on the one hand, a conception of the moral point of view as bound up with the universalizability of maxims and, on the other hand, the substantive assumptions in the light of which the universalization test is carried. As Hegel has shown in his critique of Kant's moral philosophy, the formal process of generalization of which the categorical imperative consists only works in conjunction with substantive assumptions about the desirability of ends. For example, a deposit entrusted to me cannot be appropriated by me because if everybody did so under comparable conditions then the institution of promising—which independently we prize as a valuable one—would be undermined. However, argues Hegel, if a beggar asks me for some change, the obvious fact that if everybody gave liberally poverty, and with it begging, would be undermined does not make my act immoral, for the generalization–independent reason that we don't prize poverty as a valuable thing to be preserved.[7] Applying this point to our example of radical evil, we could say that the Nazi conception of the moral point of view is vitiated, indeed perversely corrupted, by its implicit assumptions concerning the nature of the moral life—to repeat: the idea that the moral life amounts to a struggle for survival and the idea that the right to life is contingent on the possession of the power to assert it.

Brief Excursus on the Banality of Evil

This distinction between the generalizability of a set of moral norms and the assumptions against which the generalization test is carried out somehow also explains how evil could appear "banal." When questionable assumptions are accepted—and we have seen that segments of them can be found in other moral conceptions that have nothing to do with Nazism—they can congeal into a shared lifeworld and sustain a sense of "normality" in perpetrating the horror. If the source of evil lies not in the transgression of a moral point of view, which cannot be grasped from outside a conceptual schema, but must—consistently with the Linguistic Turn—be traced back to a moral culture called evil only from the observer's point of view, then it follows that *evil is no less intersubjectively constituted than the good*. This intersubjective character of evil—shared assumptions, shared values, a common vocabulary of moral relevance—in turn accounts for its banality, namely, for the *everyday* and *low-key* as opposed to the *grandiose* and *heroic* quality that evil takes on in our times. In fact, under different substantive presuppositions, we have witnessed the resurgence of the "banality of evil" again and again in Cambodia, in Rwanda, and in former Yugoslavia—meaning by the phrase *banal evil* not horror that is any less horrible, but horror that becomes entwined with everyday life, *horror as a temporarily shared form of life* rather than as the dramatic rupture of a form of life or, using yet another formulation, evil that has lost the quality of being a temptation and has turned into a habit.

So the problem of radical evil raises a challenge for us in the sense that even evil of the magnitude of the Holocaust does not take the appearance of an *intentional* violation of the moral point of view but merely comes to us as a perverted application of it in light of assumptions rooted in a misguided view of the moral life. Yet here is the rub. Within the horizon of his *Subjektsphilosophie*, Kant could believe that his own reconstruction of the moral point of view and his way of applying it in light of the assumptions typical of his philosophical horizon—assumptions that allowed him to conclude, among other things, that the death penalty is the only appropriate punishment for murder, that a child born outside of marriage, being born "outside the social contract," could be suppressed, and that women should be barred from suffrage[8]—was neutral with respect to all diversity of opinion and a direct reflection of normative structures and intuitions deepseated in the moral constitution of all human beings. We cannot. We live within a philosophical horizon based on the assumption of a plurality of language games or conceptual schemes. This is why even our condemnation of the Nazi view of the good as conducive to evil cannot proceed from the idea of its violating a moral point of view located *outside* all language games and conceptual schemes. Hence the difficulty: if, perverted though it appears to us, the Nazi view of the good constitutes a "comprehensive conception of the good," on what ground can we condemn it as "evil," as opposed to merely confining ourselves to the sober realization that its basic assumptions lie beyond all possibility of an "overlapping consensus" with our own, without violating the pluralistic premises of the Linguistic Turn?

It is at this juncture that an understanding of normative validity based on authenticity, exemplarity, and judgment can be helpful. The horizon inaugurated by the Linguistic Turn contains conceptual resources that can help us draw the line between ordinary and radical evil on a new and thoroughly postmetaphysical basis. Ordinary evil—the bank robbery taking place around the corner, the episode of political corruption reported in the local newspaper, the marital violence occurring next door—can be conceived as intraparadigmatic evil, namely, evil as the failure to live up to a set of shared normative assumptions embedded in a moral culture. When Himmler deplored the stealing of even a cigarette from the body of an exterminated Jew, he was pointing to an instance of ordinary evil from within a Nazi conception of morality. *Radical* evil, instead, is the name that we give to paradigmatic evil, namely, to a *moral culture taken as a whole* and to acts representative of or rooted in this moral culture.

Before Nazism became the ultimate term of comparison for evil, Oriental despotism played an analogous role in the social philosophy of Montesquieu, Hegel, and Marx. It constituted a *radically evil* moral culture. The culture of the plantation in the South of the United States represented another case to the eyes of the Northern republicans. However, the individualist way of life of the postindustrial societies of the West represented a devilish embodiment of ultimate evil to the eyes of Ayatollah Khomeini during the 1980s and today continues to represent an embodiment of evil in the eyes of the Taliban and thousands of Islamic fundamentalists. Thus we are confronted with the following questions: what does it mean for a moral culture as a whole to constitute an instance of radical evil? What does it mean for a moral culture to constitute an instance of radical evil "in the eyes of everyone" and not just in our own or our neighbor's eyes?

What Does It Mean for a Conception of the Good to Be Evil?

A reconceptualization of radical evil that avoids construing it as the violation of a transcontextual standard inconsistent with the Linguistic Turn can take its bearings from a judgment view of justice according to which evil, no less than the good, is always *evil for someone*. We call the Nazi view of the good as racial purity evil in that it systematically, and not just occasionally, violates the principle of equal respect for all human beings regardless of their ethnic ancestry. The grounding of such a principle rests on nothing other than the fact that we could no longer regard us as ourselves   as Western moderns of the twenty-first century—if we embraced a view of the moral life that did not include equal respect at its core. After all, the Nazis were Western moderns as well, and we can legitimately challenge their interpretation of the moral point of view as the ultimate betrayal of the values that constitute us as the kind of human beings *we* would want to be. We can claim that their "evil view of the good," if successfully institutionalized, would turn our history—the history of the West—into a tale of moral horror where human dignity, the idea of equal respect for all human beings and the critical spirit ("Hier ist kein Warum" was the standard answer given by the supervisors of the Nazi concentration camps), would all fade away to leave us in a Darwinized moral world.

At the same time, when we claim that the Nazi view of morality is evil we claim something more than that. We claim that *no one*, not just we the Westerners of the twenty-first century, could embrace it and still remain faithful to herself. How is it possible to vindicate this claim without invoking some Archimedean point and thus falling back into a kind of fundamentalism of equal respect or of human rights? It *is* possible, if we rethink the point of view of justice violated by the Nazi understanding of the good as the point of view of the good for humanity as such. Without repeating here a possible argument in support of a judgment view of justice,[9] let me recall one aspect of it.

There is no human political community whose members are not part of humanity as well and, for this reason, a political conception of normative validity that failed to include some reflection, however minimal or implicit, of an understanding of the good for humanity would thereby also fail to be true to that part of the community's collective identity that overlaps, however minimally or implicity, with the (for the time being still embryonic) identity of humanity in its entirety. It does not matter how thinly anticipatory this notion of the realization, fulfillment, or flourishing of humanity is at present. There is little doubt of the fact that the Jewish people's survival would be jeopardized by the affirmation of a Nazi ethical conception. A Nazi, however, could reply by questioning the moral import of the survival of an inferior race: he could claim that the lot of humanity would in fact be improved by that disappearance.

We have two options open at this juncture if we want to challenge this claim without essentializing or fundamentalizing our egalitarian intuitions and without ending up in the same position as fundamentalists who indict the Western way of life from the standpoint of their own comprehensive conception of the good. One line of response could be to point out that a view of the good for humanity that did not include the equal dignity of all human beings and all peoples would be a view that ultimately betrays all that *we*—we Western moderns—think should be part of the notion of realizing the good for humanity. In so arguing, however, we could not appeal to a superordinate standpoint that adjudicates the case between us and the Nazi, but would simply have to be ready to fight for preventing the narrative of that identity of humanity in which we also participate to become tainted by the horror of a Nazi view. While I think that *politically* there might be no serious alternative to this sort of stance, I am philosophically uneasy with this line of response. Let us assume counterfactually that the Nazi regime had not been imperialistically aggressive, but had tried to carry out its program of exterminating the Jews only within the boundaries of post–World War I Germany. While war should still have been waged in order to prevent genocide, even in the absence of expansionistic aggression, our justifying war on that basis would not put us in a significantly different position than a hypothetical contemporary theocratic state that waged war against the West in order to prevent our secularized, plural understanding of the good from leading to what from their point of view looks like the ultimate corruption of humanity's identity.

A second line of response, instead, deconstructs the Nazi's view immanently, so to speak, by pointing to the inconsistency of claiming that the right to life exists only for those who are in position to assert it and at the same time calling this a *moral* vision. If there is one place where one could say that the right to life is subordinated to the factual power to assert it, it is the symbolic location called the state of nature. It appears to be self-contradictory to state on the one hand that one people deserves to survive only if it is able to physically defend its existence with military force and, on the other, that this evaluative statement is a *moral* one as opposed to one that belongs in the state of nature. This is the basis on which it could be claimed—*without invoking contested values*—that a Nazi view of ethics would fail the test of constituting a viable reconstruction of the point of view of the good for humanity.

But why should the idea of the "good for humanity" represent a cogent normative standpoint for all the local moral cultures? Why couldn't we in principle conceive of a moral culture shared by a community that on the whole refuses to care for the good of humanity?

At this juncture the judgment view of justice mentioned above comes into play. Given an *intersubjective* understanding of the nature of identity, as always bound up with mutual recognition on the part of other identities—a recognition that, in turn, is made possible by the existence of some, however minimal, intersection of shared values and beliefs—for a collective identity to seek its own good or fulfillment at the expense of, or even simply overlooking, the fulfillment of the larger identity of humanity means to reduce the degree of fulfillment attainable by that identity. More precisely, it means to reduce the scope of that fulfillment by comparison with the degree of fulfillment attainable by the same identity if it were to take *into full account* all its constitutive interconnections with the other identities with which it entertains relations of recognition.

To conclude this section, because no political community exists whose members are *not* part of humanity, any community that in its conception of normative validity failed to include some understanding, however minimal or implicit, of the good for humanity would thereby also fail to be true to the part of its own collective identity that overlaps, however minimally or implicitly, with the identity of humanity in its entirety. Only the "race of devils" hypothesized by Kant could set a radical opposition of justice as the anticipated good for their race as a whole and the affirmation of the political identity of one specific sub-community of devils—provided that such a race decided to live in a political community. Only devils, in fact, could conceive of the pursuit of their own local good as the undermining of the good for the race of devils as a whole. But even the Nazi were not devils. They were all too human humans. Thus "authentic evil" is not a human, but a devilish possibility. More modestly, humans pursue what they believe to be the good and only subsequently turns out to be evil, and evil, including radical evil, thus always fails to be authentic in that it always includes a moment of self-deception—at the very least in the form of misconstruing the relevance of certain constitutive relations with other identities.

The Radicality of Radical Evil

Obviously there exist thousands of different ways of violating the moral point of view, reconstructed as the point of view of the good for humanity, that nonetheless cannot be put on a par with Auschwitz. Sexist talk in everyday informal conversation violates the ideal of equal respect, free riding on public transportation violates legal provisions, but no one calls that *radical* evil. We are still in need of a postmetaphysical definition of what radical evil on a human, as opposed to a devilish, scale could possibly mean. Where are we to locate the threshold between ordinary and extra-ordinary or radical evil? Intuitively, genocide seems to always fall under the category of radical evil, while the death penalty—which is morally repulsive to the public culture of certain, though not all, democratic societies—does not.

One of the reasons why the distinction between ordinary and radical evil is of the greatest importance in the world of the twenty-first century is that the line that separates legitimate and illegitimate interference in the internal affairs of a sovereign state could very well rest on it. Notice first of all that the line that separates ordinary and radical evil cannot be equated with the line that separates the violation of human rights from the violation of other rights. There are countless violations of human rights in many countries that, unfortunate and morally condemnable as they are, would not justify the waging of the kind of military action we have seen taking place as a UN-mandated sanction against states that repeatedly make themselves guilty of crimes against humanity. If we mentally survey the cases that most univocally fit the category of radical evil—and again we immediately think of the killing fields in Cambodia, of the events in Rwanda, of mass rape and ethnic cleansing in Bosnia—the decisive trait seems to be not so much the violent quality of the event per se, because many instances of political conflict or civil war also exhibit the characteristic of being extremely violent, as the deliberate quality of the attempt to annihilate a helpless collectivity, a group of people singled out on account of some shared characteristic: being born in the wrong ethnicity, in the wrong religion, in the wrong ideology. Constitutive of radical evil seems to be the unleashing of violence on a victimized collectivity unable to adequately react and on individuals only insofar as they belong in that collectivity: the unleashing of a violence aimed at erasing all that is human in helpless human beings, including the physical individuation of the body. Radical evil, finally, seems to possess a characteristically systematic quality that episodic violence—for example, linchings and pogroms—does not possess. It is violence exerted by a majority on a minority by means of state power.

But conceptual difficulties await us here as well. The Night of St. Bartholomew, when thousands of Huguenots were killed in France, in addition to countless episodes of ancient, medieval, and early modern history, also exhibit ferociousness against a scapegoated and defenseless minority on the part of a religious or ethnic majority. Yet somehow we realize that those episodes horrify us less, not because on some objective scale less evil occurred, but rather because the actors involved are further removed from our own moral world. The closer to home, the more radical evil arouses moral horror. Nazism horrifies us because it occurred in the very midst of one of the most developed and civilized parts of Europe. Ethnic cleansing in former Yugoslavia elicits moral sentiments of horror also in relation to the fact that it is taking place *after* we all thought that the lesson of

Auschwitz had been thoroughly metabolized on this continent. This fact of our moral life suggests that perhaps our perspective ought to change. The criterion for the radicality of radical evil ought perhaps to be internal to us, the moral community, rather than external, objective. Evil then is perhaps best conceived as a *horizon* that moves with us, rather than as something that stands over against us.

In order to further unravel this initial intuition concerning radical evil, we can go back to Durkheim. An inspiring perspective can be found in his discussion of the sacred.[10] In his writings on religion—the 1898 essay "On the Definition of Religious Phenomena" as well as his 1912 book *The Elementary Forms of Religious Life*[11]—Durkheim has always stressed the difficulty of connecting the sacred to some kind of essential, objective dimension.[12] All human collectivities share some sense of the sacred, but what is deemed sacred varies in the broadest imaginable way. Yet the sacred cannot be defined with reference to some general principle. For example, it cannot be associated with the supernatural, because cultures exist that do not incorporate the distinction between what is natural and what goes beyond the natural. The sacred cannot be associated with the idea of divinity, because there exist religions that do not presuppose the notion of an individuated divine figure. Nor can it be associated with a hierarchy of what is "high" and what is "low" on a scale of value. For many conceptual dichotomies exist—rich and poor, master and slave, rulers and ruled—that we associate with the idea of a distribution in terms of high and low, but where the superordinate category by no means appears closer to the sacred than the lower.

The innovative conceptual shift introduced by Durkheim was to conceive of the sacred in a thoroughly relational or oppositional way and to give that relational definition a certain expressivist twist. The sacred is defined as that which is radically opposed to the profane. But also health is radically opposed to disease, and so is progress with respect to decadence. According to him, the sacred is anything that we are repelled at the idea of seeing indiscriminately mixed up with the profane, anything that we think should ideally be kept insulated and protected from the profane, but also something that somehow expresses crucial aspects of ourselves.

Thus it is not enough, for something to count as sacred, that it be perceived as endowed with value and that such perception be shared across a community. What is needed in order to turn something collectively prized into something sacred is a certain *exemplariness* of the sacred thing, namely, its capacity to bring to expression some dimension of the group that at the same time is unique and is located at the symbolic center of the group's identity. No phrase better captures the spirit of Durkheim's understanding of the sacred as the experience of collective authenticity than Giorgio Agamben's aphorism: "That the world does not reveal any divine plan, that is truly divine." [13] Just as authenticity—now understood as the specific dimension of modern individuation discovered by Diderot and Rousseau—is somehow the equivalent of the sacred on the scale of individual identities, so the sacred is anchored to the authenticity of a collective identity. It captures the uniqueness of the collectivity and objectifies that uniqueness in shared symbols, which—by virtue of their being objectified in religion, lithurgy, tradition—are always exposed to the wear and tear of shared symbolism and sometimes, like worn-out metaphors, lose the power to evoke that uniqueness, to move the imagination, to elicit loyalty and awe. From another perspective, the Durkheimian notion of the sacred can be said to represent the non-negotiable normative core of a collective identity, the symbolic locus where commitments are enshrined that cannot be disattended without an ensuing perception, on the part of the members of the collectivity, that their collective identity is being betrayed, their integrity as a collectivity is thrown into question, and they are in the process of ceasing being who they are and becoming another.

Developing this reconstruction of Durkheim's notion of the sacred one step further, we could ask the question "Which society is being represented in the sacred symbols that religious rituals always try to pin down and systematize into materials for theological speculation and ritual practice?" If what Durkheim calls the sacred is somehow an objectification of the "individual law" of an entire society, a representation of that which in the eyes of its participants constitutes that given society's unique identity, what is really meant by "society"? Certainly not society as it really is, meaning by that the society we encounter everyday. But neither is the society underlying the production of the sacred an ideal or perfect society in the sense of being a product of the mind of a philosopher. For Durkheim the society we presuppose in our experience of the sacred is the *actual society idealized*—namely, a society that neither is taken "as is" nor gets transfigured into some transcendent ideal no longer connected with who we are. It is our actual society as it *could* be if all its positive potentials were to unfold, thus a society that does not exist here and now and yet does not fade into utopia: a society that maintains all those characteristics that make of it *the good society for us,* namely, *our own* ideal society, different from other peoples' ideal societies. The society idealized in the symbols of the sacred is a "concrete universal," so to speak, that exerts an orienting function similar to the aesthetic idea an artist follows in giving shape to her materials or the concrete ideal self by which an individual tries to shape his life. In the sacred we can always discern the contours of what we collectively want to be, and that image is as individuated as we are.

Finally, the production of these symbols is not something that happens to society or its members. In Durkheim's words, "A society can neither create itself nor recreate itself without at the same time creating an ideal. This creation is not a sort of work of supererogation, by which it would complete itself, being already formed; it is the act by which it is periodically made and remade."[14] Durkheim's understanding of the sacred helps us understand the radicality of radical evil in a way that is consistent with nonfoundationalist premises. First, just as the production of the sacred is part and parcel of social life and cannot be eradicated from it—secularization, in other words, affects the religious sedimentation of collective experiences of the sacred and the role of religion in social life, but not the production of the sacred— so radical evil is best understood as the polar opposite of the sacred. If the sacred is a projection of us *at our best,* and the world of the profane a representation of us *as we actually are,* including the manifestations of ordinary evil we experience, radical evil can be conceptualized as a projection of "us *at our worst,*" the worst that we can prove to be at exceptional moments while still maintaining those characteristics that make us—as a community, as a society, or as humanity—what we are.

In that sense evil, even radical evil, can never be overcome. *Concrete manifestations* of it can be overcome—Auschwitz can be driven out of this world, ethnic cleansing hopefully can too—but if evil is a horizon that moves with us then there will always be a collectively shared symbolic representation of what we, we as a single moral community or we as humans, can be at our worst. The idea of a society where evil has been eradicated is, from a postmetaphysical standpoint, as meaningless as the idea of a pacified moral world where no conflict of value exists any longer. It is as meaningless as the wish of Kant's dove that no air existed to obstruct its flight. Just as Kant's dove failed to realize that the same air that obstructs its flight also sustains it, so those who think that idealized conditions could in principle exist under which no evil affected the human world fail to understand the extent to which the constitution of ourselves as moral subjects requires that we distance ourselves from our shared images of radical evil.

Building on this notion of radical evil as the symbolic horizon where the image of "us at our worst" is inserted, let us return to the question "What distinguishes ordinary from radical evil?" Ordinary evil is evil whose existence is understood as somehow part of the normal fabric of social life. Radical evil, instead, is evil that we think should never have occurred—evil that changes the relation of the moral subject to itself.

Ordinary evil exemplifies what ought not to be done and by contrast points to what should be done, radical evil is what should never have happened, and it is repugnant for us to think that it should be connected in any way—even by exemplifying what ought not to be done—with a worthy human life. Auschwitz marks a discontinuity that is best conceptualized in terms of identity. Ordinary evil is like the countless events that affect our lives peripherally. Auschwitz, instead, is one of those events that does not allow an identity, individual or collective, to remain impassive. The radicality of the evil that took place at Auschwitz vis-à-vis the ordinary quality of, say, the evil embedded in an episode of robbery or political corruption is reflected in our perception that the relation of humanity to itself and its own past and future history has been changed in the former case but not in the latter. Just as, on an individual scale, after having committed a murder we can no longer think of ourselves in the same terms, whereas when we are caught free riding on public transportation we by and large can, in the same way after Auschwitz we cannot think of humanity in the same terms as we do after having learnt of yet another episode of electoral fraud or bribery. The same idea has been cast in theological terms by Hans Jonas when he affirmed that after Auschwitz "Eternity looks down on us darkly, itself wounded and disrupted in its depths." [15]

But what can explain the horror aroused by radical evil, if we don't want to link that horror with the transcendent nature of that which is violated by radical evil? If we accept Plato's and Kant's idea that no human being acts in a deliberately immoral way, following a principle aimed at destroying the moral point of view, then the horror aroused by radical evil comes, among other things, from the realization of the extreme extent to which our representations and moral judgments may, when wrong, lead us to lose touch with reality. Moral communities always discover *afterward*—ex post facto—that what was done by their members in pursuit of shared views of the good was radically evil. The horror we experience when thinking of the Holocaust or of other episodes of radical evil is linked with the horror aroused by the abyss of psychosis—the same horror at the idea of total loss of touch with reality as seen by other human beings or total encapsulation into a world no one understands, of total unrelatedness between the meaning we assign to our actions and the meaning they acquire in the world of all other human beings. When we look at radical evil from the perspective of the victims, the horror is aroused by the abyss that separates their innocence from their fate, again, the meaninglessness for them of the destruction they had to suffer or the total unrelatedness between their deeds and their fate.

This brings me, in closing, to the issue of the moral sentiment of compassion for the victims of radical evil. It has been said that somehow a theological framework is called for, whenever we think of radical evil in history, if anything for the reason that only such a framework allows us to restore some kind of hope that the victims of evil will at some point be compensated for what they suffered. What seems lacking in a postmetaphysical understanding of radical evil is the possibility of envisaging this moment of "undoing" or remedying the injustices of the past. The suspicion remains that "the result of this avoidance of the theological dimension is a tendency for the notion of anamnestic solidarity to become instrumentalized." [16]

Once again, Durkheim's approach to religious life and in particular to the significance of mourning could be of help. We could say that the "instrumentalization of memory" to the interests of the survivors could be avoided if we think that the sacrifice undergone by victims of radical evil, though not voluntary, has not been in vain insofar as they continue somehow to live implanted in the moral fiber of a democratic community that remembers them, honors them and feels indebted to them for its existence. When the Italian Constitution was being framed, in 1947, after the fall of Fascism, there was a proposal to dedicate it to the memory of all those who paid their resistance to Fascism with their life and whose sacrifice had contributed to make today's democratic Italy possible. The proposal did not go through (some Catholics wanted a reference to God instead, and the Communist leader Togliatti suggested that the issue be put aside), but had that intention ever materialized in the form of a preamble to the Constitution, it would have embodied a kind of noninstrumental and secular anamnestic solidarity with the victims of Fascism.

As Shakespeare's character Mark Anthony puts it, indeed the evil that men do lives after them, but the relation that successors form to the evil passed onto them by previous generations is quite peculiar. Evil does not really survive as such except in disguise. Because a deliberate and authentic pursuit of radical evil is not a human possibility, when something is recognized as evil it means that we are already distancing ourselves from it, that the darkness of the night is over and a new dawn is beginning.

5 Political Republicanism and the Force of the Example

Political traditions and philosophical conceptions differ on the extent to which they allow the force of the example, and judgment, to play a role within their framework. Only the most extreme embed the ambition to filter out any and all possible role that judgment and exemplarity might play—game theoretical approaches to political choice are of this kind, for instance—but by and large all conceptions of normativity do attribute to judgment a role at least in discerning the correct and appropriate application of independently established principles of a more general nature. Republicanism, among the various traditions in political philosophy, constitutes an exception. In some of its versions, especially the one that I will call political republicanism, it places exemplarity and judgment at center stage as the fundamental source of normativity and conceives of principles and norms as derivative.

In this chapter I will first offer a differentiated reconstruction of republicanism and, using it as a backdrop, outline the contours of what I will call political republicanism. Second, I will contrast political republicanism with *liberal* liberalism and will question the idea that the difference is best captured on the terrain of the notion of freedom. Third, I would like to offer some reflections on the centrality of judgment and exemplarity as the feature that makes republicanism a persistently relevant tradition in our historical context.

Republicanisms

Republicanism is fundamentally a child of historical scholarship rather than a product of a theoretical mind. The political doctrine that we call republicanism is the outcome of two important interpretive endeavors by historians of political thought, which have produced two kinds of republicanism quite different from one another. The first of these reconstructive interpretations is connected with the names of Hannah Arendt and John Pocock.[1] Aristotle and Machiavelli are identified as the creators of a view of politics according to which participation in the political process—the so-called *vita activa*—is understood as participation in the consensual determination of a common good pursued by the polity as a telos that outranks all individual ends. The political sphere is then envisioned as the one sphere of action that mostly allows individuals to attain the good, what Aristotle called the good life or *eudaimonia*.

The antagonist of republicanism so understood is then the privatism typical of the modern mainstream liberal conception of politics, a conception in which the normative core of politics is constituted by a set of procedures or rules of the game aimed at regulating the interaction and conflict between the interests pursued by individual citizens or associations of citizens who strive to attain a kind of "private" good, defined outside the political sphere—for example, prosperity.

If considered in this Aristotelian variety, republicanism today exerts only a limited influence in the political debate. We live in a world that is simply too deeply enmeshed in the experience of pluralism to find the celebration of just one way of life—the life of active involvement in the affairs of the republic—attractive at all. Powerful echoes of this view, however, survive within another contemporary tradition that only occasionally presents itself as a kind of republicanism and does not even understand itself as a specifically *political* tradition. I'm thinking of *communitarians*, such as Michael Sandel or Alasdayr MacIntyre, who explicitly criticize the insubstantiality of a "private" ideal of self-realization and emphasize the indispensability of "civic virtue" for the functioning of a modern democracy.[2]

The second variety of republicanism, originating in the historical work of Quentin Skinner, does not identify the vita activa as a privileged path toward eudaimonia.[3] From a normative point of view, it is a more "modest" conception, and it relates to neo-Aristotelian republicanism in the same way as the political liberalism developed by Rawls relates to the perfectionist liberalisms of the past, including the comprehensive liberalism of *A Theory of Justice*. At its core lies the opposition between living in freedom and living in a condition of servitude. The canonical authors, in this case, are Polibius and Cicero and, in partial overlap with the first variety of republicanism, the Machiavelli of the *Discorsi*. Within this second version of republicanism there is no emphasis on collective ends of a substantive nature, but only on those "thin" ends on which liberals also converge—ends such as the protection of life, liberty, and property. For example, in his *De Officiis,* Cicero identifies the secure enjoyment of property as the fundamental motive that leads men to associate in political communities and Machiavelli in his *Discorsi sopra la prima deca di Tito Livio* defines the so-called *vivere libero* (life in freedom) or *vivere civile* (civil life) as "the possibility of enjoying what one has, freely and without incurring suspicion, for instance, not to fear for the honor of women, and of one's children, not to fear for oneself."[4]

The defining trait of this more Roman than Aristotelian version of republicanism is a certain concept of liberty—a concept that makes of it a particularly insidious competitor of liberalism. As Maurizio Viroli, one of the proponents of this political republicanism, has observed, liberalism has often been criticized in the name of social justice, of tradition, of communitarian or participatory ideals, but rarely—with the notable exception of Hegel—has it been criticized for the notion of liberty. The special quality of the challenge posed by republicanism consists in this: it questions the liberal understanding of liberty.[5]

This competing republican notion of freedom is elucidated in one of the most interesting books of the last decade, *Republicanism*, by Philip Pettit.[6] Pettit begins by contrasting Hobbes and Harrington on the notion of freedom. Ironically comparing Constantinople and Lucca, in *Leviathan* Hobbes pointed out that, in spite of the large inscription "Libertas" visible on the city walls, the citizens of Lucca are no less bound by the laws of his state, no less subjected to rules and regulations, than the citizens of

Constantinople are to the will of their sovereign. The laws may be different, the political regime may be different, but the subjects are equally submitted to the will of the sovereign and to the law.[7]

In *Oceana* Harrington takes issue with this view and points to what in his opinion is a crucial difference. The citizen of Lucca may well be just as bound by the laws of Lucca as the citizen of Constantinople is by the laws of Constantinople, yet he certainly has more freedom by virtue of his concurring in the making of these laws. What we observe in this controversy is the clash between two equally negative conceptions of freedom. One is the conception, inaugurated by Hobbes and then appropriated by the mainstream of the liberal tradition until the second half of the twentieth century, according to which to be free means that no one interferes with our own will and we are therefore in a position to do whatever pleases us. The other is the conception according to which to be free means to act in accordance with laws that we ourselves have contributed to create. To be free is different from being emancipated from interference, from this republican perspective, in the sense that we can continue to be dominated even when no one actually interferes with us. For to be dominated means to be bound by rules and norms not of our own making, to depend on the will of somebody even if this will does not manifest itself. On the other hand, the free person does not experience unfreedom when obeying laws that she has contributed to frame: for these laws are not external limitations but are rather the conditions of her freedom, the bricks and stones with which her freedom to act in society, as opposed to her freedom in the state of nature, is built.

The distinction between these two concepts of freedom—freedom as *absence of active interference* and freedom as *absence of domination*—is not the same as the famous distinction between "negative freedom" and "positive freedom" articulated by Isaiah Berlin.[8] Republican freedom, understood as freedom from domination or as the condition of not depending on someone else's arbitrary will, cannot be equated with the notion of "positive freedom" that Berlin attributes to Rousseau and Marx. The republican freedom from domination is rather a variety of negative freedom. It presupposes neither substantive values nor any notion of a collective self to whose realization the individual should feel obligated to contribute.

Insofar as it is a form a negative freedom, republican freedom is perfectly suitable for constituting the normative core of a political order respectful of modern pluralism. In his essay "Republican Liberty and Contestatory

Democratization,"[9] Pettit outlines a model of democracy centered around the twin ideas of freedom as absence of domination and of legitimacy as "contestability." The principle of contestability draws its relevance from the implausibility of the assumption, underlying much contemporary political theory, that, for the individual citizen, participating in self-government or having autonomy requires scrutinizing every single preference or belief in a sort of a *Bildungprozess* size large. Were it so, no individual would qualify as being autonomous. On the contrary, what does make sense is to conceive autonomy as the possibility for an individual to throw into question and revise any previous decision. As Pettit puts it, the notion of individual autonomy is a modal and counterfactual notion, not a historical one.[10] If we conceive of democracy as self-government on the part of a collective subject, by analogy we can also understand democratic autonomy or the autonomy of the democratic citizen as a counterfactual and modal, as opposed to historical, notion. Both individuals and peoples can rely, in their deliberation, on beliefs and preferences whose origins sink their roots in a remote and forgotten past and which in any case have not been the object of conscious choice in the here and now. Also the self-governing *demos,* no less than the individuals who compose it, often acts automatically, on the basis of decision-making processes that proceed in a kind of mechanical way or from force of habit. What makes of this process a democratic one is the *contestability* of these decisions as well as their *revisable* quality.[11] Thus the republican idea of freedom as absence of domination translates—when we contextualize it to a contemporary complex society—in the proposal of a *contestatory democracy.*

This is not the only example, however, of an attempt to adapt republican concepts to the reality of complex societies. Let me briefly review a few other cases of what we might call republican liberalism and then cursorily mention a number of proposals that I will call occasional republicanisms.

Another example of republican liberalism is offered by the work of Cass Sunstein. In "Beyond the Republican Ideal" Sunstein tries to articulate a version of republicanism capable of bridging the gap that traditionally separates it from liberalism and even "incorporates essential elements of the liberal tradition."[12] A republican regime so conceived rests on four basic principles: 1. the civic-virtue basis of all public deliberation, 2. the equality of political actors, 3. the universalism of practical reason, and 4. citizenship as defined by a set of rights/duties of participation. Truly essential is the first principle, which is connected to the deliberative moment underlying the conceptions of democracy developed by Habermas, Joshua Cohen, Amy Gutman, and Dennis Thomson and should be understood in the sense that all prereflexive preferences should be scrutinized within a public space in the light of reasons. The deliberative-republican intuition is that until politics will address the satisfaction of extrapolitical preferences not filtered through the exchange of reasons it can never be expected to overcome the atomization of political constituencies that often ushers in the tyranny of the majority. In this sense, Sunstein's work draws on the Rousseauian and Tocquevillian idea of *civic virtue* and actualizes it as the necessity to strengthen the ethos of participation, turning it into a counterforce that balances the influence of special interest groups. And in his effort of translation Sunstein can find valid support in other like-minded theorists. More specifically, within the field of social theory, the work of Robert Bellah and others—documented in the two volumes *Habits of the Heart: Individualism and Commitment in American Life* and *The Good Society*—aims at reconstructing the social requisites for the rise, within the inhospitable conditions of complex societies, of a public culture centered on "commitment." [13]

A third example is offered by Frank Michelman. According to Michelman a defensible notion of deliberative democracy must necessarily strike a balance between the classical liberal emphasis on "government by consent" on one hand and the republican and democratic emphasis on "government by the governed" on the other. The starting point of Michelman's theoretical effort is not, as in the case of Habermas, the classical opposition between Locke's liberalism and Rousseau's republicanism, but rather two conflicting intuitions, both deeply embedded in American constitutional culture, namely, 1. the idea that people are politically free insofar as they are their own governors and 2. the idea that people are politically free insofar as their government is one "of laws and not of men." [14] The tension between these two notions can be easily grasped as the tension between freedom as free exercise of the sovereign will and the idea of limits to that freedom. Even if we conceive these limits as "rights" that ultimately derive their legitimacy from the sovereign will—as conditions for its free exercise, as Habermas among others has suggested, or as self-imposed limits—the tension cannot be entirely eliminated. For the limitations that, at a given point in time, the citizens accepted as sensible and justifiable at a later time, in a different historical context, may turn into unacceptable burdens. If we consider this tension from a republican perspective, Michelman suggests, we can also identify a possible way for allaying it. This republican solution consists in conceiving politics "as a process in and through which private-regarding 'men' *become* public-regarding citizens and thus collectively a 'people.' It would be by virtue of this people-making quality that the process could confer upon its law-like issue the character of validity, of law binding upon all as self-given."[15] To this process—which constitutes a condition of the possibility that a "government by the governed" be at the same time a "government by the law"—Michelman gives the name of *jurisgenerative* politics. In common with civic republicanism, this view of politics has a certain notion of "circularity" or "reciprocal influence" that presumably connects the "idea of a citizenry that acts politically as the only legal source and the only guarantee of its own rights" with the idea "of good laws and good legal rights as prerequisites for good politics." Michelman goes at great length to distinguish his own conception of jurisgenerative politics both from the communitarian overtones that Habermas attributes to him and from the classical republican idea of politics as the bringing to expression of a previous, latent, and in any event prepolitical commonality of substantive strong evaluations. What the proponent of jurisgenerative politics emphasizes is not so much the sharedness of substantive normative orientations, as a kind of "weaker" partaking of the historical experiences deposited in the collective memory of the citizenry—a shared political past that survives in the form of "collective memory."[16] Such a shared memory could suffice, according to Michelman, to "supply participants with identity 'as' a people or political community" and to set limits on what could otherwise take the form of an infinite variety of interpretations of the communal ends and meanings.

In "Traces of Self-Government" Michelman demarcates his position from classical republicanism.[17] Classical republicanism as exemplified by James Harrington embedded an emphasis on self-government, on practical deliberation as dialogue, on the equality of the rulers and the ruled, on a realistic notion of the common good, on virtue, on proprietary independence as the social basis of virtue. The fundamental principle, however, is the idea of positive freedom as consisting of self-government. The other notions are conditions of the possibility of positive freedom so understood.

Important modifications are needed if such a principle is to be adopted by a contemporary republican approach. Differently from Renaissance and Harringtonian republicanism, in fact, the republican-liberal view propounded by Michelman portrays self-government not only in a "negativized" way, as aimed merely at the preservation of rights—in this being the heir to the post-Harringtonian development of republicanism—but also as an institutionally channeled form of *self-government* or government *by the people*, mediated by the role of the Supreme Court: "the courts, and especially the Supreme Court, seem to take on as one of their ascribed functions the modeling of active self-government that citizens find practically beyond reach." [18]

The fourth example of political republicanism is offered by Bruce Ackerman. It may at first sound strange to list the author of *Social Justice in the Liberal State* among the proponents of republicanism. Yet Ackerman over the years has come a long way from the abstract liberal model of an egalitarian polity outlined in that early work. He has undertaken a complex reconstruction of the crucial turning points in the constitutional history of the United States—the first two published volumes of the trilogy *We, the People* are the product of this investigation—and, more recently, he has ventured on the terrain of formulating concrete institutional proposals on the separation of powers in complex society and rethinking emergency powers, in the face of the terrorist threat, along democratic lines. What is of interest, in the context of our discussion, is Ackerman's effort to envision ways of injecting a republican, deliberative, and participatory moment into the normal political process of contemporary democratic societies.

Ackerman's proposal is outlined in *Deliberation Day*, a volume coauthored with James Fishkin (the author of *Deliberative Polling*).[19] The idea is to use one of those civic holidays (e.g., President's Day), which presently mainly serve the purpose of creating business opportunities for the benefit of the tourist industry, for a republican experiment conducted on a continental scale. The experiment would involve all the citizens who wish to participate: for a symbolic per-day honorarium of $100 (roughly the per diem amount paid to citizens who serve as jurors), willing citizens could be asked to participate, with the assistance of experts and political leaders, in intensive, in-depth discussions on an agenda previously predetermined in a consensual way among the government and the opposition and widely publicized.

The basic idea is to create a "political market" for deliberation and discursive reflection. As things stand now in our societies, political elites find it convenient to mold their political communication along marketing lines. They storm the electorate with emotionally marked expressions and images aimed more at capturing a distracted attention than at sustaining reflection. The institutionalization of a "deliberation day" would put this kind of communication at a disadvantage with respect to a less advertising and marketing oriented kind of political communication. It is simply impossible for representatives of political parties to face ten hours of in-depth discussion with citizens if armed only with slogans or catchphrases or sound bites to be repeated obsessively: above all, it is impossible to try to do so without paying a heavy price the next day, when the newspaper will report on what has gone on during the discussions of deliberation day. Thus a powerful incentive would be created for all the political parties to adopt a more reflective and deliberative style in political communication.

This innovative proposal within the deliberative-republican strand of political theory would not require excessive costs in terms of participation and remains quite in line with the Madisonian precept of economizing on virtue. Even more important is the potential, inherent in Ackerman's proposal, for leaving behind all the trite debates on the liberty of the ancients and the liberty of the moderns, all the stale complaints about declining participation and the generic invocations, often heard in deliberative democratic circles, of more participation, of a more vibrant public sphere, and of a more robust public dialogue. With respect to Habermas's notion of the public sphere, Ackerman's proposal of a deliberation day somehow allows and encourages a state-originated and state-directed development of the public sphere. The so-called weak publics become a little bit stronger than they are in the Habermasian account: now they have an institutional channel for having their voice reach the strong publics and a secured media coverage. On the other hand, however, the filtering provided by candidates and parties perhaps will limit the agenda-setting function ideally exerted by the Habermasian public sphere: any new proposal for the agenda will have to be approved by the existent political elites and their pollsters and advisers before gaining access to the stage. With respect to the Rawlsian view of political liberalism, in Ackerman's and Fishkin's project public reason gets a larger stage than just the institutional forums that Rawls sees as its natural settings. Deliberation day activities fall in between the public forum proper—namely, the institutional publics formally constituted—and the background culture ongoingly brewing in the debating activities of churches, universities, research institutions, professional and scientific associations, and the like.

Finally, for the sake of completeness, let me just mention those positions that I have called occasional republicanisms, namely, single statements and moments within the intellectual itinerary of authors who by and large have not identified with republicanism and yet at times have vigorously emphasized republican themes. Two important examples in this category are the so-called Kantian republicanism at times advocated by Habermas and the liberal civic-republicanism defended by Ronald Dworkin in his essay "Liberal Community."[20] These further details, however, though contributing to the completeness of the picture, would not add much novelty. It is more important, in my opinion, to take up the task of situating republicanism within the larger horizon of the other contemporary political conceptions and of identifying the peculiar challenge that it poses to liberalism.

The Republican Difference

Reconstructing the republican difference with respect to the whole range of traditions of political thought presently living would require an entire volume. I will confine myself to a much more modest task: namely, to outline the specificity of republicanism relative only to the liberal tradition.

From a historical point of view, the relation of republicanism to liberalism has a univocal vectorial quality: modern liberalism is the heir of the republican tradition, which it further develops along individualistic lines, and not the other way around. Liberalism, in fact, has not created but has *inherited* from republicanism the idea of limiting the power of the state— according to Machiavelli, for example, "absolute power" is synonymous with "tyranny"—even if subsequently liberalism has originally developed the republican idea of "limiting the power the state" into that notion of inalienable individual rights that we never find in the republican tradition. Liberalism has also inherited from republicanism the (Ciceronian and Machiavellian) idea that the end of political community must be a "neutral" and uncontroversial one and that the set of ends that best approximates this quality is the protection of life, liberty, and property.

Over and beyond these central ideas, other republican motifs survive and are further developed within liberalism. Republicanism has as strong an aversion as liberalism against all utopias, conservative and revolutionary, of an entirely reconciled and pacified society. Machiavelli is keen on showing us, in his *Discourses*, how the endemic and never solved conflict between the nobility and the plebs in republican Rome contributed crucially to keeping Rome free. In fact, the lesson to be drawn from republican Rome is that "in every republic there are two humors, that of the populace and that of the nobility, and that all legislation favorable to liberty is brought about by the clash between them."[21] Once again, the appreciation of institutionally mediated conflict as a factor of stability is quite in line with the quintessentially liberal, Madisonian idea of "checks and balances."

Finally, the doctrine of the separation of powers also has republican predecessors, for example in Machiavelli's reflections on the distinct functions of sovereignty, as well as the use of the contract metaphor in accounting for political legitimacy and political obligation. Locke's liberal account of legitimate government draws on that metaphor just as much as Rousseau's republican account of the general will.

Yet it is essential to keep in mind that traditions of political thought such as republicanism and liberalism are extremely complex and internally differentiated. The *libertarian* inspiration of Nozick or Hayek is extremely distant from the liberalism of Kant or Rawls, just as the neo-Aristotelian republicanism of Pocock or Arendt is quite distant from the Roman and Machiavellian republicanism of Skinner and Pettit. It makes no sense to compare theories that are internally so diverse. Least sense of all would it make sense to mix theories located at a different level of differentiation and compare one strand of republicanism, say political republicanism, with liberalism as a whole.

If we proceed to a comparison of specific subtraditions, then, I would like to defend the claim that the observable distance between the proponents of "political republicanism" and *liberal* liberals such as Rawls, Dworkin, and others is indeed inferior to the conceptual distance that separates *liberal* liberals from *libertarian* liberals.

To make this point, let me go back to Pettit's distinction between two conceptions of negative freedom—*freedom from interference* and *freedom from domination*. According to Pettit, these two conceptions are representative of the liberal and the republican understanding of freedom. With a modicum of notable exceptions, we should be able to observe the recurrence of the first notion of freedom in the work of liberals and the recurrence of the second among republicans.

This is far from being the case, however. Not only contemporary liberal authors such as Gaus and Raz constitute exceptions, as Pettit explicitly acknowledges,[22] but a whole area of liberalism—probably the one most representative and dynamic in our times—cannot be easily situated on the same side of the dichotomy.

I will leave aside the case of Habermas—an author whose work is receptive to many liberal themes but who has always resisted being labeled a liberal—and will briefly consider aspects of the work of Rawls and Dworkin in order to show how, in their case, we find undisputably liberal authors whose notion of freedom cannot be easily reconciled with Pettit's idea of "freedom from interference."

In § 32 of *A Theory of Justice* we find an account of freedom that seems to fit Pettit's hypothesis.[23] As some critics have maintained, to separate conceptually—as Rawls undoubtedly does when raising the question "why should we want that liberty be equally distributed?"—"liberty" from the "equal distribution of liberty" means to allow for the sensibleness of speaking of liberty also in the presence of an *unequal* distribution of it, when some enjoy more and others less of it. If so, then freedom precedes politics and it can be "distributed" by a regime according to one more or less just scheme or another. Instead, it is distinctive of republicanism to assume that freedom— understood as freedom through or within the law and not as freedom from the law—does not exist for *anybody* unless it is equally distributed. No one is free unless *all* are free. We could jettison *A Theory of Justice* overboard, concede to its intrinsic old-fashioned liberal atomism, and maintain that this error is subsequently corrected by Rawls in *Political Liberalism*. I wonder, however, whether this move is really necessary. Perhaps the republican critics of Rawls look for his notion of freedom in the wrong place.

A Theory of Justice, as it is well known, has the structure of an account of a mental experiment—the deliberation in the original position, under a veil of ignorance, on the part of the representatives of citizens, concerning the fair and just basic structure for society. The standpoint of justice, of *justice as fairness,* is emulated by the device of the veil of ignorance, but this standpoint, which guides deliberation concerning the basic structure and thus also the fair distribution of freedom, in turn presupposes the equal freedom of the representatives of the citizens. It is in this indubitable and non-negotiable equality of the "coauthors" of the choice concerning the basic structure—in the unjustifiability of attributing more influence and weight to the opinion of one over the other among the participants in the original position—that lies the most important but not the only "republican moment" in *A Theory of Justice.*

As a matter of fact, it is possible to find more argumentative junctures in *A Theory of Justice* that fly in the face of attributing to Rawls a view of freedom as freedom from interference. For example, among the primary goods we find something like "the social bases of self-respect." How can it even be suggested that freedom as freedom from domination—freedom from subjection to someone else's arbitrary, albeit perhaps not manifested, will—is bound to be something alien to the liberal spirit of Rawls's framework, when one of the primary goods whose distributive scheme is explicitly thematized in the original position is the set of necessary preconditions for a future citizen to develop self-respect?

Political Liberalism then simply reconfirms the indefensibility of an interpretation of Rawls's political philosophy that would equate his implicit notion of freedom with the notion of freedom as freedom from interference. Against such interpretation speaks the initial and overarching question to which the entire book constitutes an answer: "how is it possible for there to exist over time a just and stable society of free and equal citizens, who remain profoundly divided by reasonable religious, philosophical and moral doctrines?"[24]

The idea of equal respect, presupposed by the conception of freedom as freedom from domination, is also presupposed by many among the crucial notions that sustain the conceptual structure of *Political Liberalism:* for example, the idea of "fair cooperation" or the "duty of civility," which enjoins the citizens to provide each other reasons and justifications for their choices, or the idea of "overlapping consensus" or that of "public reason" would not make sense if we did not subscribe to an underlying principle, which Charles Larmore has rightly identified as the ideal of equal respect due to all citizens, according to which the fundamental political principles should be rationally acceptable to those who will subsequently be bound by them.[25] In fact, the reason why we do not consider just the acceptance of political principles on the basis of force is not that the use of force is always unjust. If so, then—as Weber teaches us—the very idea of political association, never to be disjoined ultimately from the possibility of the legitimate use of force, would have to be considered intrinsically unjust. The reason is rather to be found in the fact that to obtain obedience through the use or threat of the use of force, without engaging the other person's capacity to think autonomously or by engaging it only in the reductive sense of an assessment of the costs and benefits of obeying, is equivalent to treating that person in a different, and certainly demeaning, way with respect to the way in which *we* wish to be treated. Thus, Larmore concludes, "to respect another person as an end is to require that coercive or political principles be as justifiable to that person as they are to us."[26] These considerations suffice to exclude that *Political Liberalism* might be interpreted as a work of political philosophy that rests on a notion of freedom as freedom from interference.

Dworkin provides us with an even clearer example on the unamenability of contemporary liberal liberalism to the reductive notion of freedom attributed to it by Pettit. Not only is Dworkin the author of "Liberal Community," the 1989 essay cited above in which he outlines a liberal position that includes important aspects of "civic republicanism," but at the center of his philosophy of law he places "the sovereign virtue," equality understood as equal respect—a notion evidently in dissonance with the idea of freedom as freedom from interference.[27]

In "Liberal Community" Dworkin takes distance from the communitarian idea of a general primacy of the common interest or good over individual interests in all spheres of life as well as from the traditional, atomistic-liberal view, according to which nothing exists that deserves the name of the common good over and beyond the sum total of the individual—possibly converging, more often diverging—interests. Dworkin defends the thesis that each political community has a life of its own, which is qualitatively better or worse depending on how certain choices are collectively made, but confines the scope of this communal life to the sole sphere of *political action*, where *political* really means "institutional" and denotes the set of all legislative, executive, and judiciary acts that can be imputed to the political community as a whole.[28]

The meaning of the phrase *political action* is elucidated by Dworkin with reference to the famous example of the collective life of an orchestra. To the extent that an orchestra has a collective life, argues Dworkin, this life is limited to the set of those acts that current social practices and current expectations identify as typical of an orchestra, e.g., to rehearse and perform a symphony. Acts such as performing a symphony are then perceived both by the members of the orchestra as well as by the spectators as single acts imputable to a collective actor. There is then a connection between the quality of individual competence and the quality of the overall performance of an orchestra, and this connection authorizes the collective actor to inspect and exercise authority over the individual, but only insofar as the institutional aim of delivering a good performance is concerned.[29] I may be concerned if the first violin gets into a drinking habit that leads her to come to the concert hall "under the influence," I do not have a right to question her private sexual choices. The Dworkinian position is clearly a liberal one, but at the same time indistinguishable from the value core that Pettit attributes to republicanism.

In fact, Dworkin defines his "liberal civic-republicanism" as a third course between the *atomistic liberalism*—according to which an individual "will not count his own life as any less successful if, in spite of his best efforts, his community accepts great economic inequality, or racial or other forms of unfair discrimination, or unjust constraints on individual freedom"[30]—and a *fervent communitarian* outlook, according to which the quality of individual life is threatened by *any* violation whatsoever of the communal norms. What better instantiation, from within the work of an indisputably liberal author, of the republican idea that there exists no real freedom for anybody, within a given political order, unless there exists a real and equal freedom for all? The kind of citizen that Dworkin takes as exemplary, in his words, "will count his own life as diminished—a less good life than he might have had—if he lives in an unjust community, no matter how hard he has tried to make it just. That fusion of political morality and critical self-interest seems to me to be the true nerve of civic republicanism, the important way in which individual citizens should merge their interests and personality into political community."[31]

Over and beyond this essay, however, it must be noted that the theme of freedom from domination underlies the whole of Dworkin's work in the form of the leading value of equality. That the state speak to all its citizens with one voice is the principle that guides not just constitutional interpretation—"making the most" of the Constitution for Dworkin means, in fact, to choose the interpretation that most enhances its egalitarian inspiration—but also the correct institutionalization of rights and the justification of democracy. In *Freedom's Law*, for example, democracy is presented not just as a procedure valid in itself, or as an end in itself, but as a means, namely, as the procedure that under normal conditions best ensures the realization of the ideal of political equality.[32]

Finally, even in those of Dworkin's writings that lend themselves more easily to the cliché of "abstract" and "ahistorical" liberal thought we find emphases that run against Pettit's hypothesis. Even in the distributive model based on an auction conducted on a faraway island with seashells replacing money, the ultimate standard according to which the fairness of the final distribution ought to be measured is nothing but the *absence of envy* on the part of each member of society relative to the set of resources that his neighbor has secured through the auction.[33] Needless to say, absence of envy is a reflection of absence of domination.

To conclude this section, not only the relation of republicanism to an important area of contemporary liberalism cannot be conceived as an antagonistic or competitive one, but the dichotomy of "freedom from interference" and "freedom from domination" fails to neatly sort out liberals and republicans even if we look at *previous* historical contexts. Figures like Dewey e Roosevelt can hardly be described as liberals who understand freedom as freedom from interference. In *Liberalism and Social Action,* for example, Dewey credits the idealist strands of British liberalism for having criticized the idea "that freedom is something which individuals can possess" and having instead suggested that the function of the state is to create "institutions under which individuals can effectively realize the potentialities that are theirs."[34] And Dewey's famous work, *The Public and Its Problem,* would make no sense if interpreted in light of a notion of freedom as freedom from interference. The public can only be important if freedom is freedom from domination. "Liberty," as we hear from this champion of liberalism, "is that secure release and fulfillment of personal potentialities which take place only in rich and manifold association with others."[35]

Roosevelt, in a famous address to the Democratic Convention of 1932, states that "liberty requires opportunity to make a living—a living decent according to the standard of the time, a living which gives man not only enough to live by, but something to live for. . . . If the average citizen is guaranteed equal opportunity in the polling place, he must have equal opportunity in the market place."[36] Had Roosevelt understood freedom along the lines that Pettit describes as typical of liberalism, we would have never had a New Deal, for his view would not have differed in any important way from the laissez-faire view of economic freedom shared by the leading entrepreneurial groups and for a long time also by the Supreme Court.

Going further back in time, in chapter 3 of John Stuart Mill's essay *On Liberty*, we find a view of liberty as the securing of the possibility of cultivating the uniqueness of the person, and this conception of liberty, once again, is hard to reduce to the notion of freedom from interference. The fulfillment and bringing to expression of one's potentials, to which freedom of expression and cultural pluralism are argued to be conducive, is not something that can take place within relations of domination.[37] Also Benjamin Constant's quintessentially liberal conception of the "liberty of the moderns" can be argued not to be exactly coextensive with Pettit's notion of freedom from interference.[38]

The list could continue even further back. Locke's critique of Hobbes's notion of freedom as the freedom to do without impediments whatever pleases us could not be more typical of what Pettit sees as the quintessentially republican view of freedom. In the *Second Treatise of Government* we read that "the Liberty of Man, in Society, is to be under no other Legislative Power, but that established, by consent, in the Common-wealth, nor under the Dominion of any Will, or Restraint of any Law, but what the Legislative shall enact, according to Trust put in it." In the end, Locke concludes, using words that might feature in any republican manifesto, that freedom in society means "not to be subject to the inconstant, uncertain, unknown, Arbitrary Will of another Man." [39]

In sum, *pace* Pettit, I believe that the examples provided suffice to show that the republican difference, with respect to liberalism, cannot be captured adequately on the terrain of the conception of freedom. Least of all can the specificity of republicanism be captured in terms of the dichotomy of *freedom from interference* and *freedom from domination*—which is not to say that a difference between liberalism and republicanism does not exist or that it could not be captured on a different basis. In fact, in the next section I will suggest that such difference is best identified as a methodological one and, more specifically, as one linked with a diverse way of understading the relation of normativity to exemplarity.

The Republican Challenge

In the preceding sections I have questioned the thesis that republicanism poses a challenge for other conceptions of politics by way of articulating a distinctive notion of freedom called "freedom from domination." I took it for granted that the other aspects of the republican tradition—such as the glorification of vita activa as the best form of human flourishing—do not pose a great challenge to our pluralistic understanding of politics. Thus the question must now be addressed: does republicanism still retain a relevance for us in the twenty-first century over and beyond its unquestionable merits as the breeding ground for liberalism, and, if so, in what sense?

The relevance and value of the republican tradition, in my opinion, are best captured as an elective affinity of the republican perspective with a more general philosophical perspective that hinges around the normativity of situated identity. No thinker in the republican tradition has ever been attracted by abstract schemes, universal principles, or demonstrations *more geometrico*. Instead, a distinctive propensity for "rhetorics" has emerged among republican authors, in the positive sense that today would translate as "dialogue" or "discourse," where rhetorics means the attempt to argumentatively woo the consensus of citizens in a context where the best solution to a given problem cannot be known a priori.

Republicanism is inherently equivalent with the exercise of public reason and judgment, almost coextensive with situated *historical* judgment and *political* judgment. When we read a text by Machiavelli, we are struck by the absence of any abstract speculation: the basis of his arguments is constituted entirely by an interpretation of historical facts—facts that may be remote from our perception but that must have been quite vivid in his contemporaries' minds. This methodological choice is often portrayed—by critics and defenders of republicanism alike—as a prevailing of the "rhetorical moment," as opposed to "rigorous," i.e., "abstract," theorizing, within republican thought. This description, however, renders a bad service to republicanism, in my opinion.

The enduring relevance of republicanism for political theory in the twenty-first century, and the challenge that it implicitly poses to liberalism, can be better understood as a propensity toward a form of universalism where the cogency of general principles is replaced by the force of the example and the argumentative cogency of exemplarity: the exemplarity of institutions, political arrangements and regimes, norms and the like that demand our consent, no less than works of art, by virtue of their capacity to set the (in this case, political) imagination in motion by virtue of their exceptional self-congruence.

As we have argued in chapter 2 in the context of a critical examination of Hannah Arendt's interpretation of Kant's *Critique of the Power of Judgment*, in politics no less than in art the exemplary provides guidance and exerts cogency beyond its immediate context of origin *not* as *schemata* do, by providing prior cases to which we can assimilate the present one, but as works of art do, namely, by providing outstanding instances of authentic congruency that are capable of educating our discernment by way of exposing us to selective instances of that special pleasure called by Kant the feeling of the promotion and affirmation of life.

Its historicist inclination leads republicanism to develop quite naturally a taste for exemplarity, where for something—a "constitutional essential," a policy decision, a legal brief, a new form of organization, an orientation of public opinion—to possess exemplarity, as argued in chapter 3, does not mean "to be an example of" anything else but rather to be a law unto itself: namely, to require us to forge a new concept and search for a new linguistic term, rather than apply the ones we are familiar with.

If, as the *Critique of the Power of Judgment* suggests of the aesthetic exemplarity of the work of art, this new political concept—the New Deal, the New Frontier, sexual harassment, multiculturalism, politics of memory, identity politics—has the ability to set our political imagination in motion and our mental powers "into a swing that is final," thereby producing an experience linked with the feeling of having gained a new vista on political life, then we are faced with exemplarity.

In the case of the New Deal, for example, the received laissez-faire wisdom of the past was challenged first by the need to respond to economic emergency—the Great Depression—but then from that response a whole new view of the meaning of equality began to develop. Some among the government initiatives stimulated by Roosevelt—the National Industrial Recovery Act (NIRA) of 1933, providing for control of the market dynamic of prices, the Civil Works Administration and the Public Works Association, protecting millions of workers from the tragedy of unemployment, the Fair Labor Standards Act, providing for minimum wage and banning child labor, the Federal Securities Act and the creation of the Securities and Exchange Commission, protecting publicity in the stock market, the Social Security Act, providing among other things for old-age pensions, survivor's benefits, unemployment insurance—have now lost their revolutionary quality and seem almost commonplace in the world they helped to create. But the vision underlying them presupposed a thorough rethinking of freedom and equality and of "what we owe each other" as citizens. Roosevelt justified the gist of those provisions by tracing an analogy between the 1776 struggle against "the tyranny of a political autocracy," against the royalists who "governed without the consent of the governed," and the need for a new struggle against *new* dynasties and kingdoms—more impersonal but no less pervasive—that are "built upon concentration of control over material things" and tend to create "a new despotism" wrapped "in the robes of legal sanction." Roosevelt creates a standpoint that reshapes our perception of freedom:

> The hours men and women worked, the wages they received, the conditions of their labor—these had passed beyond the control of the people, and were imposed by this new industrial dictatorship. . . .

Throughout the Nation, opportunity was limited by monopoly. Individual initiative was crushed in the cogs of a great machine. The field open for free business was more and more restricted. Private enterprise, indeed, became too private. It became privileged enterprise, not free enterprise.[40]

And in the same speech we see equality being rethought: "for too many of us the political equality we once had won was meaningless in the face of economic inequality. . . . If the average citizen is guaranteed equal opportunity in the polling places, he must have equal opportunity in the market place."[41] The point is that the appeal of the New Deal rests less on the cumulative justification of the single policies included within it than on the extent to which the new perspective that it opens on equality, and on the nexus of political and economic freedom, elicits a sense of the enhancement of our (political) life by virtue of adding a new dimension to it and launching our political imagination onto unexplored new paths.

It remains to be worked out, however, what it means for any element of our political life—now taken as a special area of life, distinct from aesthetics—to attain exemplarity and exert the force thereof: to move the imagination, to disclose a new political world, are still terms borrowed from aesthetics, but political philosophy is faced with the task of producing its own distinctive vocabulary for addressing exemplarity. It does not start from scratch. Charisma and mobilization are two obvious candidates for being key entries in this vocabulary.

Charisma is defined by Weber as the belief in our obligation to obey an authority who is such not by virtue of rules that apply to its case, not by virtue of tradition and mores, but by virtue of nothing other than its exceptional powers or qualities—where exceptionality of course is relative to a dimension of values and is ultimately regarded either as "of divine origin" or "exemplary."[42] When Napoleon used nothing other than the widespread acceptance of his exceptional talents to elevate people of humble origin to thrones and position of military responsibility, when Francis of Assisi would address the well-to-do youths of his town by saying "Sell everything and come with me," they were obeyed solely in recognition of the exceptional exemplarity of the one who issued such commands. Charisma is to politics what genius is to the production of works of art. For both what Weber said of charisma holds: they can only be "awakened" or "tested," not "learned" or "taught."[43] Genius and charisma carry no guarantee of aesthetic or political success: the works and deeds they inspire have to pass the inspection of taste and of political judgment, but works of art and political enterprises where genius or charisma is totally absent strike us as spiritless or dull.

Mobilization is another fundamental term of the political vocabulary. Why do certain ideas, proposals, slogans, manifestos mobilize people and political energies while others fail at that? One obvious explanation is that the mobilizing element meets with the *interests* of the mobilized constituency. But history offers plenty of examples of movements, groups, peoples, classes, nations that at certain points in time get mobilized for things that run contrary to their interests. One could easily make sense of instances such as these in terms of mistakes that political subjects make in the assessment of their short- and long-term interest. But things are more complicated. Often, in fact, we perceive policies, objectives, proposals, or rallying cries as being in our (class, national, symbolic) interest, but we fail to get moved by them. We distractedly acknowledge their existence, but no enthusiasm is aroused in us and we don't deflect from our normal routines. Again, they are another political equivalent of the spiritless works of art. What truly mobilizes us, instead, is something not only that meets our interests but also stirs our imagination and carries with it the promise of a "promotion, affirmation and furtherance" of our political life as well as the idea of a communicability of this experience. We do not think of something that mobilizes our political enthusiasm as something that merely meets our *preferences*: we think that the "vision" enshrined in that proposal, slogan, objective can potentially promote, affirm, or further everybody's life. The ability to mobilize politically rests on the force of the exemplary to inspire conduct.

To conclude, the complex societies in which we live are democracies. This means that they have to preserve some kind of unhypocritical, nonillusory sense in which the citizens are not just the addressees of the laws but also their authors. But, as one of the republican-liberal authors mentioned above, Frank Michelman, has observed, they are also societies that confront democracy with inhospitable conditions. Among these inhospitable conditions there certainly is an unprecedented degree of cultural pluralism, which makes the convergence of all citizens on a single set of political principles, even procedural ones, more difficult than ever in the past. In this context, which we have all reasons to believe will persist throughout the new century, the enduring relevance of republicanism consists in its affinity—unparalleled within any other tradition—with a model of normativity based on judgment and exemplarity. This affinity puts republicanism in the best position for providing us with a view of political justification that does not the depend on the questionable assumption of transcultural principles.

6 *Exemplarity and Human Rights*

Exemplarity can be shown to be a useful notion not only for making sense of the normativity of the reasonable, the radicality of radical evil, and the specificity of the republican tradition but also for the grounding of human rights within a larger conception of justice on a global scale.

Here again a word on our present predicament may be in order. Never in history has the need for a global rule of law based on a universalist understanding of justice been more acutely felt and yet at the same time perceived as an elusive chimera. On the one hand, the long-awaited freeing of international relations from the strictures of the post-Yalta bipolar order, the ever accelerating process of globalization, and the intensification of migratory flows have all increased the sense of urgency associated with our aspiration to a genuinely transcultural notion of justice. On the other hand, the effects of the Linguistic Turn have contributed to a growing awareness of the constitutive role of life forms and vocabularies vis-à-vis our conceptions of justice. The difficulties of articulating a single persuasive view of justice for the globalized yet pluralized world are rooted in this combination of factors.

Were the perception of an irreducible plurality of life forms, conceptual schemes, paradigms, traditions, and cultures not accompanied by a belief in their constitutive role for our thoughts, or were such a belief in turn associated with an unshaken faith in the identifiability of a core of universals underlying all cultures, no difficulty would arise. Instead, our philosophical difficulties stem from the persistence of our universalistic aspirations combined with the feeling that such aspirations can no longer be satisfied through traditional philosophical means, namely, through recourse to universal principles established as valid antecedently to their being rooted in one of many life forms—the so-called principles from nowhere that utilitarian, deontological, and, more recently, procedural approaches to justice have been postulating.

The justification of human rights is one of the areas in which this problematic constellation has made its effects most visibly felt. I will begin by briefly reconstructing some difficulties in Rawls's and Habermas's accounts of human rights and then will suggest a tentative alternative solution to the problem of justifying the universal cogency of human rights in those local legal contexts where they are not codified into positive law—an alternative solution based on the judgment view of justice that I have outlined in *Justice and Judgment*. In the context of presenting the main lines of the judgment argument for human rights, I will draw a distinction between two normative notions of humanity that become relevant respectively in a *political* and a *moral* understanding of justice on a global scale. Such a distinction is important, in the context of an argument on the grounding of human rights, because it allows us to avoid the pitfalls of either reducing human rights to the articles of a pact among existing states or reducing them to just one more "comprehensive" moral-philosophical doctrine among others. Finally, I will recall an aspect of one of the most inspiring philosophical sources for anyone who wishes to conceive of normativity as translocally cogent yet as *situated,* rather than "from nowhere," namely, Hegel's line of thinking about justice and law. No one more than Hegel, in fact, has put at the center of his philosophy the aspiration—shared today by those who, in the light of the critique of foundationalism, wish to reconcile universalism and pluralism in a not merely formalistic or procedural way—to articulate a form of normativity that combines universal significance with its possessing a *historically* concrete and particular, as opposed to a (procedurally, transcendentally, naturalistically, or ontologically) decontextualized origin.

Rawls and Habermas on the Universality of Human Rights

Human rights are at the center of both Rawls's and Habermas's arguments about international or global justice, and it is crucial to examine some of the difficulties incurred by their accounts before discussing how the judgment paradigm can contribute to overcoming them.

For Rawls the protection of human rights is a necessary condition in order for a regime to be counted as at least "decent" and for the people living under it to be worthy of acceptance within the "Society of Peoples." Severe and continuous violations of human rights constitute a sufficient condition for legitimately suspending the duty of nonintervention in the internal affairs of a country and authorizing sanctions and military action aimed at reestablishing their observance. However, the centrality of human rights as "a limit to the pluralism of peoples"[1] does not seem to be accompanied by an adequate articulation of their normative status. Rawls builds his catalogue of rights by drawing mainly on the Universal Declaration of Human Rights of 1948. More specifically, he selects only *some* of the rights listed in the declaration as "human rights proper": the rights mentioned in article 3 (rights to "life, liberty and the security of person"), in article 5 (the right "not to be subjected to cruel, degrading treatment or punishment"), and, more generally, the rights mentioned in articles 3 through 18. Furthermore, Rawls mentions other human rights that follow from the first group of rights and are the object of certain special conventions on genocide and apartheid. The whole group of rights listed in articles 19 through 30 of the declaration, however, is not included by Rawls within human rights. Some of them—e.g., the right to social security (article 22) and to equal pay for equal work (article 23)—are explicitly denied that status because they seem to presuppose specific types of institutions.

What is the basis for singling out a subset of rights as properly "human" within a legal document like the Universal Declaration? Rawls's selection certainly cannot rest on *legal* grounds, insofar as nothing in the document approved in San Francisco in 1948 suggests that the rights mentioned in articles 19 through 30 should be attributed a status different from that of the rights mentioned in articles 3 through 18. Rawls's grounds then must be grounds of a *moral-philosophical* nature.

Elsewhere the universalistic status of this subset of rights is explicated by Rawls in the following terms: "they are intrinsic to the Law of Peoples and have a political (moral) effect whether or not they are supported lo-cally." He then states: "the political (moral) force [of these rights] extends to all societies, and they are binding on all peoples and societies, including outlaw States."[2] In no other passages is the issue examined in greater de-tail. This formulation obviously generates a host of difficulties, related ulti-mately to the fact that human rights appear to be beyond the contractarian framework of the Law of Peoples in at least three senses. First, in the sense that the eight principles approved of in the original position do include the duty to protect human rights, but do not contain a specification of which rights are to be considered *human rights.* Second, the parties thus appear to be approving of a principle whose content remains totally unspecified. Third, because rights are declared to be binding also for those states that do not and cannot have representatives in the original position and thus cannot be said to have subscribed to them, their bindingness appears to be evidently of a noncontractarian nature.

Clearly Rawls is leading us back to a traditional framework within which there exist moral rights, independently grounded, that set external limits to the sovereign will of peoples. Furthermore, in *The Law of Peoples,* Rawls does not offer any argument for grounding these moral rights, but merely invites us to presuppose their being justified. Even his appeal to documents such as the Universal Declaration does not help insofar as the content of these docu-ments is not accepted in its entirety but is submitted by Rawls to the assess-ment of a moral reason assumed to be in a position to identify the core of "hu-man rights proper." This substantial retreat from the position he defended in the context of his rejoinder to Habermas on the pages of the *Journal of Philosophy*—a position within which Rawls fully subscribed to the thesis of an intrinsic connection between rights and democratic self-determination[3]—is one of the major problems that haunt *The Law of Peoples.*

The discussion of human rights is framed under quite different premises in Habermas's view of international justice. Habermas points out the pres-ence of a certain ambiguity in the notion of human rights. On the one hand, qua norms explicitly occurring in given constitutions, human rights are rights in the positive, legal sense of the term. On the other hand, because of their universalistic formulation—i.e., because of their being cast as rights of any human being regardless of her citizenship—these rights are also norms endowed with an "extrapositive validity" (*überpositive Geltung*).[4] According to Habermas, this "extrapositive validity" of human rights, understood in the sense of their having a special sort of cogency on the local constitutional lawmaker, has often been misunderstood (e.g., by Rawls) as an indicator of their being *moral* rights antecedent to any act of constitutional lawmaking, i.e. rights that can only be protected or disregarded, but not granted or denied, by the lawmaker. However, the idea of an extrapositive dimension of human rights is, according to Habermas, only a projection of the universality of their *scope* and of their being addressed to the citizens of a certain state not qua citizens, but qua human beings, under a description that applies equally as well to all those who are *not* citizens of that state. As a matter of fact, for Habermas "human rights are from the beginning (*von Haus aus*) rights of a legal nature."[5]

Their specificity, relative to other kinds of rights (e.g., political rights), consists of the fact that their legitimation can be based on purely moral arguments—which take as their object what is equally good for everyone—and requires no additional ethical or pragmatic considerations. The right to life and the right to freedom of conscience, for example, are justified just by virtue of their being in the equal interest of each person qua human being. This capacity to be justified on the simple basis of moral considerations and nothing else has generated the wrong impression that human rights are best conceived as moral norms; however, the peculiarity of their needing only moral considerations for their grounding does not, in and of itself, modify the *legal* nature of these rights.[6]

From this perspective, human rights are to be understood as legal norms with a moral content, norms that remain subjective and actionable rights. Now this certainly holds true for the human rights included in concrete constitutions: but what about the status of human rights as rights that all the existing states *ought to* include in their legal order? According to Habermas, when considered at this level human rights have an *ambiguous* status: they still await a full legal status that will materialize only in the form of a cosmopolitan legal order yet to come. We must not, however, take this hopefully transient state as a definitive one—as Rawls seems inclined to do—but we should rather think of human rights at the level of international justice as rights on their way to acquiring a full legal status.[7]

In "Remarks on Legitimation Through Human Rights" Habermas has discussed again the cooriginality of rights and popular sovereignty and has argued that human rights institutionalize the communicative conditions for a reasonable political will formation. Because rights enable the exercise of democratic popular sovereignty, they cannot be understood as mere constraints on this will.[8] Now this is certainly true of *political* rights, but as far as *human* rights are concerned it is only possible either to hope that each state in the world will eventually become a constitutional democracy that includes human rights—a far from realistic prospect—or to envisage a way of assigning such rights "immediately to each individual, *qua* citizen of the world." Who is to be the agent effecting such assignment? It must be that cosmopolitan institution barely prefigured in the General Assembly of the United Nations as it exists now—an institution that should in principle mark the definitive leave-taking from the partially modified and mitigated state of nature within which international relations still find themselves. At this juncture Habermas mentions article 28 of the Universal Declaration, in which the realization of a social and international order is called for, where the "freedoms set forth in this Declaration can be fully realized," as a source that could somehow establish the *legal* status of human rights.

This line of reasoning has to face the same objection raised against Rawls: the rights listed in the declaration are not ranked in a hierarchy of importance; moreover, they cover too broad a spectrum, including, for example, the "right to leisure and rest." Habermas's position, however, points in a promising direction. What we have to do is to specify "what conditions might allow us to think of human rights as rights that are *legally* and not just *morally* binding for all States, whether or not they have embedded them in constitutions" without presupposing that a positive answer is already embedded in legal documents such as the Universal Declaration of 1948.

As I will try to show, the judgment view of global justice is in agreement with Habermas's proposal to consider human rights legal rights, even when they are not included in specific constitutions, but it is in disagreement with the idea that this legal nature could be made to rest on legal documents such as the Universal Declaration of 1948 or the Covenants of 1966. The reasons for this divergence are that if we want to have a definition of human rights as actionable, even when they are not embedded in the constitution of the country where they are being violated, and if we want our definition of human rights to be capable of sorting out violations that can legitimately be stopped if necessary through the use of international military force, we must adopt a much narrower definition than the one included in those documents. For some of the rights mentioned in the Universal Declaration (think, for example, of the right to "social security" or the right to "equal pay for equal work") indeed presuppose, as Rawls points out, the existence of institutions that are not present in every country. Others (for example, the right to "rest" and "leisure") seem to presuppose certain levels of material affluence and in any event appear less "urgent" than the rights to life and liberty.[9] Whatever the merits of these sources of international law may have been in promoting a culture of human rights worldwide, their failure to distinguish rights that have strict priority over state sovereignty and rights that, despite their being no less "human," do not have priority in the same sense, makes these sources inadequate to the task of legally grounding human rights endowed with legal actionability and military sanctionability. A key question for the judgment perspective will thus be how it can be of help in envisaging a *legal* grounding of human rights so conceived.

Let me start, however, by showing why a couple of initially tempting answers are unsatisfactory. The first temptation to be avoided, according to Frank Michelman, is to consider the phrase *legally grounded* as synonymous with *democratically grounded*, where *democratically grounded* roughly means something like recognized as binding—through some unanimously agreed procedure—by those to whom such rights will apply. Were we to choose this strategy, the posited equivalence of legal grounding and democratic grounding would once again raise the suspicion of ethnocentrism regarding rights. And human rights are a notion that we certainly, following Rawls, cannot but wish to be "political," i.e., acceptable also to those who do not take democracy to be the only legitimate procedure for shaping a collective will.[10] Therefore we cannot take *legally grounded* as meaning "approved as legally binding by the representatives of the citizens of all the countries of the world." We must think of human rights as "democracy-independent" and thus as "not contingent on the performance or outcome of any democratic procedure," even of an ad hoc global democratic procedure.[11]

If we reject the temptation to equate the grounding of human rights with their *democratic* grounding, the other alternative that we have is to think of actionable and enforceable human rights as rights agreed on, and reciprocally granted to one another, by representatives of all the states in the world convened in a special convention called for in order to deliberate precisely on the following question, which represents an extension of the Habermasian cooriginality approach to the postnational and global level: "Which rights do we want to reciprocally grant one another for the purpose of regulating our communal life according to the form of law?" The fact that the participants of such a convention would be state delegations appointed by the local governments through a variety of procedures, on the model of the General Assembly of the United Nations, is designed to ensure that the legal grounding of human rights be independent of democracy without, however, having to pay the price of their "moralization." But more on this subject will be said in chapter 7. What is relevant here is that this solemn resolution, which could take the form of a Charter of Fundamental Human Rights—different from the 1948 Universal Declaration in its being aimed no longer at the "pedagogical" goal of stimulating the growth of a culture of human rights but rather at explicitly limiting the sovereignty of states—could wield an undisputed *legal,* not just moral authority, and could enable us to identify with clarity and through *legally established criteria* that human rights violations constitute a sufficient ground for a legitimate military intervention, instead of leaving that open, as it is the case today, to a variable mix of moral and pragmatic considerations.

However, to use a Rawlsian phrase, this is just "ideal theory." What about the status of human rights up until the time when the coming into being of a global rule of law has arrived at completion? It seems to me that up until then human rights will continue to possess an essentially *moral* nature, where having a "moral" nature is understood as pertaining to the domain of what human beings owe each other simply by virtue of being humans, as opposed to what they owe each other by virtue of their being citizens of the same state, members of the same community, believers of the same religious or secular faith.[12] Today then—and with this we have already entered the discourse of "nonideal theory"—we must conceive of human rights as rights *provisionally* justified on moral grounds, though hopefully later to be justified in full legal terms. If this view is plausible, then we are faced with the question: what is the best way to proceed to such *moral* justification, if we want to avoid the ambiguity of Rawls's formulation and the deficit of pluralism inherent in Habermas's proceduralist perspective?

To answer this question, we need to briefly recall the basic aspects of the judgment paradigm and to articulate the distinction between two normative notions of humanity needed in order to avoid conflating the political and the moral justification for human rights. Then we will be in a position to resume the discussion from the point where we are leaving it now, in order to show how the judgment view can be of help.

Judgment, Justice, and the Global Rule of Law

The judgment view of justice is meant as a response, in the realm of political philosophy, to the change of horizon originating in the Linguistic Turn that is discussed in chapter 1. The judgment view of justice builds on the idea that the kind of universalism compatible with our pluralistic intuitions and our belief in the constitutive role played by life forms is the *exemplary* universalism of a self-congruent symbolic whole. What emerges from a historical and cultural context is capable of exerting a cogency *outside* its original context not by virtue of its reflecting some kind of context-transcending principle, antecedently and independently established as valid, but rather by virtue of its exceptional congruency with the subjectivity, individual or collective, that brought it into being. Through the notion of reflective judgment, this form of exemplary universalism, typical of the realm of aesthetics, can be exported into the domain that is of interest to us here. The ideals put forward by the abolitionists, the New Deal, and the civil rights movements, for example, can all be conceived as deriving their cogency not so much from their following logically from constitutional principles as from their presenting us with creative expansions of constitutional ideas and from their opening up new political vistas on the dignity of the person and the substance of rights. They were no less "political" world disclosing than works of art are "ordinary" world disclosing, and they set the imagination in motion no less than works of art.

A view of justice anchored in an exemplary, as opposed to principle-based, kind of universalism starts from the assumption that whenever two parties come into conflict, the requirements of the flourishing of the new communal identity formed at the intersection of those in conflict help us to adjudicate the controversy in much the same way as context-transcending principles such as the happiness of the largest number or the categorical imperative were supposed to do.[13] This view allows us then to conceive of the universalism of justice as originating in an *oriented reflective judgment* concerning what the fulfillment of that superordinate identity requires—a judgment oriented not simply by common intuitions concerning what it means for an identity to attain self-realization (the dimensions of *coherence, vitality, depth,* and *maturity*) but also by the ideal of *equal respect.*[14] Much as Kant argued that reflective judgment, when it considers natural beauty, can be oriented by the notion of *finality,* which works like a guideline (*Leitpfad*) and not as a principle, so we can imagine that *other* notions exert that guiding or orienting function in other domains. When we conceive justice as the optimal fulfillment of a superordinate identity that contains the identities in conflict—then the guiding function exerted by the ideal of equal respect preempts the potentially oppressive conclusions that could follow if the well-being and affirmation of the superordinate identity were envisaged without keeping the needs and legitimate aspirations of the parties in equal consideration.

The judgment paradigm, when applied to questions of justice, thus allows us to conceive of the moral point of view as the vantage point of the *fulfillment of humanity*, taken as the most inclusive imaginable human identity. However, because the fulfillment of humanity is not an abstract formula but a substantive, concrete construction of reason that rests on historically variable presuppositions, the judgment as to which solution to a practical conflict best serves this idea is a *situated* yet universal, reflective judgment, and the moral point of view appears to be equally substantive and situated yet universal.[15]

Two main problems attend a notion of justice conceived along these lines. First, how to account for the normative cogency possessed by the standpoint of the realization of the superordinate identity? Second, how to account for the capacity, on the part of such a standpoint, to play the ordering function expected of every notion of justice?

In chapter 1 our reconstruction of the Kantian notion of sensus communis served the purpose of establishing why it is that I can anticipate a universal consensus concerning the potential for something to make not just me, but all of us, experience aesthetic pleasure. Based on that, we can suppose that our sensus communis accounts for the cognitive expectation that everybody will agree to the statement that the fulfillment of humanity in its entirety is best advanced by a certain solution to the controversy at hand. We need now to address a different question: Why should we, the participants in one of the local identities implicated in the controversy, care at all, from a practical point of view, about the fulfillment of the superordinate identity within which we and our contenders are equally included? Why couldn't we cognitively concede that the fulfillment of such an identity is best served by a specific solution yet practically resist bearing the costs of adopting it? Why should we *care* about the fulfillment of the superordinate identity, over and beyond cognitively acknowledging what it requires? And, conversely, in what sense does the fulfillment of the superordinate identity place a normative demand on us?

The normative pull of the superordinate identity rests on the eudaemonistic self-reflection of the actor. On an *intersubjective* view of subjectivity—such as the one presupposed by the judgment paradigm—it is assumed that all identities, individual and collective, are constituted by relations of recognition, and that in the case of conflict these relations continue to bear a significance for the constituted identities. For an identity to take into consideration that moment of overlap, and the requisites of the maintenance of those relations of recognition then by definition, means to gain access to a *more complete* fulfillment than the one obtainable if those aspects were deliberately or unwittingly ignored. In this sense, acting according to justice can be said to improve the life of the actor, just as it was the case within the framework of classical ethics. In sum, the question "Why should we care about the realization of the virtual identity within which both our opponents and we are included?" is answered by the judgment view of justice in the following terms: "Because this virtual identity contains a piece of our own identity as well, its failure to come to realization dooms our own separate identity to experience a *lesser* degree of realization than it could attain if the superordinate one were also to flourish."

Moving on to the problem of how a judgment view of justice could provide us with a way of ordering rival solutions to a conflict on a scale of acceptability, we must now turn to an analogy with aesthetics and, more particularly, with the kind of judgment by means of which we settle aesthetic controversies concerning the best way of bringing a work of art to completion. In the case of the production of a work of art—for example, the production of a movie, the staging of a drama, the construction of a cathedral or an auditorium—our controversies concerning the best way to complete our work can be settled by reference to an *aesthetic* project that, despite the differences of interpretation, is to some extent shared. Similarly, in controversies concerning what justice requires, the political project embedded in a constitution can play an analogous role.[16] In the case of controversies over justice on a global scale, however, we obviously cannot rely on a nonexistent world constitution. Thus our reflective judgment must fall back on an *idea of humanity* that only now, in our epoch, can acquire the status of a concrete universal and denote a concrete identity, which, by definition, includes all other identities. It is by reference to this idea that the merits of the different solutions to a controversy are assessed. Yet the idea of humanity turns out, on closer inspection, to be twofold. Before discussing it more closely, however, we need to mention in passing three further points and introduce two new distinctions.

First, the ideal of equal respect, mentioned above as an additional orienting factor (beyond the four guidelines for the realization of identities) for reflective judgments in matters of justice, has the advantage, over other possible competitors, of an unsurpassed inclusiveness. It provides a terrain of overlap among all the modern conceptions of justice—whether deontological or consequentialist.[17] Second, the notion of equal respect possesses a potential, unparalleled by any other notion of our moral vocabulary, for affecting the formation of a great number of neighboring concepts, which could not be conceived in the way they are if we did not presuppose the ideal of equal respect: for example, our concept of the person qua source of autonomous action, our idea of human dignity as a focus of recognition and respect among individuals, or the idea of democracy. Third, the ideal of equal respect is bound up with fundamental formative experiences of the modern Western consciousness, notably the end of the religious wars; moreover, it has been at the center of the most important social movements, starting with the labor movement and continuing with anarchism and radical unionism, the abolitionists, the suffrage movement, the civil rights movement, the feminist movement, the gay movement, up to today's multiculturalist sensibility. In short, equal respect is so bound up with who we are that we can't disregard it without at the same time losing touch with crucial aspects of who we, as modern Westerners, have come to be.[18]

Finally, two distinctions need to be briefly discussed before addressing the grounding of human rights on a judgment view of justice. In the first place, we need to distinguish between justice in a *political* sense and justice in a *moral* sense. From the perspective outlined here, the same judgment-based notion of justice can operate both in the realm of *political* philosophy—where it designates that which is required in order for the identity of a political community to attain fulfillment—and as a broader reconstruction of the *moral point of view* as such. The moral point of view can then be understood as a way of assessing practical controversies based on what is requested by the optimal fulfillment of the largest imaginable identity: the identity of *humanity*. The good-of-humanity standpoint possesses the desired characteristics of being *impartial* with respect to the particularism of the single contending identities and yet, at the same time, it is not an abstract principle. Rather, the good of humanity is a *concrete universal* whose substantive content varies over time. It was arguably different, for example, before nuclear weapons or when the total aggregate output of the production processes still posed a limited threat to the integrity of the natural environment or when science was in no position to interfere with genetic processes. One could wonder, at this point, why only the fulfillment

of *humanity*, as opposed to the fulfillment of all organic life, or the fulfillment of the will of a divine entity, is supposed to orient our judgments.
The reason is that humanity's is the most inclusive imaginable identity that
remains characterized by the most salient trait of all *human* identities, individual or collective. In fact, differently than a purported identity of sentient
life or than the identity of a divine figure, the identity of humanity remains
within the circle of recognition. Recognition on the part of humans—in ways
in which more will be said below—remains a salient aspect of its coming
into being and gaining a sense of progression toward fulfillment, just as it is
of more restricted human identities, in a sense that cannot be predicated of
organic life or God—two entities, so to speak, respectively located below or
above that horizon where recognition becomes constitutive.

The second point that needs to be addressed is the distinction between
an *elementary* conception of justice, in which the parties share only a minimal interest in the preservation of the overall thin area of intersection or an
interest in the avoidance of conflict, and a *full-fledged* conception of justice,
in which the parties have an interest in the *expansion* and optimal fulfillment of the overarching identity.[19] It is the difference between dividing a
cake in equal shares by having one person cut it and another choosing the
portions and dividing goods on the basis of a thicker view of justice that
does not flatten but enhances differences—for example, the Marxian ideal
"to each according to their needs, from each according to their abilities"
taken as a general principle of distributive justice.

When considering justice on a global scale or the justice dimension of
a global rule of law, the judgment perspective offers the advantage of not
forcing us to choose, as both Rawls's and Habermas's perspectives do, one
particular unit of analysis—individuals or peoples—as the ideal addressee
of justice. The judgment perspective, on the contrary, is equally useful in
determining "what justice requires" both when we wonder what an individual is owed by a collective identity and when we wonder what peoples might
owe each other. The potential for being applicable both to relations among
demoi organized as states and to domestic relations between minorities and
majorities, as well as to relations among diverse minorities (where minorities
can be identified along ethnic, political, religious, or gender lines), enables
the judgment view of justice to realistically take the status quo as its point
of departure without remaining entrapped within it. One and the same
model tells us both how the *demoi* are supposed to relate to one another
and how they should relate to the *ethnoi* out of which they are made.

Humanity: The *Political* and the *Moral* Notion

Let us now go back to the twofold nature of the notion of humanity that
we presuppose. To be sure, the idea of humanity that ultimately orients our
judgments concerning justice on a global scale must be neutral with respect to the locally prevailing articulations of the meaning of "the human,"
just as any notion of the aesthetic well-formedness of the work of art must
obviously remain independent of any specific poetics. The two notions of
humanity introduced in this section are designed to attain neutrality in
political and *moral* justification and are both necessary if we wish to avoid
a conflation of these two levels of normative argumentation. According to
the first of these notions, humanity is to be taken *as it is*—or, better said, as
it appears to us from a chosen interpretive perspective. We then conceive of
humanity as a "society which comprises in its scope all others" and consider
the "component societies" as they really are, i.e., as the concrete societies known to us, with their name, structure, geographical location, GNP,
institutional order, natural resources, past history, and so on. What we do
when thinking of humanity along "political" lines is to imagine an aggregate that contains all these single, discrete societal units, each of which in
turn includes millions of individuals. This is the *society of peoples* envisaged
by the representatives in Rawls's original position when they interrogate
themselves about the principles that could regulate the coexistence according to justice of all the peoples of the earth.[20] From the standpoint of the
paradigm of judgment, the good of humanity, when understood in a *political* sense, amounts to a notion of the good of a global society composed
of all the other societies *taken as they are*. Cultural pluralism is then clearly
paid its dues in the construction of such a "political" idea of justice among
societies—an idea, furthermore, that does not amount to the notion of a
mere modus vivendi. In fact, from the beginning, the coexistence of peoples is conceived from the perspective of the optimal flourishing of such a
society of societies—where "optimal flourishing," in turn, is a normative
construct that includes not merely the prudential avoidance of conflict but
also the protection of human rights as well as other substantive aspects,
like the protection of the environment and the regulation of the global
economy. For example, its being something more than a modus vivendi is
what allows the adherents of a *political* conception of international justice
to legitimately exclude those which Rawls calls "outlaw States."[21] If we

define "outlaw States" as regimes that pursue their expansion with all possible means and refuse to protect human rights, then to allow the peoples governed by such regimes to be part of the formation of an overlapping consensus on a political idea of justice would be tantamount to downscaling such an idea of justice to that of a mere truce or a modus vivendi.

In this political conception of global justice, however, there remains an ineradicable residue of "facticity," insofar as humanity is conceived as the sum total of existing societies *as they are,* with all their injustices and vices. For this reason we need to make use also of another, more critical or normatively demanding, concept of humanity in thinking of what it means for humanity in its entirety to attain fulfillment of the good. When we understand humanity in light of this normatively more demanding concept, we conceive it as the set of all human beings who have lived, are living, and will be living on the earth.[22] Among them, presently living ones are the only human beings endowed with *agency,* yet this does not make them the sole arbiters of what constitutes the flourishing of humanity so understood. The flourishing of humanity, in fact, consists among other things in bringing to fulfillment projects, aspirations, and values typical of the past generations and in preserving the future generations' chances to live a life of quality not inferior to that of their predecessors. Such a normative idea, concrete and based on a reconstructible narrative, of a humanity fulfilled brings to articulation the intuition of a normative valence possessed by the highest achievements of the past generations—an intuition enshrined, for example, in the notion of a "mountainous crest of humanity" mentioned by Nietzsche in the second of his *Untimely Meditations*—and constitutes the basis for the *moral* idea of global justice.

In this context societies, peoples, states, *demoi* and *ethnoi,* majorities and minorities are no longer relevant: we are left with the idea of a community of all human beings "as such," that is, of all the beings who have been living, are living, and will live within what we call the *human condition.* This community is held together both by the *human condition* as a common condition and by the precipitate, narratively reconstructed, of the best that has been achieved within this common condition.[23] Such an idea has become thicker and thicker in the course of history, from the very thin Kantian idea of a "Realm of Ends," populated by all human beings qua moral subjects endowed with autonomy, all the way to the contemporary idea, on its way to becoming more concrete and thicker precisely by virtue of the process of globalization, of a global human community characterized by a reflexive attitude and capable of understanding itself as the heir of past generations and the trustee of future ones.[24]

We can now combine the two distinctions I have drawn. Within the *political* conception of global justice we can further distinguish an *elementary political* conception and a *full-fledged political* conception of justice. Elementary is a political conception of justice on a global scale that starts from the idea of humanity as a confederation of the existent and recognized peoples and according to which the aim of justice is simply the identification of the principles potentially capable of averting conflict. This view of justice—*political* and *elementary* at once—differs from a modus vivendi insofar as the orientation of the actors is not prudential or self-interested but rather moral in nature, namely, an orientation toward the identification and the realization of the requisites for the fulfillment of a superordinate identity: humanity understood as a society of the existent peoples. Nevertheless, this remains an *elementary* conception of justice insofar as the good or realization of this superordinate identity is conceived solely in the minimal terms of the avoidance of conflict.

A *full-fledged political* conception of global justice, instead, focuses not only on the avoidance of conflict but also on the realization of other requisites of the fulfillment of humanity in its entirety—for example, the requisite of protecting the ecosystem or of having a minimal threshold of material well-being for all human beings. *Full-fledged* conceptions of international justice do not cease to be "political" in Rawls's sense; they lend normative relevance to the requisites of the identity of humanity only insofar as this relevance is recognized by each of the partial identities considered.

Needless to say, the above-mentioned distinctions are merely analytical. They are ideal types of conceptions of justice on a global scale that serve the purpose of *orienting* us within the large variety of existing doctrines. For example, it is clear that Rawls's conception cannot be considered a merely elementary conception of justice, since he links his principles of international justice not only with the function of avoiding conflict but also with that of guaranteeing the protection of human rights and with a minimal redistribution of economic resources (under the heading of a "duty of assistance"). Rawls, however, remains closer to the extreme of an elementary model of international justice than Habermas, who is more open to broader considerations of not just minimal economic redistribution but also environmental protection.

Exemplarity and the Justification of Human Rights

Let me now move on to examine the way in which the judgment paradigm can be of help in justifying the universal cogency of those human rights that constitute the deepest core of the normative notion of humanity both in its political and in its moral version. On the basis of the judgment approach to justice we can articulate, in three steps, the following justification, which can avoid the difficulties incurred by Rawls's and Habermas's respective arguments.

The first step consists of reaffirming that the "standpoint of humanity" to be used in assessing the controversy between different modes of understanding human rights—say, the ones embedded respectively in the Universal Islamic Declaration of Human Rights (1981), the Bangkok Declaration on Human Rights (1993), and the Universal Declaration of Human Rights nb(1948)—cannot itself be seen as simply a projection of Western culture. Rather, it constitutes a logical presupposition without which we cannot make full sense of the confrontation between different cultures and different understandings of human rights. The "standpoint of humanity" is the common denominator that enables us to understand cultural controversies like the one between the Western, the Islamic understanding of human rights, and so-called Asian values as a controversy *about something*. We are then faced with the task of formulating an oriented reflective judgment on what is most conducive to the realization of humanity now understood not as "a society that comprises in its scope all others," but as a communitas of all those who have been living, are living, and will be living in the human condition.

The second step consists of affirming that we Westerners, qua members of humanity—and provided that our internal pluralism allows us to come up with just "one" such idea, but I will leave this problem aside here—are entitled to put forward *our own* idea of what it might mean for humanity to realize itself and to oppose those self-declared conceptions of the good that, by allowing or even calling for genocide, ethnic cleansing, or the systematic elimination of political dissidents, irreversibly foreclose the possibility for humanity to attain a form of realization that includes the ideal of human rights. As indicated in chapter 4, the Holocaust marks a point of nonreturn in this respect: as in the construction of an individual identity it is impossible to overlook, bypass, or ignore moral violations of the magnitude of murder, so the history of humanity, despite the many massacres and persecutions of the past, is traversed by a fracture called the Holocaust, whose symbol is Auschwitz, after which it has become impossible to think of a future for humanity that does not take what happened at Auschwitz into account. The anticipation of a future identity of humanity predicated on the assumption that "Auschwitz doesn't matter" is foreclosed to "us" not just qua Italians, Europeans, or Westerners, but qua members of *humanity*—once again a humanity understood as a community of all human beings that have gone, are going, or will go through a human life. In this statement, as in all identity-grounding narratives, descriptive and normative elements are intertwined. To say that humanity cannot project a future identity of its own based on the assumption that "Auschwitz doesn't matter" is the same as saying that someone who's killed her children cannot live the rest of her life as though that event "didn't matter." On the one hand this is a fact of psychology: the person will always remain, to her own eyes, someone who committed a horrendous crime. On the other hand, this is also an event that *ought*, in a moral sense, to be addressed one way or another, as opposed to being ignored, in the context of the rest of that person's life.[25]

Returning to the plane of justice on a global scale, the perpetration of new holocausts under different names (be they the extermination of the Tutsi, ethnic cleansing, the Cambodian killing fields) is to be rejected as something that undermines humanity's possibility of maintaining a sense of self-respect, that is, each member of the human family regarding humanity within and without as worthy of respect. Whoever then is in a position to stop such crimes renders a service to humanity not so much in the sense of affirming with the force of weapons one conception of the good against another, but in the sense of keeping open for humanity a plurality of self-representations and avenues of fulfillment all compatible with a defensible sense of self-respect.

The third step consists in affirming the thesis—for the time being specifically Western, but in principle susceptible of being shared by all—that the anticipation of an ideal identity of humanity that includes human rights is capable of bringing humanity to a fulfillment *more complete* than other ethical ideals that do not comprise human rights, relativize, or deny them explicitly. This thesis cannot proceed from axiomatically posited principles, but must proceed immanently, by way of deconstructing each conception of the good that calls or allows for the violation of human rights and by way of showing the implausibility of the inequality among human beings, which constitutes one of the central presuppositions of such conceptions. In chapter 4 I have shown how this deconstruction could proceed in the case of the Nazi view of the good. When subordinating a people's *right* to life to the *contingent* ability to defend it,[26] Hitler affirms a contradictory proposition: he is purporting to offer a moral vision, but at the same time understands the moral life as a mere duplicate of the state of nature in turn understood as the theater of an evolutionary struggle of peoples against peoples for survival.

We are then back to the notion of a fulfilled identity of humanity as a source of moral normativity. This *moral* normativity should not be understood as a comprehensive conception of the good of humanity, like the Christian, the Islamic, or other conceptions. Rather, it must be understood as a "noncomprehensive" or "thin" conception of the good of humanity.[27] The basis for the inclusion of human rights as an ineliminable part of that identity is that while our pluralist intuitions enjoin us to believe that no culture, including Western culture, can claim to possess a definitive vision of what it means for humanity to fulfill itself, the same pluralist intuitions allow us, at the same time, to defend our entitlement to make sure, with all available means, that at least the *possibility* of a universal affirmation of the vision of human fulfillment centered on human rights, which we Westerners see as unrenounceable, not be jeopardized by crimes that may mark the identity of humanity in irreversible ways.

Humanity, Judgment, and "Cosmopolitanism as an Existing World"

In that it posits the standpoint of the realization of humanity as the situated source from which both the political and the moral conception of justice derive their normativity, the view of global justice based on the paradigm of judgment revives the train of thought contained in Hegel's *Elements of the Philosophy of Right.* Needless to say, such a revival takes place in light of an entirely new constellation, but two aspects of Hegel's philosophy of right that today retain their relevance are his idea of a post-traditional *Sittlichkeit,* or moral life, and his insight into the necessity of institutionally anchoring that *Sittlichkeit.*

To rethink justice as loyalty toward as large a community as one coinciding with humanity implies a revisitation of the Hegelian idea of a *situated* normativity. For Hegel, the normativity enshrined in the classical concept of ethos undergoes a radical change in modern times. Modernity begins where the naive *Sittlichkeit* that constrains the individual within a local tradition is dissolved by the *principle of subjective freedom* or of *autonomy,* according to which the normatively valid is only what proceeds from the human subject's reason.[28] One of the consequences of this process is the rise and affirmation of that modern individual who acknowledges no other normativity beyond freedom itself and whose sole identity rests on "his freedom, his capacity for self-reflection and self-determination."[29] This idea of freedom and autonomy, however, far from being a kind of decontextual-ized freedom of a transcendental subject, soon becomes an ethos of its own, a peculiar ethos coextensive with modernity. It becomes "the moral life [*Sittlichkeit*] of the moderns, a moral life grounded on taking distance from any tradition other than the tradition of freedom itself."[30]

This new and peculiar *post-traditional ethos of freedom,* however, can become a real alternative to the classical one (based on the immediacy of being part of a tradition) only when it ceases to be a merely *subjective* ori-entation and becomes, in Hegel's words, an "existing world" (*vorhandenen Welt*) as well as coextensive with the "nature of self-consciousness"[31] or, in a vocabulary closer to us, when it becomes a life form with its own specific institutions as well as a second nature "modeled after liberties."[32] The so-called moral point of view, for Hegel, sinks its roots in this concrete modern constellation. It is neither a "construction of reason" nor a counterfactual hypothesis; rather, it is part and parcel of a form of life that arose in modern times.

The interesting point is that this modern form of moral life (*Sittlichkeit*) is far from being a *reconciled* one. On the contrary, it is traversed by severe tensions, which Hegel understands as fundamentally linked: 1. with the inability of the modern *Sittlichkeit* to constitute an "individuating dwell-ing" for the individual who inhabits it and 2. with the inability of modern civil society to really integrate the individual's empirical particularity into a totality not foreign to her. The modern culture of liberty, of autonomy, and of self-determination—to use once again a vocabulary more familiar to us—leads its adepts to devalue every given, every immediate substance, including one's own subjective substance. The modern individual who finds his own essence in freedom shares in common with all other individuals something that is *not* ultimately his own. The modern individual, then, understands his own individuality as a mere *application* of the principle of autonomy and in so doing he witnesses the vanishing of what today we would call his *difference*. Consequently, according to Hegel, we the children of modernity are certainly at home in the realm of subjective freedom that has meanwhile become "a world" for us, but not exactly at home in the same sense as the premodern individual was at home in the moral life of her community.

At the same time, modern civil society—being based on that "system of universal dependency"[33] captured by Smith with the metaphor of the "invisible hand"—is not in a position to truly integrate within itself the particularity of each individual. In Hegel's words, it is not really capable of mediating universality and particularity. The reason for this unsatisfactory predicament is that functional dependency is not yet complemented, before the *Rechtstaat* is founded and fully operative, by a coordination of individual autonomy through political institutions wherein each single citizen can recognize the reflection of her own will. Functional interdependency, at this stage, exists in the context of a thorough *atomization* of the political will.

Hegel sought a solution to these tensions inherent in modern ethical life not along the lines of a return to premodern forms of normativity, but in a *self-reflexive radicalization of the process* that gave rise to these tensions in the first place. The *Entzweiungen* or fractures of modernity, for Hegel, originate in the still quite limited extent to which the principle of subjective freedom has up to now been able to become an "existing world" or to become institutionalized. Here is the point of origin of the philosophical figure of thought that urges us to bring to completion a modernity that has not yet been modern enough—a figure of thought rescued and reconstructed along postmetaphysical lines by Habermas in *The Philosophical Discourse of Modernity*.[34] However, this is also the point where the limits of the relevance of Hegel's framework for us become evident.

Hegel identifies the *nation-state* as the ideal locus where these fractures—between individuality and universality, between the inwardness of subjective intention and the externally objectified character of the norm, between the subject's freedom and the freedom objectified in institutions—can finally come to a reconciliation. As one Hegel scholar perceptively suggested,

> the *loci* where the modern individual is educated to autonomy, reflexivity and respect for the other are no longer the specific and particular traditions or the traditional communities, which are irreversibly wiped out by the grand march of abstract freedom and survive only as

a nostalgic yearning, but rather the institutions of the modern State. The dwelling that the modern individual perceives as truly his own is no longer his fatherland or his home but rather an abstractness that has turned into a world, a universality that has turned into history, into a legal code and into the idea of the rule of law.[35]

Formally "free and equal" citizens, in sum, are able to find themselves at home in their predicament if and only if an entire institutional order sustains the exercise of their freedom. The fact that this institutional order takes the form of a nineteenth-century nation-state is something best explained as a feature of the historical horizon within which Hegel is immersed, rather than as an internal necessity of his argument. Now, it is exactly at this juncture that our discussion of the normative foundations of justice on a global scale and their relation to international institutions can be connected with Hegel's train of thought.

De nobis fabula narratur—the story is ultimately about us. We are today, as far as the international scenario is concerned, exactly like those citizens of modern civil society described by Hegel. Our lives are unequivocally tied up with global processes and with the actions and strategies of global players, as well as with the unintentional effects of actions that take the whole world as their theater. Our lives depend on economic processes, on migrations, on cultural currents of global import, on markets of primary goods, on currency rates, and so on, but who could recognize herself in this universal dependency, who could interpret the outcomes of these forces as the product of one's own intentions, who could detect in that universality even a trace of one's own particularity? Our lives depend on the ups and downs of Dow Jones and Nasdaq and of oil prices and of the main currencies, yet, again, who could see in these forces the sign and the projection of one's own will?

As Hegel's citizens did on a *national* scale, so we too aspire, on a *global* scale, to complement this "universal dependency" of a merely functional nature with some kind of thicker political will capable of becoming law and within which our individual will can finally recognize itself. In this aspiration we are again at one with Hegel's effort to conceive of a universal that does not impose itself from without, so to speak, but can be reconciled with particularity and can do so in the medium of law.

The reconciliation of subjective freedom with the universalistic normativity of law, however, for Hegel is to be expected only within the bounds of a single state. The Hegelian individual is unable to recognize his own subjectivity in the universality of world-history. This is the case because for Hegel *Weltgeschichte* always takes place behind the backs of its protagonists, and thus the individual can never recognize his own subjectivity in the *Weltgeschichte* in the same sense that he can in the objectivations of a political will collectively formed together with other citizens in the context of one nation-state.

A crucial difference, however, separates our horizon from Hegel's. We have begun to witness the coalescing of a universal history now deflated from philosophical concept to empirical reference, from *Weltgeschichte* to *global history*. The rise of institutions like the UN, the IMF, OCSE, the World Bank, the International Court of Justice, FAO, UNESCO, UNICEF, the WTO, the High Commissioner for Human Rights, and many others testify to the ongoing transition from a mere "global civil society"[36] populated by global economic actors, such as the multinational corporations, by NGOs of global scope, like Greenpeace or Amnesty International or the Catholic Church as well as by classic transnational powers like the EU or NATO, to a global society endowed with political institutions within which the subjective freedom of state actors can finally find a reconciliation through a truly universal body of laws. Under such conditions, cosmopolitanism can now turn from a philosophically "abstract" idea to an "existing world."

However, in order to provide a postmetaphysical version of the Hegelian idea of anchoring the moral point of view in a "futurized community" characterized by a situated post-traditional moral life, it is necessary to articulate more carefully the notion of the identity of humanity. Is it possible to attribute an identity to humanity as such? Despite an almost instinctive reaction of skepticism, two factors seem to suggest a positive answer.

First, the processes of economic and cultural globalization and the beginnings of a supranational politics seem to suggest that increasingly the global horizon is no longer a horizon just for philosophical reflection but also for concrete actors. And the action of global actors arguably gives rise to a global history whose subject is humanity no less plausibly than the action of traditional actors—classes, parties, movements, minorities, interest groups, and so on—gave rise to a historical horizon centered around the nation.

Second, whereas in the case of collective actors, like national political communities, it is possible to speak of identities proper, because the collective quality of the identity in this case leaves the need for recognition and the dynamics of relations of recognition intact, it has been objected that in the case of humanity it is unclear how we could speak of an identity that, as desirable, remains within the circle of recognition. It is hard to imagine which "other of humanity" could provide recognition.

This objection can be met, however, if we think of the possibility of *virtual recognition*. Every theory of recognition is at least partially also a theory of the *virtual recognition* that the actor "anticipates" or "expects" to receive from other actors. The establishing and maintenance of a sense of the self presupposes an internalized construction that *only at its ontogenetic beginning* maintains a link with the reality of a concrete act of recognition on the part of significant and equally concrete others. Mead's theory of the social genesis of the self testifies to this: the mature individual stabilizes her self-representation through the anticipation of a *virtual* recognition by a "generalized other" who is entirely a construction of the mind (albeit of the "socialized" mind), though it certainly is somehow related to the reality of the average individual of that society.[37] What is truly peculiar to applying this understanding of subjectivity to humanity in its entirety is the fact that, differently than it happens with all other individual and collective subjects, *the concrete and the generalized others do merge* in one and the same figure: they are no longer distinguishable.

If we accept the idea that any identity can be stabilized through virtual or anticipated recognition in at least one possible world, we will not find it difficult to accept the idea that we, both qua single individuals and qua collective actors, can attribute to humanity an identity susceptible of being recognized either by other intelligent species that might be present in the universe (in which case the concrete and generalized others will separate again) or by the generations of human beings who will live in the future. The second alternative is the one most often operative: we think of fulfilling or betraying the identity of humanity with a view to how posterity will interpret what humanity does at a given point in time. If we irresponsibly let the ecosystem deteriorate, nuclear weapons proliferate beyond control, energy sources be depleted before alternatives are available, we immediately think of a silent reproach from the yet unborn.

Toward a Principle of Intersubjective Freedom

To conclude, the philosophical agenda of the paradigm of judgment requires that when we think of justice on a global scale, our conception of justice 1. be "political," in the sense of avoiding presuppositions whose acceptance is coextensive with accepting the foundations of liberal-democratic constitutionalism; 2. not sanction, through its being addressed to an implicit set of "recipients of justice," a merely contingent international status quo; 3. include the protection of human rights within the subject matter of justice, albeit without dedifferentiating the spheres of morality and law or returning to a postulated priority of morality over politics; and 4. articulate at least in general terms the nexus of justice on a global scale and the kind of institutional order presupposed by it.

The judgment view of justice—which hinges on the idea that justice can be equated with the requirements of the fulfillment of a superordinate identity originating, albeit only potentially, from the interaction of the contending parties—reflects these ideal desiderata within its structure. More specifically, because it refrains from privileging any given class of entities as the prototypical addressees, recipients, or subjects of justice, it can be applied equally well to the determination of what is owed to individuals qua citizens of the world no less than to the determination of what is owed to the peoples included in the "society which comprises in its scope all others," the judgment view of justice does not fall prey to the contingency of the international status quo. By using both concepts of humanity outlined above, the judgment view qua "political" conception of justice on a global scale may well take that status quo as its point of departure, because it can also transcend it when it functions as a "moral" conception of justice.

Second, because both in its "political" and "moral" version the normative cogency of the judgment view of justice is anchored in the overlapping of collective identities—peoples and societies—based on diverse cultural presuppositions, the judgment view remains consistent with our pluralist intuitions and at no juncture requires that nonliberal or non-Western individuals and peoples embrace assumptions that are not their own.

Third, in its "political" version my view of justice embeds a conception of human rights as rights not only of a moral but potentially of a *legal* nature; in other words, as *rights in the process of acquiring a fully legal nature*. It is of crucial importance that human rights not just be "moral" rights. We want them to be "higher law" in order to withdraw them from the contingencies of political confrontation and local majorities—basically for the same reasons why on a domestic scale we want certain essentials of political life removed from the arena and secured as "rights." The judgment view, however, does not share the optimistic view that this legal nature of human rights already *is* established by the existing legal sources, but rather outlines an institutional process that—through a Charter of Fundamental Human Rights, on which more will be said in the next chapter—could lead to the *undisputable* acquisition of such a legal status on the part of human rights.

Fourth, following in the footsteps of Hegel, the paradigm of judgment inclines us to understand the relation of justice on a global scale to the rise of cosmopolitan institutions as a *constitutive* relation. Just as economic and cultural globalization is producing the first indicators of a burgeoning global civil society, from within which also an incipient global public sphere is taking its first steps, so the building of international and cosmopolitan institutions is gradually generating an actual "world" in which the idea of humanity can at last be understood as a *concrete universal* and no longer merely as a regulative idea. Furthermore, by virtue of its being based on a twofold normative concept of humanity—humanity as the society of all peoples and humanity as the set of all human beings who have lived, are living, and will be leaving within the human condition—the view of justice outlined here brings to expression a new "principle of *inter*subjective freedom" that underlies the cosmopolitan institutional order in the process of being formed. The articulation of this principle is one of the contributions that philosophy can offer to the pursuit of the Kantian *Weltrepublik*.

7 Enforcing Human Rights Between Westphalia and Cosmopolis

The threats to peace and security in the twenty-first century include not just international war and conflict but civil violence, organized crime, terrorism and weapons of mass destruction. They also include poverty, deadly infectious disease and environmental degradation since these can have equally catastrophic consequences. All of these threats can cause death or lessen life chances on a large scale. All of them undermine states as the basic unit of the international system.
—Kofi Annan, *In Larger Freedom*

The UN exists in a world of sovereign states, and its operations must be based in political realism. But the organization is also the repository of international idealism, and that sense is fundamental to its identity. It is still the main focus of the hopes and aspirations for a future where men and women live at peace with each other and in harmony with nature. The reality of human insecurity cannot simply be wished away. Yet the idea of a universal organization dedicated to protecting peace and promoting welfare—of achieving a better life in a safer world, for all—survived the death, destruction and disillusionment of armed conflicts, genocide, persistent poverty, environmental degradation and the many assaults on human dignity of the twentieth century.
—International Commission on Intervention and State Sovereignty, § 6.25

Let me start with the abused metaphor of the wade. At the present stage within the so-called global age we find ourselves at an indeterminate point in our wading between two shores that are conceptually quite clear and distinct: namely, the one constituted by a Westphalian system of sovereign states that relate to one another as if they were in a state of nature, only sporadically interrupted by alliances and pacts entered voluntarily and always rescindable, and the opposite shore constituted by a hypothetical cosmopolis where the different parts of the globe, be they traditional nation-states or postnational entities of various kinds, relate to one another according to some kind of law in a way not dissimilar from the manner in which the regional and local segments of a nation-state relate to one another.

We have left the pure state of nature, as symbolized by the Peace of Westphalia of 1648, behind us ever since the League of Nations, after World War I, radically questioned the right of a sovereign state to initiate a war according to its own perception of political expediency and the Briand-Kellog Pact of 1928 banned aggressive war as an instrument of normal politics. The inefficacy of sanctionless norms such as these was manifest from the beginning, yet from their ashes the Nuremberg Trial was born, as well as the idea of a right of the international community to protect peace not just through norms but also through sanctions decided and enforced by the Security Council. And from this initial core of cosmopolitan law that body of legal sources has been generated which includes the Charter of the United Nations, the Universal Declaration of Human Rights, the Additional Protocols to the Geneva Conventions, the 1948 Convention on the Prevention and Punishment of the Crime of Genocide, the Covenants of 1966 on civil, political, social, economic, and cultural rights, and the Rome Statute of the International Criminal Court drafted in 1998.

Furthermore, also the notion of security—originally understood as the absence of regularly declared conflicts among sovereign states or, in other words, no men in uniform fighting other men in uniform—has evolved into a much more differentiated concept, defined in the following way by the secretary-general of the UN:

> The threats to peace and security in the twenty-first century include not just international war and conflict but civil violence, organized crime, terrorism and weapons of mass destruction. They also include poverty, deadly infectious disease and environmental degradation since these can have equally catastrophic consequences. All of these threats can cause death or lessen life chances on a large scale. All of them undermine states as the basic units of the international system.[1]

I will not deal with such a large range of possible threats to security and human life, but would like instead to focus rather narrowly on the one question that in my perception stands out as the most fundamental, namely, how the line ought to be drawn between the sovereignty of single states and the sovereignty of the international community as reflected in its cosmopolitan institutions.

Despite the indubitable progress made by international relations along the way from the initial state-of-nature condition to a fully fledged rule of law, that transition is far from having been completed. No world-state is in sight nor will be for a long time, if by this expression we mean an organization endowed with the Weberian "monopoly on the legitimate use of force"—and few people agonize over that. What might very well be in sight, however, are cosmopolitan institutions endowed with a functionally equivalent monopoly: the "monopoly over the attribution of legitimacy to the use of force." In order for such a prospect to materialize we need to presuppose the acceptance of a normative framework capable in turn of generating what used to be called the certainty of law, capable of regulating the relations among existing and persisting states and susceptible of defining the sovereignty and jurisdiction of new cosmopolitan institutions, such as the most recent international criminal court. My topic is the contribution that political philosophy can offer to the articulation of such a normative framework.

The Terms of the Problem

From a historical point of view, the first limitation of the sovereignty of states has come from the normative understanding of the idea of international security, according to which no state can jeopardize peace through aggressive actions and by so doing may be subject to sanctions that include a military intervention on the part of the international community. Ever since 1945 this understanding is embedded, as a specific provision, in the Charter of the United Nations.

Needless to say, however, the most horrible violations of human rights may take place—and indeed have taken place in Cambodia or Rwanda—without necessarily endangering international security, on account of the geopolitical import or location of the country where they occur. The sovereignty of states must then be bound by limits more stringent than the endangering of international security as traditionally understood. I would like to develop some reflections on the nature of these limits and the rules according to which they can be reestablished once they have been trespassed.

Under what conditions are the international community and its cosmopolitan institutions entitled to intervene—directly or entrusting the intervention to one or more willing states—in the internal affairs of a sovereign state? In paragraph 126 of the secretary-general's report *In Larger Freedom* the definition of this aspect is presented as the question most urgently in need of an answer if the United Nations is to continue to exercise any appreciable role on the world scene. In the absence of such a universally acceptable clarification of the proper limits of state sovereignty, the charters and declarations of human rights are destined to play a merely pedagogical role. As Kofi Annan aptly put it,

> Villagers huddling in fear at the sound of Government bombing raids or at the appearance of murderous militias on the horizon find no solace in the unimplemented words of the Geneva Convention, to say nothing of the international community's solemn promises of "never again" when reflecting on the horrors of Rwanda a decade ago. Treaties prohibiting torture are cold comfort to prisoners abused by their captors, particularly if the international human rights machinery enables those responsible to hide behind friends in high places. A war-weary population infused with new hope after the signing of a peace agreement quickly reverts to despair when, instead of seeing tangible progress towards a Government under the rule of law, it sees war lords and gang leaders take power and become laws unto themselves.[2]

We thus reason and argue on the basis of a different unit of analysis—the globalized world rather than the nation-state—but the fundamental question to be considered remains the same: under what conditions is the use of force legitimate, what makes the supranational authority of a cosmopolitan institution different from the assertiveness and arrogance of a global power?

What kind of criterion can we use in order to answer this question? The first thing we might want to emphasize is that the basic principles underlying a universal jurisdiction—namely, one that can be enforced independently of the local existence of a norm that prohibits the violation of certain human rights—cannot be less than universally acceptable. These principles cannot be subscribed to by only part of the peoples that human-ity comprises. Were it so, the capacity of these principles to legitimate the use of force would be null as the legitimating capacity of a fatwa issued by a religion in which we do not believe.

Let us examine a number of criteria for justifying military interven-tion that at least prima facie might be plausible candidates for universal consensus.

A first family of proposals embeds an appeal to the moral conscience of humanity. An example of this way of approaching the problem comes from Michael Walzer, when in *Just and Unjust Wars* he states that "humanitarian intervention is justified when it is a response (with reasonable expectations of success) to acts 'that shock the moral conscience of mankind.'"[3] One limitation of this approach is the difficulty of operationalizing the notion of a moral shock. Who is to say when the moral conscience of humanity is shocked enough to justify interfering with the sovereignty of a state? In the past, the execution of a king has certainly been cause of enough moral shock as to induce the powers of the day to intervene against France, but, on the contrary, we Westerners almost unanimously connect that dramatic occurrence with a true example of moral progress. Thus it can hardly be acceptable that the prevailing state powers of the day be entitled to decide on the occurrence of moral shock, if anything because—as Michael Walzer reminds us—intervention and annexation often proceed hand in hand.

The teachings of Machiavelli are helpful in this respect. In his *Discourses* he shows how the imperial expansion of Rome was linked with an innova-tive modality that the contemporary reader may not be altogether unfa-miliar with. In the ancient world a republic was known to be able to ex-pand in two distinct ways. One was the "federal" mode, exemplified by the Achaians in Greece (and by Switzerland in Machiavelli's times). It consisted of joining more republics together in a league in which no single partner outranked the other. The other was the "annexive" mode, exemplified by the Spartans and the Athenians. It consisted of acquiring "subjects," not partners, through military victory.

The Romans invented a third mode: "to make associates of other States; reserving to themselves, however, the rights of sovereignty, the seat of em-pire, and the glory of their enterprises."[4] In other words, they always pre-sented themselves as a "stronger ally," as *senior partner*, so to speak, in a relation that was never formally one of sheer domination. Thus the Romans were always careful to establish a strong relation with an ally internal to the province to be acquired—an internal ally who would provide a formal legitimacy to intervention as well as decisive political and logistic support for the Roman armies. As Machiavelli notes, "by the aid of the Capuans they entered Samnium, and through the Camertini they got into Tuscany; the Mamertini helped them into Sicily, the Saguntines into Spain, Masinissa into Africa, and the Massilians and Eduans into Gaul."[5]

Machiavelli extols this third modality by comparison with the previous two. The annexive mode requires the forceful domination of entire cities: this proves especially difficult when the subjected cities are used to live in freedom and, furthermore, creates the imposing need for ever more numerous armies as the expansion proceeds. The federal mode, on the other hand, hardly allows a large-scale expansion, insofar as the decisional center becomes dispersed across a plurality of locations. The expansive mode invented by the Romans, instead, afforded political unity—the "seat of empire" would always remain in Roman hands—and yet would not require the deployment of large Roman armies in order to control and rule the newly acquired provinces, insofar as these were often spontaneously eager to orbit around Roman power.

The lesson to be drawn from imperial Rome then is that the interpretation of what offends and shocks the moral conscience of humanity cannot be left for powerful and potentially hegemonic states to articulate.

Perhaps the role of interpreter of the moral conscience of humanity could be attributed to the Security Council in a new composition, or to a court, such as the International Court of Justice, or to a special branch thereof, in any event to an institution that incorporates the general guidelines for limiting state sovereignty and then on their basis be able to formulate a judgment wherein the moral element, the juridical element, and, inevitably, the political moment as well are balanced against each other. In fact, the legitimate entitlement to enforce respect for human rights has to be balanced, along consequentialist lines, against the costs and benefits of intervention for the global collectivity. There is undoubtedly a realist residue in this position, but in my opinion the metabolization of such a residue is the necessary price that a theory of the limits of sovereignty has to pay in order not to turn into the caricature of ethics that Max Weber captured in the formula, typical of all ethics of ultimate ends: *fiat justitia, pereat mundus.*

A second type of criteria for justifying military intervention pivots instead around the notion of "suffering"—which is obviously more indirectly connected with a moral horizon. Again, Kofi Annan sums up the goal of the Charter of the United Nations as the protection of the individual human being and calls legitimate the intervention of the international community, even against the political will of the state where the intervention takes place, "when death and suffering are being inflicted on large numbers of people, and when the State nominally in charge is unable or unwilling to stop it."[6]

Among the advantages provided by this second criterion is its relative independence from moral categories, always potentially controversial, and its relying on the single most widely shared assumption within the history of political thought. Whether we conceive of the ultimate end served by the state as the promotion of eudaimonia (as in Aristotle), the cultivation of the *vivere civile* (as in Machiavelli), or simply the preservation of physical life (as in Hobbes), there is little doubt that included within that which the state owes its citizens must be the protection of their lives. The protection of human life is then the most uncontroversial standard on whose basis we can make sense of the line that separates the sovereignty of states from a kind of supranational, international, or cosmopolitical sovereignty—and as such has been articulated by the International Commission on Intervention and State Sovereignty (ICISS), chaired by Gareth Evans and Mohamed Sahnoun and sponsored by the government of Canada in 2001 to develop with the least controversy a much needed normative framework for rethinking the limits of sovereignty. To engage the final report issued by this commission provides a promising way of addressing the question of the proper limits of the sovereignty of nation-states in the global world.

A Copernican Revolution

The key contribution to be found in the Report of the International Commission on Intervention and State Sovereignty consists of a reformulation of the terms of the problem from the more traditional notion of a "right to intervene" to the new concept of a "responsibility to protect." We are then transfered from a conceptual territory characterized by the contest of two rights—the right of a sovereign state not to suffer external interference in its domestic affairs as pitted against the right of the international community to intervene in order to prevent grave violations of human rights from being committed or to prevent peace from being endangered—to a new conceptual territory where only one fundamental "responsibility" exists, namely, the responsibility to protect each single human life, and a plurality of institutions variously capable of discharging this duty. Among these institutions the nation-state remains the default one, but no longer the last on a scale of inclusiveness. Above the nation-state there exists today cosmopolitan institutions that can exert this function whenever the states lose, for reasons dependent or independent of their will, their own capacity to discharge it.

The point is that the legitimacy of the function is beyond dispute, as anticipated above. Even Thomas Hobbes, the advocate of absolutism, had no problem in acknowledging that the authority and legitimacy of the sovereign stands or falls with the sovereign's capacity to protect the lives of the citizens. No obedience is owed to a sovereign who neglects to or becomes unable to protect.

Aside from its indisputability, this formulation is characterized by an exceptional inclusiveness: it becomes irrelevant whether a state actively persecutes part of its citizens or fails to prevent formally private "death squads" from committing the crimes, whether a state becomes incapable of protecting its citizens' lives out of deliberate choice, negligence in predicting risks, fortuitous contingencies, or other causes. Whatever the reasons, if a state becomes unable to fulfill its life-protecting function or intentionally threatens the lives of its citizens, the international community can legitimately take over this function in lieu of the local state. The idea of a responsibility to protect is not exhausted by the mere dimension of military intervention—this is another important element of the proposal put forward by the Evans-Sahnoun commission. The more general responsibility to protect includes three distinct more specific responsibilities: 1. the most important "responsibility to prevent," understood as the responsibility to intervene preemptively on the background and immediate conditions that may generate the risk of a loss of human life; 2. the "responsibility to react," which includes a whole gradient of measures, ranging from economic sanctions to military intervention proper; and, finally, 3. the "responsibility to rebuild," both in the material sense of restoring destroyed infrastructure and in the nonmaterial sense of promoting processes of societal reconciliation after the external intervention. The decisive problem, however, for the purposes of rethinking the limits of sovereignty is constituted by the definition of the threshold of human rights violations that warrants and legitimates a military intervention. This issue is decisive in the sense that if no satisfactory solution is given to the problem of defining when intervention is legitimate, then overall we still have no solution to the problem of re-defining sovereignty in the age of human rights where insights into the requirements of prevention and rebuilding won't help us.

Defining the Threshold

For the purpose of defining the appropriate threshold of human rights violations that legitimates intervention, the commission spells out the notion of a just cause and complements it with a number of concomitant conditions that I will discuss in the following sections. Just cause is specified as the necessity to stop or avoid

- large-scale loss of life, actual or apprehended, with genocidal intent or not, which is the product either of deliberate state action, or state neglect or inability to act, or a failed state situation; or
- large-scale "ethnic cleansing," actual or apprehended, whether carried out by killing, forced expulsion, acts of terror or rape.[7]

The commission's report then proceeds to discuss in detail the kinds of acts that are to be included in or excluded from this list.[8] For instance, those violations of human rights that fall short of mass killings or ethnic cleansing, as well as cases of racial discrimination, jailing, or persecution of political opponents, do not constitute a just cause for external military intervention. Similarly excluded are those cases in which the will of a population to create a democratic regime is smothered by a military coup and neither massive loss of human life occurs nor a regional political destabilization with potential risks for international security ensues.

The commission, while referring several times to a "large-scale" loss of human life, has deliberately chosen not to quantify this specific aspect of the threshold for legitimate intervention, in the anticipation that no radical disagreement will take place in this respect. It has chosen instead to emphasize the legitimacy of preventive action aimed at avoiding the occurrence of the threshold conditions for intervention. As it puts it, if this kind of preventive action was not considered legitimate, "the international community would be placed in the morally untenable position of being required to wait until genocide begins, before being able to take action to stop it."[9]

Additional Criteria

The legitimacy of the use of force within the internal sphere of the sovereignty of a state is not defined solely by the notion of a just cause for intervention. The commission identifies five further criteria. Two of them seem in all respects of self-evident acceptability. The second, after "just cause," is the criterion of last resort, that is, the idea that before a legitimate military intervention is launched all other alternatives, which are less intrusive and pose less risks to human life, must have been tried or at least considered and found unsatisfactory.[10] The third is the criterion of proportionality of means, which obviously precludes legitimacy from being attributed to interventions of disproportionate amplitude relative to the violations or risks thereof that are taking place. The fourth, fifth, and sixth criteria deserve closer inspection.

The fourth criterion is that of right intention. Given that the UN does not have armies of its own available for certain interventions, but will, within the foreseeable future, have to delegate the use of force to single states or coalitions of states willing to bear the costs of operations, a crucial importance is assumed by the issue of the permissible aims and objectives these states may pursue in carrying out the mission called for by the UN. Starting from the realistic assumption that totally disinterested motives are not to be expected, the commission suggests a number of interesting guidelines: for example, it is legitimate for a state to aim at stopping or preventing migratory waves of refugees near its borders, to aim at preventing the formation of sanctuaries for criminal and terrorists in its vicinity. On the contrary, it is inadmissible for a state to pursue the goal of altering the existing borders or the balance of force among competing factions within the target country or of changing the existing regime. According to the Canadian proposal, cosmopolitan institutions embrace democracy but do not impose it. For they embed the presupposition that a regime can be changed only by its citizens and therefore do not seek to overthrow political regimes through military force. One of the methods to ensure that the criterion of right intention be fulfilled is for the UN to delegate intervention, whenever possible, to a plurality of states rather than to one state only and, furthermore, to obtain clearance for the composition of the intervening force from both the "country of destination" and the neighboring countries.

The fifth criterion concerns reasonable prospects of success. The idea of a responsibility to protect becomes self-defeating if it is not accompanied by a careful assessment of the foreseeable geopolitical consequences of intervention. Also at this juncture the commission strikes a realistic chord. No legitimacy can be attributed to a use of force that in the end generates a result worse than inaction would have produced, for example, force that threatens to ignite a conflict in the region or throughout the world. In such cases we cannot but soberly accept the sad reality of the helplessness of a certain number of human beings: we simply do not know, in the given condition, how to bring them relief without endangering the lives of an even larger number of human beings. The use of force then cannot be legitimate.

As a consequence, all intervention is excluded against the five permanent members of the Security Council as well as against other powers that are not members of the Security Council, for "it is difficult to imagine a major conflict being avoided, or success in the original objective being achieved, if such action were mounted against any of them."[11] A double standard? Impunity for *global players*? Impunity for China in Tibet and Russia in Chechnia? Here the commission impresses a consequentialist rather than deontological trajectory to its argument. The fact that it is impossible, or rather counterproductive, to intervene against certain strong powers does not detract from the rightness of intervening in those other cases where no prohibitive negative consequences are to be expected. The argument makes perfect sense, and one could add the consideration that the strengthening of cosmopolitan institutions, which would most likely result from a consolidated practice of the "responsibility to protect," would in turn create favorable conditions for the public opinion of the great powers—some of which are democracies—to also accept the limitation of sovereignty that the international community is imposing on the less powerful states. Furthermore, all the great powers that hold seats in the Security Council, regardless of their democratic status, have large economies intertwined with the global economy. Therefore nonmilitary sanctions adopted with the support of democratic public opinions might have a greater impact on them than on authoritarian countries with a more autarchic kind of economy.

Another set of considerations to be addressed concerns the context of international relations within which the development of a cosmopolitical form of governance is envisaged. The war in Afghanistan and the war in Iraq are reshaping this context along lines that are far-reaching. These two recent wars are redesigning a world in which there is basically no geopolitical counterweight to the interpretation of the situation that is given by the U.S. administration in charge at the time—not in the sense that there cannot be criticism or a diversity of intepretation, some of which may even be influential, but in the sense that the balance of military force is inevitably tilted. After the end of the cold war, and with no nostalgia for it, we live in a world where no country has the force to oppose the United States and where any country that were to come into conflict with the United States could only count on its own, easily overpowered, force. This is a basic fact of the world we inhabit. The "new constellation," tendentially postnational, described by Habermas in 1998 has already yielded to an even "newer" constellation, born after 9/11. It was one thing to envisage the possible transition toward a cosmopolitan rule of law, as Habermas did, against the backdrop of a post-bipolar world characterized by an unstable equilibrium between regional powers, some of which were of a postnational nature while others were of a more traditional national nature, and it is quite another thing to envisage the same transition against the backdrop of a world where only one global superpower with no match or check (other than its own internal democratic process) exists and various regional powers compete for strategic alignment with the superpower. The picture is much more complicated than the image of a contest between authoritarian regimes of various kinds (theocratic regimes, paternalistic ones, tribal regimes, regimes dominated by coalitions of warlords) on the one hand and democracies on the other. Alongside the contest between liberal democracies and nonliberal regimes there is also the beginning of a rift that separates the small and medium-scale democracies from the interests of the one democracy of imperial size. This new rift, whose manifestations are just beginning to materialize in response to 9/11, may change the way in which we want to envisage the transition from the actual predicament of international relations to a cosmopolitan rule of law. That transition, if it ever happens, will most likely not take the form of a gentle relinquishing of segments of sovereignty on the part of the nations-states (first the democratic ones, then the rest) to institutions like a reformed Security Council or the International Criminal Court or still others. The transition will rather be a much more complex process—involving the South of the world, China, Russia, India, the EU, and the one superpower left—that will resemble a negotiation of the limits of the sovereignty of the superpower, a negotiation that will perhaps remind us more fully of the classical process whereby the liberal rule of law came into being out of struggles to curb the power of kings than of the joint law making of free and equal citizens to which recent liberalism has accustomed us.

The Authority in Charge of the Decision

The sixth criterion is as complex as the just cause criterion: it concerns the identification of the authority to which the bestowing of legitimacy to the intervention is to be attributed. The commission points out that the Charter of the UN identifies in the organization itself the ultimate source of the legitimate use of force and in the Security Council the locus of all single decisions in this matter.[12] According to the commission there is no doubt as to the fact that "it is the Security Council which should be making the hard decisions in the hard cases about overriding state sovereignty,"[13] and this notwithstanding the Security Council's imperfect representativeness, internal inequalities, and record of idle discussion and stalemate at certain crucial junctures.

Therefore the Security Council, though it is by no means the only institutional actor involved,[14] remains for the Evans-Sahnoun commission the ultimate deciding body as far as the legitimacy of the use of force is concerned, and against its decisions there is no appeal. This is a level of our problem of redefining the limits of sovereignty at which perhaps it would be reasonable to envisage some solution that goes beyond existing arrangements.

For example, without entirely revolutionizing the current arrangement, it might be imagined that the General Assembly could share, if not take, the final decision on intervention, based on a proposal issuing from the Security Council. In fact, in democratic states the decision to enter war always requires consent on the part of the legislative assemblies. It might also be imagined that the conformity of such decisions with the existing cosmopolitan legal sources be subject to review on the part of a special section of the International Court of Justice.

The International Court of Justice could and should discharge a further function. Essential to any decision that concerns intervention is an assessment of the evidence for violations of human rights, and the assessment of evidence must be made independent of the dimension of political interest, as clearly suggested by the story of the alleged possession of weapons of mass destruction on the part of Saddam Hussein. The International Court of Justice should then act as the supreme arbiter of evidence, and perhaps this function by itself would counterbalance the prerogatives of the Security Council, often hostage to the power relations among its most influential members.

Finally, there is no need to recall how one of the limitations affecting the state of nature is the total absence of a dimension of thirdness in relation to the contending parties. In the Lockean version, the state of nature is not, like the Hobbesian one, devoid of all normativity—natural rights exist in it, as we know—but this normativity is always interpreted and applied to contested matters by actors who are directly involved. Everyone is judge in his own case. Similarly, in our present predicament at mid-wade between Westphalia and Cosmopolis, one of the aspects of the state of nature that awaits being superseded is precisely this lack of a dimension of thirdness or impartiality in addressing conflicts. The International Court of Justice could be the vehicle through which this dimension is attained.

The Normative Source: The Role of a Charter of Fundamental Human Rights

Once the problem of the proper authority entrusted with bestowing legitimacy on the use of force is solved, there remains the question of the normative sources that should inspire this authority's decisions. Toward the end of its report the commission recommends that the council give itself an explicit code of "principles of military intervention" and adopt a principle that might be called "constructive veto," basically a code of self-limitation in the use of veto. Furthermore, it recommends that the secretary-general implement the recommendation of the report in concert with the presidents of both the Security Council and the General Assembly.[15] The most important recommendation, however, urges the General Assembly to pass a resolution that formally establishes the responsibility to protect. Such resolution, according to the Evans-Sahnoun commission, should include the following elements:

1. an affirmation of the idea of sovereignty as responsibility;
2. an affirmation of the threefold duty, on the part of the international community, to prevent, to react, and to rebuild whenever confronted with calls for the protection of human life in states incapable or unwilling to discharge their duty to protect;
3. a definition of the threshold (large-scale loss of life or ethnic cleansing, actual or apprehended) that must be referred to when legitimating a humanitarian intervention;

4. an articulation of the precautionary principles that must be observed when using military force in order to protect human life, namely, the principles of right intention, last resort, proportionality of means, and reasonable prospect of success.

It is worth noting that this proposal of the commission cannot be derived automatically from the main legal sources of cosmopolitan law, namely, the Universal Declaration of Human Rights and the Charter of the United Nations. On the contrary, those legal sources lend themselves to a plurality of differently nuanced interpretations. The schema for a resolution of the General Assembly proposed by the commission is certainly to be shared, but it could, in my opinion, be further strengthened in light of the following considerations and integrated with a number of other points.

The legal sources mentioned were enacted in a context where the main threat to international security issued from wars among sovereign states and where such documents as the Universal Declaration responded to the purpose of favoring the diffusion of a culture of human rights worldwide, not to the purpose of drawing the line between the sovereignty of states and the sovereignty of the international community. The drawing of such line, which has become all too urgent only after the end of the cold war, requires that the violations of fundamental human rights—which warrant all forms of intervention, including the use of military force—be identified with unquestionable clarity. Given that the Universal Declaration does not posit any hierarchy among rights—nor was it sensible for it to do so given the historical context to which it constituted a response—it is of crucial importance that the attribution of a *fundamental* character to a certain set of human rights, from which its priority relative to state sovereignty follows, not be a product solely of philosophical argument and construction, let alone of political calculation, but rather be itself the product of cosmopolitan law making. The only thing that can legitimate a limitation of the sovereignty of states vis-à-vis certain fundamental human rights is a new document issuing from the convergent will of all the states of the world.

Thus I would complete the proposal put forward by the Evans-Sahnoun commission with the following additional points:

1. the public enunciation of the new limits of state sovereignty should not take the form of a mere resolution, but should rather take the form of a solemn document voted by the General Assembly or by

a global convention convened for this purpose, a document that could be called a Charter of Fundamental Human Rights and would be intended to rank at the same level as the Charter of the United Nations or the Universal Declaration of 1948;

2. the historical and political contingency of the composition of an assembly made of state delegations (only the states existent at a given historical moment would be represented) should be overcome via a special clause of the charter where all the initially ratifying states pledge to make their own recognition of any future state that forms conditional upon its acceptance of this "bill of rights" of the Durkheimian "society which comprises in its scope all others" or of the Rawlsian "society of peoples";

3. this charter of human rights that are fundamental in that they, differently than other human rights, overrank state sovereignty should be preceded by a preamble capable of connecting these fundamental human rights and the idea of human dignity in a vocabulary accessible to all the main religious and philosophical cultures of the planet;

4. this new document should also contain a synthetic but explicit and univocal specification of the structure of authority in charge of implementing the universal observance of the principles established by the assembly or by the World Convention.

Only if this course is followed will we have a fully legitimate use of military power for the purpose of enforcing respect of universal and fundamental human rights. Furthermore, the composition of the deliberating body (be it the General Assembly or a global convention) by states will ensure the independence of the consensus being formed from the hegemony of the political culture or type of regime prevailing in one part of the world, an independence from hegemony that should be a matter of concern both for Western democrats and for the citizens of non-Western states.

A few years ago, at the time of the debate on multiculturalism, the *New Yorker* published a cartoon that speaks to this point. You could see a Spanish armada on a tropical beach having disembarked from innumerable ships and a group of half-naked natives with their colorfully dressed chief coming out from the jungle. The heavily armored conquistador apparently had just stepped forward, had planted the cross in the sand, and was addressing the natives by saying "We have come from far away to talk with you about the true faith." And the chief of the natives was smiling back at him, answering: "We are happy to welcome you here: what do you want to know about the true faith?"

Few of us would feel comfortable with the idea that this picture might reproduce itself with democracy or human rights in lieu of the cross.

8 Europe as a Special Area for Human Hope

As a European, few expressions irritate me more than the so-called idea of Europe. I find the exercise of grafting a possible identity for the Europeans onto some philosophical or religious concept both futile and arrogant, indeed, a perfect example of what Europeans had better stay away from. This is not to say, however, that a reflection on what is distinctive about Europe in the larger context of contemporary Western society is purposeless. On the contrary, it is a priority, given the "constitutional" moment that the European Union has been undergoing since the formal signing of the Constitutional Treaty and the difficulties incurred in the ratification process after the results of the French and the Dutch referenda of 2005. Such reflection, however, has to be conducted in a quite different vein.

After the unfortunate, but perhaps salutary, setbacks represented by these two referenda, the hitherto followed "Jean Monnet method" of piecemeal institutional changes toward ever closer EU integration, yet without an anticipatory blueprint and without much of a public discussion except in elite circles, cannot be revived. Indeed, once the ambitious idea of a *constitutional founding* has been evoked with great emphasis and solemnity, it is not easy to turn the spotlights off the real question: what is Europe for?

What appears most in need of justification is the "ultimate project" in the service of which the constitutional agenda has been set in motion or, in other words, the *finalité* that supposedly drives the process of European integration. Whether the process of integration will eventually lead to a traditional nation-state of continental size, to a confederal arrangement, or to a postnational state may remain open[1]—though I sympathize with the last alternative, not least for its capacity to provide a viable example of the postnational sovereignty that may very well be the only form of sovereignty accessible to cosmopolitan institutions—but the attractiveness of the product of such a process will ultimately depend on what goals it may lead us to achieve.

Against the backdrop of these considerations, I'll try to reconstruct what we may understand to be the project or *finalité* underlying the process of integration and constitutionalization of the EU. And I'll try to outline it not with reference to some kind of philosophical "idea of Europe" but simply with reference to the text of the Constitutional Treaty and with reference to three background features of the current predicament of Europe that somehow qualify the way in which integration may be implemented: first, a certain inclination, imprinted in the historical experience of all major European countries, to acknowledge the ineliminability of the enemy, second, a distinctive relation of capitalism to democracy, and third, certain features of the integration process.

The aim of the considerations that I will develop, thus, is somehow much more modest than the various attempts thus far undertaken to spell out the meaning of the European identity by drawing on an interpretation of its historical vicissitudes or of its cultural heritage. Philosophers have often tried to capture the essence of Europe—an effort often signaled by the abused expression "the idea of Europe"—as located in a certain propensity to accommodate diversity, in a propensity for critical distance, in an emphatic idea of the human subject, in the depths of a multimillennial history, or in a certain notion of transcendence that chooses to embody itself in the human.[2] Fascinating and suggestive as these formulations may be, I believe that the most efficacious approach to the European identity is a Rawlsian one: there is enough substance to the Constitutional Treaty for a philosopher to reconstruct a European "political" identity—namely, an identity understood as the precipitate of the operating of public reason in what may well be the largest democratic space after India existing on the planet—without having to resort to the trite game of drawing ineluctable conclusions from comprehensive, yet controversial, premises. Where else should we look to identify the contours of an identity so understood if not at the locus where the jurisgenerative process already has operated at the highest level, namely, at that proposal for a Constitutional Treaty still in the process of being ratified?[3]

Differently than some of the most famous constitutional texts of the past, the treaty—with its 448 articles, which set it more on the side of the infamous "lawyer's contract" contrasted by Roosevelt with the "layman's document" that a democratic constitution is supposed to be—is very parsimonious with phrases capable of impressing the collective imaginary, phrases such as "life, liberty and the pursuit of happiness" or "liberté, égalité, fraternité." The only exception to this expressive restraint is the sentence that concludes the preamble where Europe is identified as a "special area of human hope."[4] What I would like to carry out here is nothing more than the semantic exercise of assigning a plausible meaning to this expression and suggesting that such an exercise constitutes the best beginning for our reconstruction of a European identity, "political and not metaphysical." In order to carry out this exercise, we need to understand, first of all, the exact nature of the hope for whose realization Europe supposedly constitutes a special area. Second, we need to make sense of the "specialness" of the European space: why is this political space so exceptionally conducive to the realization of that "human hope"?

In the course of this exercise we will then have to address questions like the following: what original elements can be found in the Constitutional Treaty? In what sense do these novel elements add up to a political identity different from that embedded in the other liberal-democratic polities thus far realized? And, furthermore, aside from the innovative quality of its main features, what is the overall political and historical significance of the treaty? The phrases "democratic deficit" and "lack of a European *demos*" are often heard. Yet to what extent does it make sense to apply traditional conceptions of a constitution and of a "constitutional moment" in the case of the European Union?

Semantics of Hope; or, the *European Dream*

When a large political unit, not simply a "country," in the case of the European Union, gives itself a constitution, by this act inevitably it enters an ideal dialogue with other crucial jurisgenerative junctures that have marked the history of humanity: the Magna Carta, the Declaration of Independence, the Constitution of the United States of America, the 1789 Declaration of the Rights of Man and Citizen, the Universal Declaration of Human Rights of 1948.

The most significant moments of this ideal dialogue are to be found in part 1 ("Definition and objectives of the Union") and part 2 ("Fundamental Rights and Citizenship of the Union") of the Constitutional Treaty.

In article 1, the constitution is presented as issuing from the will both of the citizens and of the states of Europe, a formulation that is unprecedented even if we take the constitutions of federal states into account. There are different ways of interpreting this clause. We could understand it as an adaptation to the reality of the European status quo, in other words as a reflection of the absence of a real *demos*. However, we could read in this formulation also the reflection of an entirely new reality: the reality of a constitution not just for a single state but for a postnational and poststate-like entity. Such a constitution then needs to draw legitimation not simply from the will of free and equal individuals but also from superindividual forms of political will, much in the same way as Rawls imagines that the principles regulating a "society of Peoples" be legitimated by the concurring will of the representatives of liberal and decent peoples.

Among the aims of the union, stated in article 3, the promotion of peace is mentioned twice. Incidentally, the promotion and achievement of peace on the European territory—a territory plagued by wars among all the peoples that have inhabited and inhabit it—is the real objective that has been undisputably achieved since the Treaty of Rome. So firmly and durably has this objective been achieved that today, more than half a century after that foundational moment, it appears as a banal and obvious, almost rhetorical, goal, no longer capable of mobilizing any enthusiasm. It suffices, however, to exert, just for a moment, the art of *depaysement,* and we can see things from a quite different perspective. It is enough that we look at the European Union as it is, with its quarrels on milk quotas and subsidies to agriculture, through the eyes of a resident of Srebrenica or Kossovo, in order to understand how much else Europe means over and beyond that common market to which we always fear that it could be reduced. When observed from Srebrenica or Kossovo, Europe means the embodiment of a value, the achievement of an aspiration, indeed the realization of a human hope—namely, the hope that what has been experienced by the countries that used to be part of the former Yugoslavia might no longer occur. And for those who have belonged to the European Union from day one, this means the hope that the peace achieved here might, through the force of the example, become a successful solution elsewhere as well—after all, forms of regional integration such as Mercosur, Asean, Nafta, the Andean Community, the South African Development Community (SADC), and the Economic Community of West-African States (ECOWAS) are somehow indebted to the European example and thus contribute to eradicating the phenomenon of organized warfare from this world. This objective of the promotion of peace is thus one of those tangible aspects that indicate the extent to which even now the European Union is much more than a common market.

Other salient objectives mentioned in the Constitutional Treaty are the protection of the environment, a sustainable development, full employment, the struggle against social exclusion, and intergenerational solidarity. Except for environmental protection and intergenerational solidarity, all the other objectives reflect a full acceptance, within the constitutional text, of the ideal of the welfare state or, in other words, the notion of a duty, incumbent on the state, to actively protect the welfare of the individual when it happens to fall below a certain threshold. This objective returns subsequently in article 14, clause 4, where it is stated that the Union can adopt initiatives aimed at coordinating the member states' welfare policies and thus is an active subject in the securing of social rights.

The most innovative aspects of the Constitutional Treaty, however, can be found in part 2, where the previous Treaty of Nice is integrated. More specifically, seven constitutional essentials that contribute to defining the identity of the European Union can be identified:

- The explicit prohibition against including the death penalty into penal law, in that the death penalty is understood as a violation of the right to life (part 2, article 62, 2). This clause sets the treaty on a line of discontinuity with the most important constitutions of the eighteenth century, notably the American and the French Constitutions, which contain no provision of this sort, and offers an obvious term of contrastive comparison with current U.S. legislation. The prohibition is accompanied by a further provision to the effect that the deportation, expulsion, or extradition of anyone (not just an EU citizen) "to a State where there is a serious risk that he or she would be subjected to the death penalty, torture or other inhuman or degrading treatment or punishment" (part 2, article 79) is also forbidden. The treaty thus forcefully expresses an ethical intuition that unites the whole European continent and without hesitation or reticence creates a counterpoint effect in what we call the West. On the two shores of the Atlantic the equal protection of a diversely understood human dignity may result in differences as wide as that which separates a life sentence from a death sentence as the proper punishment for the gravest crimes.

- The bioethical vein in which the right to bodily integrity is understood, as clarified in article 63. The requisite of free and informed consent, the prohibition of any eugenic practice and of reproductive cloning (which leaves open the possibility of cloning for therapeutic purposes) are explicitly constitutionalized, but even more important is the explicit prohibition, within the fields of medical science and biology, of "making the human body and its parts as such a source of financial gain."

- The constitutional codification of the right to privacy in article 67. The original formulation of a right to privacy as such, distinct from the right to the integrity of one's reputation or from the right to property, dates back to 1890, when Warren and Brandeis defended the protection, on the part of the state, of everyone's right "to be left alone" or to "privacy" on the ground that everyone has a right to the protection of the conditions for the integrity of his or her personality.[5] Only in the period between the 1940s and the 1960s, after over four decades of tormented legal debate, did the principle of a right to privacy gradually gain widespread acceptance on the basis not only of a normative understanding of the idea of the integrity of a personality—as Warren and Brandeis had already suggested—but also on the basis of a more fundamental right to obtain protection of those intimate relations that constitute the social frame wherein it is solely conceivable for us to maintain the coherence of one's identity[6] as well as the notion of a right "to develop one's own uniqueness."[7] No attempt has thus far taken place, however, to incorporate the "right to privacy" in a constitution. The Constitutional Treaty, therefore, in its providing for the right of everyone to "respect for his or her private and family life, home and communications" (article 67) opens a new chapter in constitutional law.

- The new specification of a right to "freedom of information" alongside the more traditional right to "freedom of expression" or "free speech." Pursuant article 71, freedom of expression consists no longer simply of a right of the individual to express her own thoughts without censorship but also of an obligation to respect "the freedom and pluralism" of the media. Now, while the freedom of the media is something that depends entirely on the existing law and thus lies within the reach of the legislative power of the member states of the union, their "pluralism"—understood as the existence of a plurality of media that convey differentiated currents of opinion—depends on a number of economic, entrepreneurial, and market conditions that cannot be influenced via policy with the same degree of direct efficacy. Here as well the Constitutional Treaty breaks new ground in the history of relations between the economic and the legal sphere.

- The constitutionalization of equality between men and women "in all areas." The innovative quality of article 83 manifests itself in two senses. From a historical point of view, the proposal to constitutionalize gender equality in Europe stands out relative to the failure of the last large campaign for an equal rights amendment in the U.S. in the 1970s.[8] While the protection of gender equality is entrusted to ordinary legislation in the U.S., its constitutionalization in Europe carries the historical significance of sheltering this subject matter from the normal political arena and of solemnly sanctioning its connection with the core constitutional value of human dignity. From the standpoint of constitutional politics, it is noteworthy that the second clause of the article goes so far as to explicitly provide for the admissibility of quotas, in order to avoid the risk that the actual implementation of a formally uncontested principle of gender equality might be quagmired in the intricacies of controversial policies. Whether the "measures providing for specific advantages in favor of the under-represented sex" can be reconciled or not with the overarching principle of the equality of all citizens is not left by the framers to the judgment of a court, but is rather a question to which the treaty provides a direct, explicit, and unquestionably positive answer.

- In the area of social rights we find in article 98 of the treaty a guarantee directed at ensuring "a high level of consumer protection."

In this case as well it is not difficult to detect an element of great innovativeness: namely, the constitutionalization of a tendency, inherent in contemporary Western law, to consider equality—the Dworkinian "sovereign virtue" of all liberal-democratic polities— as a principle that should inspire, if not strictly regulate, not only the public realm, for which it was originally conceived, but also the sphere of those private relations that unfold in the economy. The entire antitrust legislation is but a translation and application of the principle of equality in the sphere of economic relations. The aim of article 98 is obviously to bridge the gap between the influence of the great market players and the single atomized consumer without falling back into the regressive utopia of the abolition of the market.

- Finally, and again in the area of social rights, it is quite salient that article 85 of the treaty should mention the "right of the elderly to lead a life of dignity and independence and to participate in social and cultural life." In the famous constitutional charters of the past this idea had been mentioned only once, in article 123 of the 1793 French Constitution, where it was said that the Republic honors "loyalty, courage and old age."

In light of these seven constitutional essentials we can conclude that the human hope to which the Constitutional Treaty refers can be summed up in the following terms: the European Union, on the basis of the will of the peoples that belong to it at this time, proposes itself to its own citizens and to the rest of the world as the political space in which the dignity of the human being, not just of the citizen, is protected in the most complete way available on this planet. More specifically, to protect human dignity means to shield from the normal routine of political contestation and from the electoral fluctuation of majorities the idea that under no conditions can the state take the life of one of its citizens, residents, or temporary aliens, the idea that the genetic infrastructure of the human being cannot be a source of profit, the idea that no one should be allowed to starve without being helped by our institutions, the idea that no one should be left alone to face illness without being offered treatment by our institutions, the idea that no one should be left alone to suffer, along with the inevitable decline associated with the last stages of life, exclusion and indifference as well, the idea that no one should be left alone to defend her interests as a single individual, atom of humanity, against the interests of the economic powers that influence our lives by producing the goods that we consume and the information that we need to know in order to make our political choices, and, finally, the idea that every new human being who will enter the world through this space, even in the remote future, should be able to count on the fact that those who have preceded her committed themselves to care also for her and for her enjoying undiminished life chances. This is the European notion of human dignity—the *European dream* in the hearts of millions of citizens of the Union—and its full realization is the hope to which the final sentence of the preamble of the Constitutional Treaty refers.

Why a "Special Area"?

If this is arguably the meaning of the hope mentioned in the phrase "a special area for human hope," we can now move to the second segment of our interpretive exercise, namely, to the correct decodification of the adjective *special*. Why should the European political space be an especially propitious one for the purpose of realizing a human hope thus spelled out?

It is possible to identify three large groups of reasons that justify such a claim to specialness: 1. reasons connected with the cultural reflection of certain historical contingencies, 2. reasons connected with the relation of democracy to capitalism, and 3. reasons related to the institutional structure of the EU and to the process that has led to the Constitutional Treaty.

For each of these types of reasons, but especially for the group of historical reasons, we must carefully distinguish those reasons that characterize and set the European experience as such apart from the larger backdrop of Western modernity. Unduly equating the two has been a source of ethnocentrism, severe historical misunderstanding, and a lot of pernicious ideologies. The "special area" with which we are concerned here is something specifically European, not generically Western.

Reflections of the Frontier and of the Lack Thereof

From a historical point of view there exists one factor that sets Europe apart from other parts of the West and especially from the United States. Habermas and Derrida have discussed some aspects of it in their joint essay written on the occasion of the beginning of the attack on Iraq.[9]

The historical experience of the United States and, by reflection, its public culture has always been marked by the perception of a sort of military invulnerability—a perception whose roots date back to the absence of bellicose and threatening neighboring peoples, already noted by Tocqueville, the fact of never having experienced an invasion or an occupation, which explains the extraordinary impact of 9/11. On their territory the United States has only fought an ethnic enemy—the natives—up to annihilating it without conditions and reducing it to a state of complete political insignificance. This contingent historical situation has led to the rise of a culture of the frontier certain reflections of which still shape the American public imaginary of the present time, for all the profound changes undergone by this imaginary from the time when its public sphere was a limited and local one—the network of the thousands of *local newspapers* operating in the nineteenth century—to the present time when the infrastructure of the American public sphere is constituted by a differentiated network of large publishing conglomerates, the Internet, and currents of opinion operating and intersecting at the local, national, and global level. In its original form the culture of the frontier entailed a sense of unlimited geographic expansibility of one's own form of life, a sort of communally experienced sense of its undefeatability and of an affirmative destiny connected with it. It also means—even more important for our purposes—that our opponent of the moment can be reduced to a mere military variable and be thought of as annihilable.

The twentieth century has only reinforced this legacy. The only truly engaging challenges have come from Nazism and from the Soviet empire during the cold war, and both of these challenges have been won in a way that is, after all, not too dissimilar: they have come to an end with the annihilation and the political dissolving of the enemy. We can only be grateful, of course, for the outcome of such challenges. However, from the particular angle of the new historical context brought about by the creation of the EU and its possible projection on global politics, the blind spot can be immediately detected: the manifest annihilability of the enemy in turn entails an equally manifest superfluousness of dialogue, or a perception of dialogue as a negotiatory waystation toward the final victory, not as a stable and enduring condition never to be overcome. If the enemy can be uprooted and driven away, reduced to impotence and insignificance, then dialogue is but a symptom of weakness, irresoluteness, well-meaning but impractical idealism, and cannot but compare unfavorably with assertiveness, firmness, and tough-minded realism. Aren't these the terms of every electoral contest between Democrats and Republicans whenever foreign policy gains center stage, aren't these the psychological traits whose credible possession can make or break the electoral fortune of a presidential candidate in times when foreign policy, rather than the economy, is at the top of the political agenda?

Entirely different is the case of Europe. In the political DNA of each of its largest countries is the ineliminability of the enemy. The enemy is a competing life form, a culture just as differentiated and in all respects on an equal footing with one's own native culture. There will always be a France capable of standing up again, even after Nazi occupation. There will always be a Britain capable of resisting even Hitler. There will always be a Germany capable of resurrecting as a major economic power. The European soil has always been the stage where several peoples played their acts, and none of them has ever been in a position to prevail alone over the rest for longer than a transient moment. Today each of the most important countries—France, Germany, the United Kingdom, Italy, Spain, the Netherlands, Portugal, Greece, Austria—has a vivid memory of better days and has suffered the experience of being occupied and defeated.

Thus there is no single idea more alien to the public culture of European society than that of the frontier, namely, the notion that the enemy could be reduced to a military variable, then driven to surrender without conditions and that in this way immense new territories might be opened up for the expansion of one's own form of life. Even the temptation of an expansion southward in the age of classical colonialism soon met with the realization that neighboring countries rival in Europe were now rival competitors in the new colonial spaces, which then became just a deplaced replica of what was experienced at home. Of course each European country has had plenty of internal enemies, mostly identified on an ethnic and religious basis, but their physical near annihilation, as happened with the Armenians in Turkey, has been more the exception than the rule. Even the Holocaust cannot be taken as counterevidence. It was the product of the most horrible totalitarian regime, which lasted only twelve years, and it constitutes the backdrop against which not just the constitutional regimes of contemporary Europe, but any political movement and party within any democratic society seeks to define itself. As the embodiment of radical evil, it functions, if anything, as a powerful vaccine for immunizing the public sphere and the political imaginary of all European societies against the very idea of annihilating an internal enemy.

In politics the imaginary plays a crucial role. For politics is shot through not just with interests, conflicts, and power as a reductive view of it would have it, but also with ideas, some of which exhibit the rare quality of "mobilizing" people. What we call the "imaginary," however, works against the backdrop of historical experiences that are shared by individuals and handed down through the rituals of memory. No wonder then that all the metaphors—even the progressive ones—that evoke the idea of the frontier lose much of their appeal in Europe. The very idea of calling anything to which we simply assign political priority a "war"—as signaled by such expressions as the "war on crime," the "war on drugs," or the "war on poverty"—takes on quite different connotations when transposed to a European context.[10] The basic idea underlying the European political imaginary is the exact opposite of the frontier. If one wanted to condense it into a motto, it would be "We're stuck here." In other words, we have to make do with what we have got, we have to find a form of coexistence on the territory that we have available, we must better redistribute the resources we have, and, above all, we cannot but come to terms, enter dialogue, negotiate, with our opponent. For today's enemy will always be there, in the same political space where we are.

My hunch is that these mechanisms and constructions of the political imaginary are today undergoing a transformation in a global direction. This is not the context for assessing the merits of the policies vis-à-vis the various facets of the Islamic world—terrorism, fundamentalism, moderate Islam, secularized Islam, and the so-called Euroislam mentioned by Bassan Tibi.[11] Let me just end this section by raising a question: if by definition the global world is the world with no conceivable "outside," and thus a world where at least on certain dimensions—such as human rights, the environment, trade regulation, and so on—politics must prescind from the opposition of friend and foe, then which of the two political imaginaries constitutes a better, more adequate basis for the purpose of promoting peace and stability and of contributing to a cosmopolitan kind of governance?

Capitalism and Democracy: The European Way

A second host of considerations concerning the specialness of the European Union as an area for human hope concerns the relation of market, capitalism, and democracy. The time lapse between 1917 and 1989 has witnessed the birth, the unfolding, and the final decline of the idea of building a modern democracy on a basis other than a free market and the idea of free enterprise. The lesson to be drawn from this historical experience is all too evident: simply, we do not know of any way of structuring economic life other than capitalism, which in the long run is compatible with the protection and expansion of democratic freedom. Although it is much older than capitalism, democracy reaches its most complete flourishing thus far in the capitalist countries. Furthermore, its relation to this economic form has been very different in the course of the nineteenth and twentieth century and forms the object of everyday political contestation in all democratic countries. In fact, when the themes of security do not monopolize public attention, majorities and oppositions in the European Union countries and in the United States usually struggle over different ways of interpreting this relation and assessing its consequences. Needless to say, there exist almost as many solutions to the problem of democratically regulating the economy as there are countries to be considered—just think of the German *konzertierte Aktion,* of the Italian so-called income-policy of the 1960s and 1970s, of the Scandinavian social-democratic model, of Thatcher's and then Blair's different versions of neoliberalism, of the Spanish way, of Chinese-type capitalism without democracy, of the various types of paternalist regimes in the Southeast Asian countries and, of course, of United States "high-speed capitalism" or "turbo-capitalism." [12]

In order not to be quagmired in the extremely fine-grained detail of all the different models, however, we can highlight three main kinds of relation between capitalism and democracy: a *fusional* relation, a *metabolizing* relation, and a *paternalist* relation.

A fusional relation is one in which the capitalist ethos and the democratic ethos become one and the same form of life—a shared ethos in all respects. The most exemplary embodiment of this kind of relation between capitalism and democracy ironically comes from a labor leader such as Blair, when he suggests that everyone ought to become an entrepreneur of himself. What Weber used to call the spirit of capitalism—the pursuit of economic success through the rational use of different kinds of resources (financial capital, energy sources, raw materials, instrumental goods, human resources) acquired on the market in full respect of the law—and whose decline he observed and deplored in a world where the very success of the capitalist enterprise led to monopolistic concentrations, to the predominance of employed labor, and to the weakening of the original ethical-religious motivation toward economic success, paradoxically seems to undergo a singular rebirth and regain center stage in a new version at the dawn of the twenty-first century.

In this new and entirely secular version, each of us possesses at least one human resource—herself—to cultivate, educate, enhance, defend, and ultimately invest as best she can within that context in which fate has thrown her. "Self-reliance," the virtue of depending solely on oneself, glorified by Emerson's democratic individualism,[13] now also becomes the supreme public virtue, and the market becomes the allocator of choice for the distribution of all kinds of resources. The active correction of the distributive outcomes of the market by the state and its institutions—actually inaugurated in the United States with Roosevelt's New Deal policies of the 1930s—becomes, when considered from this standpoint, an instrument to be used as sparingly as possible and, further, an instrument that carries with it a social stigma. To be a recipient of welfare provisions means not having made it by oneself, being a loser who elicits compassion.

A long digression should be opened here on a specific aspect of the Puritan legitimation of capitalism. Over and beyond the well-known legitimation of economic success as a *sign* of salvation, equally important has been the legitimation bestowed by Puritanism, through its idea of not interfering with the unknowable divine plan for the distribution of salvation, on indifference toward the fate of those who have lost and have not managed to achieve success by relying solely on their capacities.[14]

Tocqueville also noted how the American democratic ethos could perfectly dovetail with the privatism of *homo oeconomicus* and even generate a tyranny of the majority, which in the end contains an element of indifference for the suffering of others. The events of the summer of 2005 in New Orleans, in the aftermath of Hurricane Katrina, provide a case in point: privatism, indifference toward those who suffer and toward social inequalities contribute to undermine further an already fragile social fabric, which cannot but then be lacerated by external catastrophies. When the natural disaster is over, the worst has yet to come: and that is the social disaster of a local community where the temporary suspension of external coercion immediately unleashes the resentful losers to loot the store windows gazed at in wishful admiration up until the day before, to steal from those who have already lost everything, to rob and assault the rescuers, to rape those who find themselves without protection.

Quite different is the relation that has developed in Europe between capitalism and democracy. There is no fusion between the two, often there has been quite a tension, and in any case the way in which most European societies have metabolized capitalism has consisted of considering it one of the necessary costs incurred for the sake of stabilizing and developing democracy. Whereas in Great Britain an elective affinity has always existed between liberal-democratic culture and the entrepreneurial spirit, on the continent by and large various cultural traditions—from the so-called social teachings of the Catholic Church to socialism—have always aimed at reconstituting, in the midst of a fully modernized society, that Great Community oriented to the common good whose destruction on the part of industrial society John Dewey forcefully lamented in 1927.[15]

In Europe the coming to full fruition of democracy has always been seen as entailing somehow the superseding of the spontaneous dynamics of the market and of capitalism, whether in the direction of a direct taking of responsibility for the good of the community on the part of the enterprise or in the direction of a complete overcoming of the private ownership of capital. The persistence, over several decades, of a more radical anticapitalism of socialist inspiration, along with a more moderate but no less tenacious anticapitalism of Catholic inspiration has injected a completely different ethical substance in the familiar institutions of the Western welfare state. No significant resistance has ever materialized in Europe against the constitutionalization of social rights, nor has any social stigma been attached to benefiting from welfare provisions. On the contrary, almost everywhere one can observe a great sensibility for the diffuse social suffering generated by the market processes, an ethical "ennoblement" of the welfare state as a viable and desirable second best to the authoritarian utopias of the classless society and the new man, and a perception of the market as merely of instrumental value for society, but in no sense as carrier of ethical values that are all-roundedly positive, indeed rather as the locus of dissemination of values that are ethically dubious.[16]

The third type of relation between democracy and capitalism is a paternalistic relation found especially in East Asia. In this case the market and the entrepreneurial moment enjoy a total preeminence with respect to the democratic moment and are understood as surrogates for democracy itself. A flourishing capitalism with the minimum possible amount of democracy seems to be the ideal—as in China, where even the intellectual dissenters hope that the further development of democracy might be imposed as a functional necessity by the requirements of the unbridled economic dynamics that the ruling class considers a surrogate of democracy.

In almost all of Southeast Asia—but mainly in China and Singapore, followed at a distance by South Korea and Taiwan, and with the luminous exception of the Philippines—we can observe a nexus of capitalism and democracy that runs in the opposite direction relative to that prevailing in continental Europe: not so much the acceptance with reservations and several corrections of those market and capitalist structures that are functional for democracy, but the acceptance with many reservations only of that modicum of democracy that is deemed necessary to guarantee the functioning of a system of capitalist enterprises.

Also from this second standpoint, therefore, it is plausible to hypothesize that the relation between capitalism and democracy contingently arisen in the European context is the most favorable one for the coming true of that "human hope" consisting in the historically most complete protection of human dignity.

The Postnational Constitution

Finally, a third order of reasons that characterize the European space as a special one has to do with the way in which the constitutional process has unfolded.

The Constitutional Treaty under ratification today is the end point of a multidecade evolution whose most important segments are constituted by the Treaties of Rome, Maastricht, Amsterdam, Laeken. Though some of these moments, Maastricht for example, may arguably be attributed a *constitutionale* valence, only in 2004 was the term *constitutional* used for the first time in an explicit and affirmative way. The difference with respect to the "constitutional moments" in the development of those polities that are paradigmatically taken as examples of constitutional democracies have been widely discussed. It is almost commonplace to speak of the absence of a European capable of acting as a *pouvoir constituant* and to point to the surrogate function played by state institutions that in turn are responsive to national *demoi:* a *democratic deficit* would arise as a result of the width and depth of this surrogatory function exerted by the national governments, by technocratic structures, and by European institutions whose chief officials are themselves nominated by governments.

This is not the only aspect of the European constitutional process that stands out as atypical with respect to classical constitutionalism. Also noteworthy is the fact that the constitutional document appears to be instrumental in solidifying a political reality whose *finalité* remains underdetermined in many important ways, not least the location of the boundaries of the territory whose political and social life will be regulated by the constitution. The Constitutional Treaty is the "constitution" for a political entity yet to be finallydetermined rather than for an already defined one. Finally, with respect to constitutional documents such as the Constitution of the United States or that of the French Republic, the treaty is located on a line of substantial continuity with the constitutional past of the polity and contains very few innovations: it systematizes the past more than marking a fracture with it.[17]

Valid and appropriate as these considerations might be, they cannot exempt us from the need for a further reflection, which should start from the following question: to what extent is it sensible to assess the constitutional import of a process—the one inaugurated by the European Convention, continued by the formal proposal for a Constitutional Treaty, and that will come to a close with its ratification—that has been set in motion in order to bring about a new poststate and postnational sovereignty against the benchmark of traits that instead have been distinctive of the constitutional processes of the modern nation-states? Do we not risk committing a conceptual error? Should an additional effort not be made, in order to assess the constitutional import of the ratification of the Constitutional Treaty on the basis of an ad hoc benchmark, *juxta propria principia,* or according to parameters no longer reflective of the experience of the modern nation-state? What could these new parameters be?

Perhaps also in this case we can look at the European experience and the coming into being of a special area for human hope. The European Union separates what Western modernity had united in a way that the global world now undermines: namely, the EU dissolves the unity of a state apparatus, a nation, a geographically distinct territory, and a constitution. Although some aspects of this picture remain relatively unaltered—for example, there remains the idea of a large and unified economic space, immersed, of course, in the global economy—but three other aspects are quite novel and contribute to making of the EU space a special one as far as the protection of human dignity is concerned.

The first is the loosening up of the nexus of constitution and state apparatus. The European Constitution does not purport to constitute the *Grundgesetz* of a state, but to constitute the fundamental law of a supranational legal space to which the states that we continue to be citizens of belong. Furthermore, the degree and scope of the participation of these single states to the supranational legal order is not fixed and could in the future vary even more. As of today, the citizens of some, but not all, European countries share the right to total mobility sanctioned by the Schengen Treaty, and a different set of EU citizens share a common currency. Thus the citizens of the EU may share a constitution but not fundamental aspects of the organization of a state, even of a federal state. They can learn to see themselves as belonging to the same political community, inspired by the same constitutional patriotism, united in a common destiny, without at the same time seeing themselves as being administered by the same apparatus or even—as in the classical pictures of the democratic rule of law—without seeing themselves as the authors of the laws they obey. Popular authorship of the laws—the very hinge of all democratic polity—in the European context is a much more *indirect* authorship than the one to which the nation-state has accustomed us. For a long historical period in Europe the legislative initiative will not be solely in the hands of the European Parliament, but will form at the crossroads of Parliament, the European Commission, and various intergovernmental bodies—and, in the future, especially if a certain orientation will prevail, it might always be so. One can certainly interpret this predicament as a democratic deficit, if we use the legislative authorship of the citizens of nation-states as a benchmark. Nevertheless, it seems to me at least worthwhile to address the question whether in Europe something might be in progress whose assessment calls for different parameters: perhaps a new kind of democratic authorship that might be relevant as a model for conceiving the democratic authorship of the "citizens of the world" in the context of future cosmopolitan institutions, which again will have to fit a constitutional framework already partially in place but without aspiring to constitute a world state.

The second aspect of the European constitutional process that bears some relevance for our interpreting the phrase "a special area for human hope" has to do with the indefinite quality of the borders and the self-representation of a political community in formation that emerges from the document. A constitution is—according to what the tradition of national constitutionalism has taught us—the fundamental law that governs political life within a territory whose borders are fixed and certain. Article 1 instead runs, "The Union shall be open to all European States which respect its values and are committed to promoting them together" and the subsequent article 57 emphasizes a similar point. The values to which reference is made are those spelled out in article I-2, namely, "respect for human dignity, freedom, democracy, equality, the rule of law and respect for human rights," understood as the fundamental values of a society grounded in turn on "pluralism, non-discrimination, tolerance, justice, solidarity and equality between women and men." Contemporary twenty-seven-member Europe represents itself then as a political entity "in progress," one centered around a rule of law that other "European" states—"European" then obviously on a basis different than participation in the union—will in the future be able to join. This circumstance injects part of this lack of closure to the constitutional document itself: we simply do not know today how many and who our legal consociates will be. Above all, from the treaty we glean the image of two distinct sets that will tend, but only at a point in time located in an unspecifiable future, to coincide: the set of the countries that are "geographically European" and the set of the countries that are members of the union.

Finally, the third aspect of the European constitutional process that is of interest to us is its potential for reviving the model of the *civitas,* as distinct from the model of the *demos.* Not only is there no European *demos,* but perhaps there will *never* be one in the modern and democratic sense of the term, namely, a *demos* that forms its political will in the context of a unified public sphere. There exists at least embryonically, however, a European *civitas,* formed by a plurality of *gentes, demoi, ethnoi.* This picture I see as perfectly reconcilable with an Ackermanian dualistic view of democracy. Relatively to the national version of democratic dualism, the postnational one will have to rely on a more emphatically conceived constitutional moment to compensate for the more diluted, indirect, and technocratized bent of ordinary politics in a context characterized by a multilayered governance. An example of this accentuated dualism could be seen as a possible way of solving the impasse determined by the French and Dutch "No" to the ratification of the Constitutional Treaty. While a minimalist response in an intergovernmental spirit would be to resubmit the existing document or continue the ratification with no changes, the solution consistent with accentuated dualism would be to take seriously the challenge of the negative vote, to call for a redrafting of the constitution by a real convention elected by the citizens, and to then devise a majority, no longer unanimousness-based mechanism of ratification, that involved a same-day referendum for the entire EU electorate after and adequate period of discussion and contestation.

Again, this model is perhaps the one that best allows us to consider the European Union as an exemplary embodiment of what in the future might be a *cosmopolitan civitas,* where we will have a more indirect popular authorship of the laws and a new form of governance without a state apparatus molded after the state apparatus typical of the nation-state. "Governance without state apparatus" is not a vague formula, but rather means something specific. It means that no central monopoly exists on the legitimate use of force (after all, there is no European police or army), but a functionally equivalent monopoly does exist: the monopoly on the attribution of legitimacy to the use of force. Also in this case, then, the phrase "special area" acquires a distinct sense: the European Union is the one political space on the entire planet where this separation of governance and state-apparatus, of constitution and state, of the monopoly on the legitimate use of force and the monopoly on the attribution of legitimacy to the use of force is being more thoroughly explored and put into practice—a separation that might function as an example for an even more extended cosmopolitan governance in the future.

These considerations, I hope, might corroborate the plausibility of the thesis that European identity can be fruitfully discussed not only in terms of philosophical speculation about the version of the human that has found embodiment in the history and in the cultural and religious traditions of Europe, not only in terms of the Christian roots of the European society or in terms of the "idea" that such society represents. It is possible, instead, to discuss the European identity in a Rawlsian "political" vein, as a precipitate of political and legal choices that draw their legitimacy from the area of overlap between distinct and often rival conceptions of ethics. The identity thus delimited can be shown to be—if the considerations developed above are plausible—robust enough for Europe to stand out as something specific relative to the rest of the West and the rest of the world. And yet the substantive nature of this reconstructed identity is such that what we as Europeans collectively are might not preclude the possibility that others, in the process of constructing their identities, find inspiration from this example. Often we Europeans acknowledge with a slight trace of self-pity the obvious fact that our becoming a second "superpower" with as much influence as the United States on the affairs of this world is nowhere in sight. But perhaps we underestimate the extent to which the "European form of life," the "European dream," as it can be gleaned from the texture of our constitutional law more than from the speculations of our philosophers, might constitute an attractive example, relative to what can be seen in other parts of the globe, of how diversity can be reconciled into unity without violence and without dissolving itself into homogeneity.

9 Religion Within the Limits of Reasonableness

> There is, or need be, no war between religion and democracy. In this respect political liberalism is sharply different from and rejects Enlightenment liberalism, which historically attacked orthodox Christianity.
> —John Rawls, *The Law of Peoples*

> I believe that intercultural aspects today are an inevitable part of the discussion about the fundamental issues concerning the essence of human beings, that this is a discussion that cannot be held entirely within Christianity nor simply within the Western rationalist tradition.
> —Joseph Ratzinger, "Reason and Faith"

As the title suggests, something has changed in the relation between religion and politics as the twentieth century passed into the next. What precisely has changed is the subject discussed in this chapter. Is the demand emerging within Western democratic societies for a more conspicuous and visible "public role" to be played by religious faith, or at least for deprivatization of religious affiliation and conduct, justified and legitimate? What are the implications of acknowledging this transformation of our public space for our understanding of the nexus of religion, modern society, and politics?

To start this analysis, I suggest one should concentrate on three issues: 1. the achievement of full equality between citizens who are believers and nonbelievers, 2. the different evolutionary pace of religious and secular conscience, 3. the anthropological difference between the various forms of religiosity in their adapting to the separation of church and state. In the final section of the chapter I will address the role of historical and cultural context in the implementation of the principle of the religious neutrality of democratic institutions—a subject that can be addressed using the example of the display of the religious symbols, such as the crucifix or the Ten Commandments, in public institutions.

There is no doubt that religion has forcefully returned to the political scene within the new scenario that has emerged since 1989. For some time now sociologists such as Peter Berger, José Casanova, and Adam Seligman have warned us about desecularization processes, about the "reemergence" of a need for the sacred that has in fact never really vanished,[1] about the increasing importance assumed by religious symbols and themes for a constantly growing number of individuals and groups. In the course of time, the idea of a progressive secularization of modern societies turned out to be what it effectively is: yet another philosophy of history driven by an ideological thrust. Not only has the "religious phenomenon" not disappeared, since it is embedded in the phenomenon of society as such, for which it functions both as an idealizing and integrating element, as explained by Durkheim in *The Elementary Forms of the Religious Life*, but in late modernity religion has reacquired the presence on the public stage it appeared to have lost during early modernity.

These are only, however, the facts of the matter: but the question I intend to address is instead a normative one. If our perception of the relationship between modernization and the religious phenomenon has changed, should we also reconsider the relationship between politics and religion as we have come to understand it in the modern Western world? Do concepts such as the religious neutrality of institutions or the separation between church and state need to be reassessed in view of the new scenarios that have emerged? Is the understanding of the "separation" developed when secularization was considered the destiny of modern societies still compelling when instead we come to consider the religious phenomenon as one that is here to stay and possesses intrinsic value as well?[2]

An important signal that something has changed at a deeper level than just the "political climate" comes from the fact that it is not only antiliberal, neocon, or communitarian authors who urge the rethinking of religious neutrality. Authors such as Jürgen Habermas and John Rawls wonder whether the interpretation of these concepts provided by liberal political theory was not excessively restrictive. Their most important thoughts on the subject can be found in "The Idea of Public Reason Revisited" and in "Religion in the Public Sphere."[3]

Let us first of all pin down our term of comparison: in the classical version of the separation betweenchurch and state religious faiths are protected in their freedom to articulate revealed knowledge and paths to salvation, to administer the interpretation of what is holy, to regulate rituals, to infuse transcendence in daily life, to celebrate the bond shared by the faithful, as long as they never invoke support from the state's coercive power, never pretend to turn sin into crime, and always allow their believers to change their minds and turn to another religion or no religion. What reasons might we have now to question this well-tested recipe that has permitted the creation of the democratic societies we live in today?

Taking the Equality of Citizens Seriously: The "Asymmetrical Burden"

The element that justifies a critical reassessment of the "well-tested recipe" is the awareness that in the liberal political arena only nonreligious, secular reasons are a legitimate basis for binding decisions imposes an "additional burden" in fully participating in the democratic process on those citizens authentically and totally experiencing their faith. If the only currency used in the public arena of politics is constituted by "penultimate" (as opposed to "ultimate") reasons, by the reasonable "secular" reasons shareable by believers and nonbelievers alike, then it is obvious that not all citizens are exactly equal. Due to the religious nature of their most profound beliefs, citizens who are believers are required to go an extra hermeneutic mile, compared to those embracing secular beliefs, in order to formulate reasons that can be legitimately used in the political arena. A form of redressing the balance is necessary, not as an act of homage to the changed zeitgeist but in the name of the principle of equality. Rawls and Habermas independently offer two mainly converging, but in some interesting ways differing, ideas for reestablishing the egalitarian equation that forms the normative keystone of the liberal polity.

Both offer us a bipartite picture of the public space: on the one hand the strictly public realm, in which regulations and proposals must be free from all links with religion, and, on the other hand, an equally public—in the sense that it s not restricted to the domestic walls—but not equally structured environment, in which believers instead enjoy a total freedom to express ideas based on their religious credo. Rawls calls these two parts of the public space the "public forum" and the "background culture," while Habermas instead identifies them as the space inhabited by the "strong publics" (i.e., the formal contexts such as parliaments, courts, ministries, and administrations) and a more informal "political public sphere."[4]

Furthermore, Rawls explicitly distances himself from a restrictive interpretation of his concept of "public reason" and of "reasonableness": on the basis of the so-called wide view of public political culture, citizens may *at any time* legitimately bring their most profound beliefs, inspired by religion, to the public arena on condition that when and if what they propose is formalized in a law, these initially religious grounds should be accompanied by other, secular reasons, fully shareable by citizens who are nonbelievers.[5] Furthermore, as we have seen in chapter 3, "public reason" is only *one* of the modalities of legitimate public speech, whereas "conjecture," "witnessing," and "declarations"[6] are forms of public speech in which comprehensive reasons based on religious beliefs may legitimately play a preminent role.

Finally, Rawls warns us against confusing "public reason" and "secular reason."[7] When the time comes to draft a law, even citizens who embrace *secular* beliefs, ranging from Enlightenment rationalism to Marxism—beliefs that in the past have generated forms of fundamentalism no less ruinous and oppressive than those based on religion—are asked to transform their ultimate reasons into penultimate ones, shareable also by those who do not share their ideologies. Being religiously neutral but not militantly secularist, "public reason" therefore appears as equidistant from *all* forms of reasoning that start from controversial comprehensive assumptions, be they religious or secular. Its internal standard is "reasonableness," as distinct from rationality, understood as the capacity to acknowledge the fact of pluralism, the partiality of one's own position, and the readiness to join in fair cooperation with others, a cooperation based on principles that can be shared by all.

Habermas too emphasizes how within the public sphere there cannot be restrictions placed on the kind of reasons invoked in order to justify or criticize a proposal.[8] The idea of neutrality in the strictest sense is applied only to formal decision making in the political sphere: in parliamentary records or in court rulings controversial religious references are not permitted. And Habermas too makes a distinction—fully parallel to Rawls's distinction between public reason and secular reason—between secular reason, often with a scientistic basis, and so-called postsecular reason, which results from a learning process internal to the Enlightenment tradition and is ready to accept all that religious faith can teach.[9] But he expresses greater concern than Rawls with regard to what he defines as an "undue *mental* and *psychological* burden,"[10] an asymmetrically distributed burden of translation, that aggravates the believer citizen given the fact that the currency used by democratic politics can only be that of religiously neutral reason. It is a burden that elicits pragmatic concerns—for example, the increasing alienation of large masses of religiously oriented citizens or the cultural system's lowered integrating capability when facing a split between institutionalized secular values and widespread religious ones—but also raises a genuine normative concern: whatever happened to the principle of equality?

This concern leads Habermas to formulate a proposal not to be found in Rawls's work: the additional burden of translation should be *shared* among citizens who are believers and those who are nonbelievers. This is to ensure that the believer citizens, who for reasons independent of their will should find it impossible to "translate" reasons linked to their faith into religiously neutral reasons, not be deprived of political influence. The same should apply to citizens embracing secular beliefs and unable to translate their claims into a postsecular form—I'm thinking here not only of scientistic secularism but also of those constitutional cultures in which the secular conscience of the socialist and communist movements played a role just as important as that of the Catholic conscience. But here Habermas hesitates: almost as if the citizen who believes in a secular utopia is in some way more in line with the postsecular reason that undergirds public speech than the religious citizen is.

Even a superficial inspection of the secular ideologies that raged throughout the twentieth century raises some doubts as to the superior alignment the secular citizen would enjoy with respect to the requirement of neutrality. The providentialism of the proletarian revolution, the party's messianism, the mistrust in regard to "merely formal" democracy, one-way pacifism, romantic third worldism, distance from "bourgeois justice," resistance to the "system's" oppression, the idea of a world revolution, and many other of the socialist movement's classic themes for decades formed a cultural humus in which generations of citizens grew up, coming to take them for granted. The hermeneutic task required of them in order to participate in the discourse of public reason is no less demanding than that required of the most devote Christians.

Other voices have come to enrich this debate on the changing meaning of "religious neutrality" and the separation of church and state. Charles Taylor, for example, in his essays entitled "A Catholic Modernity?" and "Religion Today,"[11] speaks of a "spiritual lobotomy" that the horizon of modern humanism, if assumed as exclusive, would impose on the Christian citizen, who does not identify with an idea of "human flourishing which recognizes no valid end beyond this."[12] This form of antitranscendent humanism of "shared political values" risks appearing to the believer citizen as "a gratuitous exclusion of religion in the name of a rival metaphysical belief, and not simply as the protecting and controlling of the borders of a shared and independent public sphere."[13] The remedy is neither univocal nor easy to identify. Taylor seems to favor a balanced combination of the "humanisms" anchored in various secular and religious visions rather than a delimitation of the public space by "subtraction" or "bracketing."

Walzer proposes a flexibilization of the line separating politics and religion. At times reasons of justice and the principle of equality outrank reasons in favor of a rigid application of the separation understood as neutrality; for example, this occurs when in a compensatory vein the state establishes quotas for disadvantaged groups who in the past suffered discrimination and are systematically underrepresented in certain positions. According to Walzer, on other occasions the state can legitimately suspend its neutrality for pragmatic reasons, without this actually counting as a violation of the principle. For example, should one wish to establish a weekly holiday, there is no need to hold a draw to decide which day it should be: the principle of separation is only applied in a flexible way, not violated, if the state chooses Sunday, adopting the tradition of the majority of its citizens. The separation would be violated if the law should forbid the believers of other religions to celebrate their festivities on other days. Another example could be the correct decision taken by the mayor of Rome when he closed all schools and offices on the day of the funeral of John Paul II, a decision dictated by obvious pragmatic reasons considering the extraordinary number of people attending the funeral, security issues arising from the presence of two hundred state delegations, and the normal problems posed by traffic in the city. Who could say that this exception violated the principle of religious neutrality?

It is interesting, however, to observe at this point the difference between the proper way to fulfill the ideal of neutrality in the context of classical liberal polities and in the Italian historical-constitutional context, where democracy is a latecomer and democratic political culture still relatively weak. Walzer excludes both the celebration of Easter and of May 1 as incompatible with the idea of the state's religious neutrality: a perfect example of neutrality understood as the "bracketing" of controversial options. In Italy both these festivities have coexisted and coexist in a public dimension without anyone perceiving this as damaging to religious neutrality, and I take this as a symptom of a different idea of neutrality—an idea perhaps more fertile and appropriate in times of massive migration and consequent reshuffling and reconfiguration of political cultures. In this case neutrality is understood not as a "bracketing" of conflicting religious or secular ideas, but as the "search for a balancing," of an equilibrium of sorts between them. Neutrality by addition, rather than by subtraction: with the pluralistic pantheon as a model and not the bare walls of public buildings from which symbols of the faith are banished.

Finally, Ronald Dworkin has recently joined the debate to question the viability of the Rawlsian model of public reason. Dworkin begins his argument by outlining two alternative models of the role that religion should play in the public space—the model of a tolerant religious nation "committed to the values of faith and worship, but with tolerance for religious minorities, including non-believers" and the model of a tolerant secular nation "committed to thoroughly secular government but with tolerance and accommodation for people of religious faith."[14] The two models are contrasted in terms of their likely response to the two clauses of the First Amendment of the Constitution of the United States.[15] Whereas the *religious tolerant* model interprets the establishment clause as merely prohibiting the favoring of one confession over another but allowing for institutional upholding of (monotheistic) religion versus agnostic attitudes, and allows the use of religious symbols and references in public ceremonies, the *secular tolerant* model strives to be equidistant from both militant atheism and religion, refuses to acknowledge a special status of monotheistic creeds and any intrinsically positive value to religious experience as such, and bars religious (or antireligious) references from public ceremonies.[16] Concerning the free exercise clause, whereas a *religious tolerant* society understands religious practices in a narrow sense and thus feels authorized to ban (even on religious grounds) such practices as homosexuality, abortion, genetic research on stem cells, a *secular tolerant* society takes a broader view of freedom of religion as aimed at protecting a nonspecifically religious capacity for autonomy and self-determination. Consequently, if freedom of religion matters to us qua instance of a more general capacity for autonomous choice—the capacity to choose one's own faith—then other practices, such as sexual conduct, marriage, procreation, scientific investigation, which also count as instances of autonomous self-direction, should also be considered as under constitutional protection and could never be banned on religious or other grounds.[17]

Dworkin's objection to Rawls's is that the religious citizens of conservative orientation often cannot separate their religious convictions from their political principles: "their religious convictions *are* political principles" and "they do not accept private observance as a substitute for public religious endorsement."[18] Given their mindset, they are not likely to accept the precepts of public reason, because they do not respect nonbelievers as people in deference to whom they should abstain from pursuing their "profound religious ambitions." Religious conservatives think that secular citizens are deliberately in error, in that "they stubbornly refused to open their hearts to the truth," and that as long as they wield a majority it is pointless for them to give up the chance to shape society by law according to their beliefs. It might be objected, against Dworkin, that his argument merely starts from a different assumption than Rawls's thesis: namely, Dworkin just assumes that, at least in the conservative wing of the religious citizens, reasonableness is not the prevalent attitude and thus the appeal of public reason will be very weak. In this sense, Dworkin's point would not be a real counterargument, but only a more pessimistic assessment of the diffusion of reasonableness among religiously minded citizens.

However, Dworkin's suggestion, interestingly, not only does not constitute a real challenge to political liberalism, but ends up unwittingly reaffirming it. For, in the end, from his negative appraisal of the appeal of public reason among conservative believers, Dworkin draws the suggestion that liberals "try to show religious conservatives that their ambition to fuse religion and politics in the way they now propose is an error because it contradicts the very basic principles that are also part of their faith."[19] Liberals should try to convince religiously minded conservatives that one of the constitutive ingredients of the idea of human dignity—namely, the requirement that we take personal responsibility for the choice of our own ethical convictions, including religious ones—is indeed common ground across the two sides and enjoins religious, no less than liberals and secular, citizens to abstain from usurping, through statutory and judicial coercion,[20] the ability of people to exert responsibility for their lives through autonomously shaping their most significant practices. More generally, secular minded citizens should confront religious conservatives with the intrinsic inconsistency of their subscribing to the principle of personal responsibility for the values pursued in one's life and at the same time aspiring to bring the culture of a complex society in line with certain controversial moral guidelines thorough coercive law.

In the end, what Dworkin urges liberals and secular citizens to do is not far from the Rawlsian idea of wide public reason: they should engage the real beliefs of their opponents by calling them to task concerning the legal and institutional consequences of the notion—shared across the divide—of equal personal reponsibility for shaping one's life.

These reflections on the "wide" concept of public discourse and reason, on the asymmetric and undue hermeneutic burden carried by believer citizens, on the selectivity of the principles of secularism, on flexibility in applying the separationist recipe, and on the inconsistency of religious paternalism somehow redefine the implications of the principle of equality for the separation of religion and politics in a postsecular society. Aside from the issue of equality among religious and secular citizens, however, two further problematic aspects of the well-tested recipe of the separation between religion and politics as understood until now need to be considered.

The first concerns the difference in the evolutionary rhythms of the religious and the religiously neutral public conscience (the difference is greatly reduced if we compare religious and militantly secular forms of conscience) and the effects of such difference on the principle of toleration.

The second aspect concerns the unequal pressure exerted by the separatist recipe on the various forms of religion, an unequal pressure that compounds the different burden inflicted on believer and nonbeliever citizens with a further, as yet unexplored, diversity of burdens among believing citizens. I will address these two aspects of the separation of religion and politics in the next two sections.

The Differential of Evolutionary Pace

What is to be tolerated, in a "religiously neutral" state, in matters of religiously motivated conduct? Suppose that a religious faith exists that orders its faithful to take drugs, for example opium or peyote, as part of the usual collective prayer rituals during certain festivities. Such a ritual would certainly not be tolerated by our current civil legislation. Religious behavior involving mutilation of the body, ill treatment of animals, human sacrifices, compulsory "holy prostitution," or other forms of forced promiscuity would be equally intolerable. Where exactly is the line separating the tolerable from the intolerable?

In this case too we nowadays find ourselves in a context in which the solution classically provided by the founders of the modern liberal state—and in particular John Locke—shows considerable limitations and calls for a reassessment.

Locke's answer to such questions is incomparably clear. Every church is free to regulate as it thinks best all practices related to the cult—place, time, and modality of these practices—on condition that these practices are legal according to civil law. Instead, a church never has the right to establish cults including acts that are against the law. Furthermore, one must introduce a distinction between what is "part of the worship itself" and what is instead "but a circumstance."[21] What is considered as specifically wanted by God belongs to the first category. For example, sprinkling holy water for benedictions, using a host in the place of the bread representing the body of Christ, the use of wine, etc. Within the second category fall instead all the things that "though in general … cannot be separated from worship" are just applications and variations of vaguely defined things and as such indifferent; these include "the time and place of worship, habit, and posture of him that worships. These are circumstances, and perfectly indifferent, where God has not given any express command about them."[22]

Now, just as a civil magistrate cannot impose the practice of a cult, it cannot forbid it either, "because if he did so, he would destroy the church itself; the end of whose institution is only to worship God with freedom after its own manner."[23] A cult, however, cannot be against the law. Should a church intend to sacrifice a child, or impose an "indecent promiscuity," or practice any other illegal act, would the civil authorities be obliged to tolerate this? Locke's answer is negative. While on one hand "whatsoever is lawful in the Commonwealth cannot be prohibited by the magistrate in the Church. Whatsoever is permitted unto any of [the commonwealth's] subjects for their ordinary use, neither can nor ought to be forbidden by [the magistrate] to any sect of people for their religious uses," on the other hand "those things that are prejudicial to the commonweal of a people in their ordinary use, and are therefore forbidden by laws, those things ought not to be permitted to churches in their sacred rites."[24]

One of the great merits of Locke's concept of tolerance—a concept, one ought to remember, created to regulate only "intraprotestant" relations, excluding Catholics, atheists, and the faithful of non-Christian religions—is certainly the extreme clarity and elegance of the criteria implied. Why does the need arise today to reassess it?

The need to rethink Locke's formula for tolerance, certainly not in order to thwart it but to adapt it to a new context, arises from the observation—after three centuries—that "secular" civil law evolves following a totally different and more accelerated pace than religious conscience. This differential in evolutionary pace is causally linked to a series of factors deserving more careful consideration at an empiric level. First of all, the religious conscience experiences a very intense relationship with its own tradition, a relationship that finds only a weak equivalent in the importance of "precedent" for legal argumentation. This applies to highly institutionalized forms of religiosity, such as Catholicism, which envisages an explicit "Magisterium of the Church" on the subject of articles of faith, cult modalities, as well as an equally explicit principle of the "infallibility of the pope," but also to those forms of religiosity that allow the believer greater autonomy. As far as the great historical religions are concerned, tradition is often the interpretative tradition of a holy text that by definition can never be corrected, let alone replaced, but only reinterpreted.

The internal structure of juridical conscience is different, and even more different from this model is *political* consciousness. There are no texts placed beyond correction. The Constitution itself is open to revision, even on fundamental issues. Juridical interpretation too is in a sense oriented at the importance of a "precedent," but only because conformity with a precedent is functional to the objective of ensuring the legal system's overall coherence and the predictability of legal consequences—what Max Weber used to call the rational calculability of the legal consequences of one's actions.

Furthermore, in a modern society the juridical conscience operates in a manner autonomous both from morals and politics, but is nonetheless always immersed within a political context characterized by the presence of a plurality of values, interests, and options finding support within a plurality of more or less organized groups. Its binding force consists more in the coherence of its pronoucements and decisions with certain basic values— freedom and equality, but not only—than in the continuity with a tradition as such: fundamental values of the polity are often better fulfilled by institutional change (for example, the abolition of forms of discrimination, the creation of new rights, of new institutions, etc.) rather than by preserving existing conditions.

Moreover, the juridical conscience in our times is naturally immersed in a democratic political context, and this obviously contributes to the dynamism and fluidity of the legal fabric itself. After all, after centuries during which the democratic form of government has remained more or less the same, in the course of the last one hundred years innovations such as universal suffrage, social legislation, laws about the public administrations' transparency, the protection of privacy, cultural rights, and the international protection of human rights have revolutionized democracy. No other form of political order has proved to be so dynamic. The effects of this dynamism intrinsic to a democratic form of government, with its public sphere and the market as natural accelerators of the renewal of traditions, are obvious.[25]

While Locke's concept of tolerance identifies what can be tolerated in the religious sphere on the basis of what is allowed by civil law, it is clear that such pronounced evolutionary dynamism—especially within a democratic context—will inevitably soon unbalance the equation. Religious customs and ritual forms of conduct, once solidly within the area of civil legality, will soon end up outside it due to changes in the law following the democratic process; immediately obvious examples are woman's inferior position in many ecclesial communities, the religious rejection of nontraditional forms of families, and discrimination against homosexuals.

The more general point is that a democratic and pluralistic context is characterized by a host of intersecting and connected struggles for recognition and by a public sphere in which the constant presentation and discussion of new expectations will most likely lead to a greater probability of social and cultural change—and hence also of juridical-legal change—than is the case with an ecclesial community bound to the continuity of one single tradition and integrated via one single source of authority. Is it fair to ask religious communities to keep pace with the democratic conscience, is it fair to move the border between the tolerable and the intolerable, strictly observing Locke's principle, at the promulgation of every new law? Is this "imperative of keeping pace" not another asymmetrical and additional burden, different than that of translation, imposed on religious traditions and not on those secular cultural traditions that share an elective affinity with the dynamism of democratic political culture? What forms of compensation can we identify for the intrinsically disadvantaged predicament of the religious conscience?

Religious Anthropologies

Finally, there is yet another reason for reassessing the traditional understanding of the principle of separation between religion and politics and the manner in which this separation has until now been institutionalized. This reason concerns the different and unequal burdens, psychological and existential, that participation in the public sphere imposes on believers whose faiths give rise to diverse anthropological profiles. In this case the issue addressed is not the equality between believer and nonbeliever citizens, but the equality between believers embracing different faiths. A typical example of this problem is the case of the Catholic and the Protestant faiths.

Does the standard recipe for separation place the two parties at the origin of this conflict effectively on an equal footing? Even considering the broad spectrum of the varieties of Protestantism—ranging from Anglicanism's greater institutionalist inclination, to Lutheranism, Calvinism, and the more radical versions of Anabaptism, Pietism, Methodism, Congregationalism, etc.—all forms of Protestantism may be said to accentuate the inwardness of faith. Emphasis is on the individual's charisma, on the authenticity of his persuasions, on the transparency and continuity of his motivations and furthermore the believer is granted the right to directly interpret, following his conscience, the doctrinal meaning and the practical consequences of the Scriptures. It is obvious that once a form of religiosity, such as Protestantism, becomes dominant in certain national contexts, it generates an anthropological scenario spontaneously in keeping with the "well-tested recipe" of the deinstitutionalization and privatization of faith.

Catholic religiosity is quite different. Here one observes the kind of relationship between the believer and his religion that Charles Taylor has called "paleo-Durkheimian." Religious faith is mediated by an institution, the Church, that has a public presence, is at the center of a community that is chorally and publicly present in the life of the individual, administers the sacraments, pardons sins, and acts as a vehicle for divine mercy. At certain times—and the collective pathos caused by the death of John Paul II is a tangible example of this—this community of believers gains the center of the public stage, attracting attention, beating the tempo of all that is social, acting as the source of a shared extraordinary meaning, a power capable of truly bridging immanence and transcendence, the inert profanity of the "here," the this-worldly, and the mystery and shrouded sacredness of "the beyond," the otherworldly.

From my point of view, as a secular person, I imagine that experiencing religion as a Catholic means precisely this: experiencing the suggestion of the great processions, the authoritative and public presence of the Church and her representatives, a close network of associations impregnating the social fabric, the separation between monastic perfectionism and the indulgence of the "we are all sinners." Catholicism reduced simply to the inward dimension of the conscience, Catholicism with a curtailed magnificence of external symbols, is a mortified Catholicism.

Once again, Catholicism's peculiarly communitarian and public vocation does not mean one should abandon the principle of separation and return to the premodern short circuit between religion and power, sin and crime, dogma and law. It only means that a "religiously neutral" but not secularist "postsecular" society must assume responsibility—in a compensatory sense, as in the case of the additional hermeneutic burden, and in any event in an institutional sense yet to be spelled out—for this different impact of the separation between the state and the church on citizens and communities embracing different religious faiths. In this case, too, it is on the ground of equality that a reassessment is needed.

Principle and Context

The relation of religion and politics in the postsecular state is not merely "a matter of principle." Until now we have discussed the relation of religion and politics in the postsecular state in general terms, and we have come to the tentative conclusion that what is in need of a reassessment is not the principle of separation as such, but rather the way in which separation has been institutionalized. It is not only a matter of choosing a more or less good principle. Given a sound principle—say, separation—there can be a good way of applying it, with judgment and appropriateness, and there can be an inconsiderate, rigid, and obtuse way of applying it. No principle is capable of regulating such a complex issue as the relation of religion to politics without the contribution of judgment, without drawing on the ability to place the principle within the context of the form of life to be regulated. I cannot discuss the diversity of models of separation or religious neutrality that can be more or less appropriate to the various kinds of historical contexts in which modern democracies are immersed. I can only show how context affects the answer that we might give to the question, debated in various countries and recently also in Italy, concerning the exhibiting of religious symbols (the cross, the crucifix, the Ten Commandments) in public places.

Let me start again from the basics. The religious neutrality of the institutions, in a liberal-democratic context, means that the people—understood here simply in the technical sense as the "holder of sovereignty"—through the constitution and the separated powers attributed to certain institutions, outline a public space for civil coexistence within which they have the legitimate and equal right to express a series of religious and "humanistic" values in forms the law establishes as acceptable. It is the "sovereign people" who through their legitimate representatives delimits the space of what is tolerable and what is intolerable, and the line separating the tolerable from the intolerable is then applied equally to all faiths, religious or secular, irrespective of their historical origins, irrespective of the number of followers, irrespective of their contents. The institutions—within this "standard" framework—are lay or neutral when the ethical substance for which they provide an expression remain on this side of the imaginary line beyond which doctrinal divisions begin—hence they are neutral when they embody ethical contents universally shared in society.

Italy's particularity certainly does not lie in contradicting this idea of the neutrality of institutions. It consists rather in the fact that historically the line of what is tolerable has been drawn with respect to one and only one faith, embraced by the vast majority of Italians, and has been drawn jointly by *two*, not one institutional actor. This particularity resulted in what I do not hesitate to define as the "concordat's distortion," namely, the idea that the neutrality of the public institutions is based on their fitting the terms of a concordat between two powers—one secular, the state, and the other religious, namely, the Church, always rigorously used in the singular—each occupying a position on either side of the dividing line between the temporal and the spiritual realm and each reigning with full sovereignty within separate realms yet on the same geographical territory. Within this framework the neutrality of the state's institutions is understood not as a function of the state's sovereign autonomy—as in Locke's account of toleration—but as a function of the more or less stable "negotiating" balance achieved by two powers, "independent and sovereign," each with its own order. This historical model in a way cuts across Dworkin's distinction of a religious tolerant and a secular tolerant society.

Obviously in other countries too there is a concordat, for example in Spain, but the crucial difference is that these other countries do not host the "concordant power," in its highest level of authority, on their domestic territory. "A Free Church in a Free State" is a formula with very different implications depending on whether the "Church" has or does not have its curial, pastoral, and economic leadership in the same territory as the state in question.

In Italy the result of this peculiar context has been a religious neutrality sui generis, achieved in the shadow of what is best described as a "special relation" between the state and the Catholic Church—a relation that only with difficulty can be reconciled with the principle of the equality of all citizens. For example, only in April 2006 the constitutional court derubricated the special crime of "defamation of the Catholic Religion" to the more generic crime of "defamation." Another result of this "abnormal" situation is the widespread presence of the crucifix in public institutions and the Italian courts' hesitation to draw and accept the consequences of the "supreme principle of religious neutrality"—identified by the constitutional court as "one of the profiles of the State outlined by the Republic's Constitutional Charter."[26] Whereas subsequently the Italian constitutional court specified the principle of religious neutrality (*laicità*) of the institutions in the sense of a proper "equidistance and impartiality" of the state's attitude with regard to all faiths "without giving any importance to the quantity or more or less widespread adhesion to this or that religious confession,"[27] nevertheless one can still read in the findings of the court of Naples on March 26, 2005, that the presence of the crucifix in polling stations cannot be considered a violation of the principle of religious neutrality "since this is merely the exhibiting of a symbol in which it is known that the majority of Italian citizens identify from a spiritual point of view."[28] It is also possible to read in the findings for an analogous case, published on March 24, 2005, by the court of Bologna, that the principle of religious neutrality is not violated by exhibiting the crucifix in polling stations since this is a "nonsymbol" for nonbelievers and nonChristians,[29] as if symbols had symbolic power only for followers and therefore a swastika or a sickle and hammer had no symbolic value for those not following the respective ideologies.

The defense of the lawfulness of exhibiting a crucifix in classrooms argued by the regional administrative court of law of Veneto seems less in conflict with the principle of religious neutrality sanctioned by the constitutional court. The regional administrative court of law recognizes as one consequence of this principle the idea that "in State schools in which the young must also be trained with regard to the values of freedom, democracy and the State's neutrality, it is not legitimate to impose any kind of religious credo and in fact it is a duty to provide an education based on maximum freedom and reciprocal respect in this sector."[30] The court, furthermore, acknowledges that the crucifix possesses value not only in a cultural sense, within the Italian context, but also explicitly as a Christian religious symbol, yet the court expresses the belief that the substantive values expressed by this symbol place it not in conflict with the principle of religious neutrality but rather in a position of congruence with the principle. Is it not the case that Christianity, argues the court, with its "strong emphasis on the precept of love for one's neighbor and even more with the explicit supremacy attributed to charity even over faith" already contains "in brief those ideas of tolerance, equality and freedom at the basis of the modern secular state and in particular of the Italian State"? Is it not the case that Christianity was one of the 'roots' of the Italian constitutional experience and played a "leading role" in inspiring the Republican Constitution? Is it not the case that "observing history, standing therefore on a hill and not confined to the bottom of a valley," one might observe an affinity "between the 'hard core' of Christianity which, by privileging charity over all other elements, including faith, emphasizes the valorization of what is different, and the 'hard core' of the Republican Constitution, consisting in the joint valorization of the freedom of each individual and in guaranteeing through the law the respect of others"? Would it not therefore be "subtly paradoxical to exclude a Christian symbol from a public building in the name of a religious neutrality (*laicità*) that certainly has one of its distant sources precisely in the Christian religion"?

In order to measure the impact of context on principle, it is sufficient to contrast the way in which the "supreme principle of religious neutrality" is understood by the Italian courts—supreme, but overshadowed by a special relation between the state, the nation, and the Catholic religion—with the way in which the same theme of the cultural continuity uniting the

Ten Commandments (publicly exhibited in some courthouses in Kentucky) with modern secular law was treated by the United States Supreme Court in an opinion of June 27, 2005.

In a country in which references to a nondenominational God open sessions of the Supreme Court, are written on banknotes ("In God we trust"), and appear in every important presidential speech, as well as in the oath taken by presidents at the inaugural ceremony, but in which the separation of religion and politics is not implemented against the background of a special relation between state institutions and one single church, the Supreme Court has no difficulty in acknowledging that the state, in expressing a preference for a religion, or in favor of religiosity compared to nonreligiosity, indefensibly sends nonbelieving citizens a message that "they are outsiders, not full members of the political community" and sends citizens who are believers the opposite message, implying they are "insiders, favored members."[31]

Plaintiffs objected that the goal of this exhibiting of the commandments, within the context of a display of other juridical sources of modern law as well, was not religious proselytizing, but simply to illustrate how the Ten Commandments provide "the moral background of the Declaration of Independence and the foundation of . . . legal tradition" of the United States and was thus well within the bounds of the Lemon test.[32] The Supreme Court, however, counterobjected that this way of presenting the initiative cannot eliminate the fact—evident to all nonprejudiced observers endowed with common sense—that "the commandments are sanctioned as divine imperatives, while the Declaration of Independence holds that the authority of government to enforce the law derives from the 'consent of the governed.' "[33] This same observer could not help suspecting that the "continuity" thesis in fact manifests the intentions of a local government to occupy with unequivocally religious symbols the walls of those halls of justice required instead by the Constitution to rigorously respect neutrality.

With this ruling, which reasserts the principle of religious neutrality—harshly disputed by those, such as, for example, the dissenting Justice Scalia, who believe that constitutional protection should be extended to citizens of the different faiths, but not equally to those "without faith"[34]—the Supreme Court proves once again to be the highest example of an idea of public reason that is the only one today capable of taming the reawakened beast of "religious divisiveness."

To conclude, something has changed profoundly in the manner in which we perceive the state's religious neutrality in the twenty-first century. The limits within which religion is permitted to inspire and guide our lives are no longer imposed by a reason that in turn knows no other restrictions than those it provides for itself, but in the twenty-first century should be, more modestly, the limits of a "postsecular" reasonableness—according to which legitimately binding and enforceable is only what is shared by everyone under conditions of freedom and equality—a "postsecular reasonableness" equally accessible to both believing and nonbelieving postsecular citizens.

Notes

Introduction

1. For a discussion of *phronesis* and reflective judgment from the angle of exemplarity, see chapters 2 and 3 of Alessandro Ferrara, *Reflective Authenticity. Rethinking the Project of Modernity* (New York: Routledge, 1998).

2. It could be argued that the *force of the example*—the contingent yet reconciliatory alignment of what is and what ought to be—is the real basis of that "decision," experienced (along with the awareness of undecidability) rather than *made*, that Derrida identifies as the ultimate source of the *force of law* and the one and only moment when the law can be "fully just." The force of exemplarity is the only force that can dispel the "haunting of the undecidable." Indeed his whole set of aporias affecting the force of the law can be shown to depend on the conflating of two models of reason—speculative and deliberative reason—that relate to exemplarity and principles in a quite different way. But this point cannot be developed here. See Jacques Derrida, "Force of Law: The 'Mystical Foundation of Authority,'" in Drucilla Cornell, Michel Rosenfeld, and David G. Carlson, eds., *Deconstruction and the Possibility of Justice* (New York: Routledge, 1992). For an illuminating

discussion see Christoph Menke, *Reflections of Equality* (Stanford: Stanford University Press, 2006), 86–103.

3. See Ludwig Wittgenstein, *Tractatus Logico-Philosophicus* (New York: Routledge, 2001), 5.6.2.

4. See Ludwig Wittgenstein, *Philosophical Investigations* (Oxford: Blackwell, 2003), § 217. Within a different vocabulary a similar point has been recently articulated forcefully by Hilary Putnam in his *The Collapse of the Fact/Value Dichotomy and Other Essays* (Cambridge: Harvard University Press, 2002).

5. See Willard van Orman Quine, *From a Logical Point of View* (New York: Harper, 1963), 24.

6. See Max Weber, "Objectivity in Social Science and Social Policy" (1904), in Edward A. Shils and Henry A. Finch, eds., *The Methodology of the Social Sciences. Max Weber* (New York: Free, 1949), 72–76.

7. See Michael Walzer, "Two Kinds of Universalism," in *Nation and Universe,* Tanner Lectures on Human Values (Salt Lake City: University of Utah Press, 1990); and Tzvetan Todorov, *Nous et les autres: la réflexion française sur la diversité humaine* (Paris: Seuil, 1989).

8. See Jürgen Habermas, *Postmetaphysical Thinking: Philosophical Essays* (Cambridge: MIT Press, 1992), *Justification and Application: Remarks on the Discourse Ethics* (Cambridge: MIT Press, 1993), *Truth and Justification* (Cambridge: MIT Press, 2003). Of the immense body of literature on Habermas's work let me mention Stephen K. White, ed., *The Cambridge Companion to Habermas* (Cambridge: Cambridge University Press, 1995); Maurizio Passerin D'Entrèves and Seyla Benhabib, eds., *Habermas and the Unfinished Project of Modernity* (Cambridge: Polity, 1997); and David M. Rasmussen and James Swindal, eds., *Jürgen Habermas,* 4 vols. (London: Sage, 2002).

9. See John Rawls, *The Law of Peoples* (Cambridge: Harvard University Press, 1999); Frank Michelman, "Human Rights and the Limits of Constitutional Theory," *Ratio Juris* 13(1) (2000); and Michael Ignatieff, *Human Rights as Politics and Idolatry* (Princeton: Princeton University Press, 2003).

1. Judgment as a Paradigm

1. For recent discussions of the fruitfulness of judgment as a general model for validity see Ronald Beiner and Jennifer Nedelski, eds., *Judgment, Imagination, and Politics: Themes from Kant and Arendt* (Lanham: Rowman and Littlefield, 2001); Frithof Rodi, ed., *Urteilskraft und Heuristik in den Wissenschaften. Beiträge zur Enstehung des Neuen* (Birkach: Velbrück Wissenschaft, 2003); and Alessandro Ferrara, ed., *The Uses of Judgment,* special issue of *Philosophy and Social Criticism* (2008).

2. Immanuel Kant, *Critique of the Power of Judgment,* ed. Paul Guyer, trans. Paul Guyer and Eric Matthews (Cambridge: Cambridge University Press, 2001), introduction, § 4, 67.

3. On this point see Beatrice Longuenesse, *Kant and the Capacity to Judge: Sensibility and Discursivity in the Transcendental Analytic of the "Critique of Pure Reason"* (Princeton: Princeton University Press, 1998), 163–65.

4. See Christine Korsgaard, *The Sources of Normativity* (Cambridge: Cambridge University Press, 1996), 49–50.

5. See Hans-Georg Gadamer, *Truth and Method* (New York: Continuum, 1975), 19–29. On the notion of "fore-understanding," see ibid., 235–53. On the notion of "horizon," see ibid., 269–74.

6. See Alfred Schutz, *On Phenomenolgy and Social Relations,* ed. Helmut R. Wagner (Chicago: University of Chicago Press, 1970), 164–65; see also his *The Phenomenology of the Social World* (Evanston: Northwestern University Press, 1967); and Alfred Schutz and Thomas Luckmann, *The Structure of the Life-World,* vol. 2 (Evanston: Northwestern University Press, 1989).

7. Some interpreters attribute this shortcoming also to Arendt's view of judgment; see Jennifer Nedelski, "Judgment, Diversity and Relational Autonomy," in Beiner and Nedelski, *Judgment, Imagination, and Politics* (Lanham: Rowman and Littlefield, 2001), 117–18. For my own view on this point see chapter 2.

8. Peter L. Berger and Thomas Luckmann, *The Social Construction of Reality: A Treatise in the Sociology of Knowledge* (Garden City, NJ: Doubleday, 1966), 13–14.

9. Henry Allison has called attention to the fact that Kant has emphasized, of his conception of *sensus communis,* that it is a *sense.* It is a "sense (or feeling) for what is universally communicable, which can also be assumed to be universally shared. Otherwise expressed, it is a shared capacity to feel what may be universally shareable." Henry E. Allison, *Kant's Theory of Taste: A Reading of the Critique of Aesthetic Judgment* (Cambridge: Cambridge University Press, 2001), 149.

10. Kant, *Critique of the Power of Judgment,* § 20, 122.

11. Ibid., § 21, 123.

12. See Stanley Cavell, "Aesthetic Problems of Modern Philosophy," in Beiner and Nedelsky, *Judgment, Imagination, and Politics,* 38.

13. Kant returns to his account of the "communicability of a sensation" in § 39, where he states that the feeling of pleasure, which aesthetic judgment anticipates to be universally shareable by all those who come in contact with a beautiful object, "must necessarily rest on the same conditions in everyone, since they are subjective conditions of the possibility of a cognition in general, and the proportion of these cognitive faculties that is required for taste is also requisite for the common and healthy understanding that one may presuppose in everyone"; Kant, *Critique of the Power of Judgment,* § 39, 173.

14. Ibid., § 23, 128.

15. See Robert Nozick, *The Examined Life: Philosophical Meditations* (New York: Simon and Schuster, 1989), 100.

16. See Alessandro Ferrara, *Reflective Authenticity: Rethinking the Project of Modernity* (New York: Routledge, 1998), 70–107.

17. For a very interesting alternative, nonreflective approach to authenticity and fulfillment, see Charles Larmore, *Les pratiques du moi* (Paris: Presses Universitaires de France, 2004).

18. Kant, *Critique of the Power of Judgment*, § 49, 191.

19. The best statement of this view can be found in Ronald Dworkin, *Law's Empire* (Cambridge: Harvard University Press, 1986), 228–38; but see also Dworkin's most recent work, *Sovereign Virtue: The Theory and Practice of Equality* (Cambridge: Harvard University Press, 2002), and *Justice in Robes* (Cambridge: Harvard University Press, 2006).

20. See Bruce Ackerman, *Social Justice in the Liberal State* (New Haven: Yale University Press, 1980); *We the People,* vol. 1, *Foundations* (Cambridge: Harvard University Press, 1991), and vol. 2, *Transformations* (Cambridge: Harvard University Press, 1998).

21. See Ackerman, *Foundations*, 23.

22. See Jürgen Habermas, *Between Facts and Norms: Contributions to a Discourse Theory of Law and Democracy,* trans. William Rehg (Cambridge: MIT Press, 1996), chapter 3.2.

23. It is understood in this way, for example, in the opening essay of Jürgen Habermas, *The Inclusion of the Other: Studies in Political Theory,* trans. Ciaran Cronin and Peter De Greiff (Cambridge: MIT Press, 1998).

24. The first interpretation of "D" provides the sharp distinction between ethics and morality that is one of Habermas's priorities; but it also generates collateral problems, notably the return to the pre–"linguistic turn" pretense of having discovered and described at least one portion of uninterpreted reality (in this case, the presuppositions of communication). The second interpretation avoids this last residue of foundationalism, but at the cost of blurring the line between the ethical and the moral. For a more detailed argument on the ambiguity built in Habermas's test of discursive generalization, see my own *Justice and Judgment: The Rise and the Prospect of the Judgment Model in Contemporary Political Philosophy* (London: Sage, 1999), 156–64. See also Frank I. Michelman, "Morality, Identity and 'Constitutional Patriotism,'" *Denver University Law Review* 76 (1999): 1009–1028, and especially 1013–14.

25. See the interesting remarks on the notion of "re-presentation" developed by Maeve Cooke in her *Re-Presenting the Good Society* (Cambridge: MIT Press, 2006), 129–60.

26. See Ferrara, *Justice and Judgment*, chapter 6.

27. John Rawls, "Kantian Constructivism in Moral Theory," *Journal of Philosophy* 88 (1980): 519.

2. Making Sense of the Exemplary

1. Hannah Arendt, *The Life of the Mind* (New York: Harcourt Brace, 1978), 192.

2. Ibid., 193.

3. Maurizio Passerin D'Entrèves, *The Political Philosophy of Hannah Arendt* (London: Routledge, 1994), 102.

4. See Hannah Arendt, "Freedom and Politics: A Lecture," *Chicago Review* 14 (1960): 28–46; "The Crisis in Culture," in *Between Past and Future: Eight Exercises in Political Thought* (New York: Viking, 1968), and "Truth and Politics," ibid.

5. Ronald Beiner, "Interpretive Essay," in Hannah Arendt, *Lectures on Kant's Political Philosophy* (Chicago: University of Chicago Press, 1982), 93.

6. Hannah Arendt, "Thinking and Moral Considerations" (1984 [1971]), *Social Research* 38(3): reprinted in *Social Research*, vol. 51, no. 1.

7. See Richard Bernstein, "Judging—The Actor and the Spectator," in *Philosophical Profiles* (Cambridge: Polity, 1986).

8. Beiner, "Interpretive Essay," 139–40. See also Ronald Beiner, "Rereading Hannah Arendt's Kant Lectures," in Ronald Beiner and Jennifer Nedelski, eds., *Judgment, Imagination, and Politics: Themes from Kant and Arendt* (Lanham: Rowman and Littlefield, 2001), 99–100, and "Rereading 'Truth and Politics,'" in *The Uses of Judgment*, special issue of *Philosophy and Social Criticism*, forthcoming 2007.

9. Arendt, *Lectures on Kant's Political Philosophy*, 63.

10. On this point see Seyla Benhabib, "Judgment and the Moral Foundations of Politics in Hannah Arendt's Thought," in Beiner and Nedelski, *Judgment, Imagination, and Politics*, 195–98.

11. Jürgen Habermas, "Hannah Arendt's Communicative Concept of Power," *Social Research*, 44(1): 22–23.

12. Albrecht Wellmer, "Hannah Arendt on Judgment: The Unwritten Doctrine of Reason" in *Endspiele. Die unversönliche Moderne* (Frankfurt: Suhrkamp, 1993), 309–32.

13. Arendt, *Lectures on Kant's Political Philosophy*, 42; further references will appear parenthetically in text.

14. Arendt, *The Life of the Mind*, 193.

15. Immanuel Kant, *Critique of the Power of Judgment*, ed. Paul Guyer, trans. Paul Guyer and Eric Matthews (Cambridge: Cambridge University Press, 2001), § 40, 173.

16. Beiner, "Interpretive Essay," 123. On the "enlarged mentality" see also George Kateb, "The Judgment of Arendt", in Beiner and Nedelski, *Judgment, Imagination and Politics*, 131–32.

17. For a very illuminating discussion of the intricacies involved in the relation of exemplification see Catherine Z. Elgin, *Considered Judgment* (Princeton: Princeton University Press, 1996), 171–83. For an interesting critique of Arendt's account as

failing to distinguish schemata from symbols in her account of exemplary validity, see Alan Singer, *Aesthetic Reason: Artworks and the Deliberative Ethos* (University Park: Pennsylvania State University Press, 2003), 55–56.

18. Genesis 22.

19. Arendt, *The Life of the Mind*, 193.

20. For a more detailed discussion of validity in interpretation, see my *Reflective Authenticity: Rethinking the Project of Modernity* (New York: Routledge, 1998), chapter 7.

21. Again, the issue is discussed in greater detail in my *Justice and Judgment: The Rise and the Prospect of the Judgment Model in Contemporary Political Philosophy* (London: Sage, 1999), chapter 3.

22. In Kant's words, "the aesthetic idea is a representation of the imagination, associated with a given concept, which is combined with such a manifold of partial representations in the free use of the imagination, that no expression designating a determinate concept can be found for it"; ibid., 194.

23. Kant, *Critique of the Power of Judgment*, § 49, 192.

24. Ibid., § 1, 90.

25. Ibid., § 23, 128. I am indebted to Rudolf Makkreel for having drawn my attention to these passages.

26. Rudolf Makkreel, *Imagination and Interpretation in Kant: The Hermeneutical Import of the "Critique of Judgment"* (Chicago: University of Chicago Press, 1994), 155ff.

27. Ibid., 155–56.

28. Kant, *Critique of the Power of Judgment*, introduction, 71.

29. Makkreel, *Imagination and Interpretation in Kant*, 156.

30. Arendt, *The Life of the Mind*, 181.

3. The Exemplary and the Public Realm

1. See Jürgen Habermas, "Reconciliation Through the Public Use of Reason: Remarks on John Rawls's *Political Liberalism*," *Journal of Philosophy* 92(3): 109–31; as well as John Rawls, "Reply to Habermas," ibid., 132–80.

2. See John Rawls, *A Theory of Justice* (Cambridge: Harvard University Press, 1971), 580–81. On this point, see Charles Larmore, "Public Reason," in Samuel Freeman, ed., *The Cambridge Companion to Rawls* (Cambridge: Cambridge University Press, 2003), 368–93.

3. Rawls, *A Theory of Justice*, 133.

4. John Rawls, "Kantian Constructivism in Moral Theory," *Journal of Philosophy* 88 (1980): 512–72. The point is subsequently readdressed in John Rawls, *Political Liberalism* (New York: Columbia University Press, 1993), 66–71.

5. Rawls, *Political Liberalism*, 213.

6. Ibid.

7. Ibid., 214. Public reason is carefully distinguished from "secular reason" by Rawls. It must not be understood as synonymous with the bracketing away of religious conceptions of the good from public life. In fact, the ideal of public reason is much more demanding. It enjoins us to keep also nonreligious comprehensive conceptions of the good out of public justification on fundamental issues.

8. See John Rawls, "The Idea of Public Reason Revisited" (1997), in *The Law of Peoples* (Cambridge: Harvard University Press, 1999), 155–56.

9. Rawls, *Political Liberalism*, 215.

10. See ibid., 220. Charles Larmore rightly suggests that Rawls should have introduced a further distinction, in acknowledgment of the fact that arguments conducted in the public forum are not always aimed at eventual decision making. Sometimes even in institutional fora we find "open discussions" where people just argue with one another, drawing freely on their comprehensive conceptions. Only in the former, perhaps more common in the public forum but by no means uniquely possible, case are the participants not supposed to exceed the limits of what is shared. See Larmore, "Public Reason," 382.

11. Rawls, *Political Liberalism*, 247.

12. Ibid., 247 (emphasis mine).

13. Rawls, "The Idea of Public Reason Revisited," 144 (emphasis mine).

14. This is in fact the fundamental difference between *A Theory of Justice* and *Political Liberalism* as Rawls himself presents it: in the former, writes Rawls, "justice as fairness is presented . . . as a comprehensive liberal doctrine (although the term 'comprehensive doctrine' is not used in the book) in which all the members of its well-ordered society affirm that same doctrine. This kind of well-ordered society contradicts the fact of reasonable pluralism and hence *Political Liberalism* regards that society as impossible"; "The Idea of Public Reason Revisited," 179.

15. In *Justice and Judgment* I have suggested that the notion of equal respect is better suited for that pivotal role. See Alessandro Ferrara, *Justice and Judgment: The Rise and the Prospect of the Judgment Model in Contemporary Political Philosophy* (London: Sage, 1999), 202–13.

16. On these three types of conflict, see Rawls, "The Idea of Public Reason Revisited," 177.

17. On related points, see David Rasmussen, "Reasonability Versus Reason: Reflections on the Reasonability of Public Reason," in Riccardo Dottori, ed., *Yearbook of Philosophical Hermeneutics* (Munster: LIT, 2003).

18. See Anthony Laden, *Reasonably Radical: Deliberative Liberalism and the Politics of Identity* (Ithaca: Cornell University Press, 2001), chapter 5.4.

19. See Rawls, *Political Liberalism*, 243, and "The Idea of Public Reason Revisited," 169–71.

20. Rawls, *Political Liberalism*, 243.

21. Ibid.

22. Rawls, "The Idea of Public Reason Revisited," 169.

23. Ibid., 170.

24. Rawls, *Political Liberalism*, 251.

25. See ibid., 49.

26. See ibid., 94, and Rawls, *The Law of Peoples*, 87.

27. Rawls, "Kantian Constructivism in Moral Theory," 519.

28. Rawls, *Political Liberalism*, 28.

29. Christine Korsgaard, *The Sources of Normativity* (Cambridge: Cambridge University Press, 1996), 136; further references appear parenthetically in text.

30. For the notion of "orientation" and of "oriented reflective judgment," see Alessandro Ferrara, *Reflective Authenticity. Rethinking the Project of Modernity* (New York: Routledge, 1998), 47–49. For an application in the area of judgments concerning justice, see Ferrara, *Justice and Judgment*, 221–22.

31. Habermas, "Reconciliation Through the Public Use of Reason," 122.

32. See Immanuel Kant, *Critique of the Power of Judgment*, ed. Paul Guyer, trans. Paul Guyer and Eric Matthews (Cambridge: Cambridge University Press, 2001), paragraphs 8 and 13.

33. Indeed, as Nancy Fraser aptly puts it, "in political discourse telling a story or adducing an exemplar is . . . itself a form of argumentation in the broad sense, another way of advancing a reason or justifying a claim. In this respect, it is entirely on a par with a deduction from principles." See Nancy Fraser, "Communication, Transformation, and Consciousness-raising," in Craig Calhoun and John Mc-Gowan, eds., *Hannah Arendt and the Meaning of Politics* (Minneapolis: University of Minnesota Press, 1997), 173.

34. This is the problem, for instance, with Arendt's use of the Kantian doctrine of judgment and with her understanding of "exemplary validity" as developed in her *Lectures on Kant's Political Philosophy* (Chicago: University of Chicago Press, 1982); see chapter 2.

4. Exemplifying the Worst

1. Immanuel Kant, *Religion Within the Limits of Reason Alone* (New York: Harper and Row, 1960), 31. Further references will appear parenthetically in text.

2. For a different appraisal of the relevance of Kant's theory of radical evil, see Maeve Cooke, "An Evil Heart? Moral Evil and Moral Identity," in María Pía Lara, ed., *Rethinking Evil: Contemporary Perspectives* (Berkeley: University of California Press, 2001), 113–30.

3. *Hitler's Secret Conversations, 1941–44,* quoted in James Bernauer, "Nazi-Ethik. Über Heinrich Himmler und die Karriere der Neuen Moral," *Babylon* 6 (1989): 49.

See also Eichmann's protestation: "Since quite a long time I have adopted Kant's categorical imperative as a norm. I have led my life according to this imperative"; *Eichmann Interrogated: Transcripts from the Archives of the Israeli Police,* quoted in Bernauer, "Nazi-Ethik," 49.

4. *Goebbels-Reden,* quoted in Bernauer, "Nazi-Ethik," 53.

5. As he put it, "We don't have the right to steal even a fur coat, a watch, a Mark or a cigarette or anything else"; *Himmlers Rede in Posen,* quoted ibid., 52.

6. *Hitler's Secret Conversations, 1941–44,* quoted ibid., 54.

7. See Georg Wilhelm Friedrich Hegel's "Über die wissenschaftlichen Behandlungsarten des Naturrechts, seine Stelle in der praktische Philosophie und sein Verhältnis zu den positiven Rechtswissenschaften," in G. W. F. Hegel, *Werke* (Frankfurt: Suhrkamp, 1971), 3:465–66.

8. See Immanuel Kant, *The Metaphysical Elements of Justice,* part 1 of tk*Thetk Metaphysics of Morals* (Indianapolis: Bobbs-Merrill, 1965), 106.

9. I have developed it in Alessandro Ferrara, *Justice and Judgment: The Rise and the Prospect of the Judgment Model in Contemporary Political Philosophy* (London: Sage, 1999), 178–230.

10. I am indebted to Jeffrey C. Alexander for having alerted me to the possibility of using Durkheim's sociology of religion in order to reconstruct a postmetaphysical approach to radical evil. See Jeffrey C. Alexander, "Toward a Sociology of Evil: Getting Beyond Modernist Common Sense About the Alternative to 'the Good,'" in Lara, *Rethinking Evil,* 153–72.

11. See Emile Durkheim, "On the Definition of Religious Phenomena," in Kurt H. Wolff, ed., *Emile Durkheim* (Columbus: Ohio University Press, 1960), and *The Elementary Forms of the Religious Life* (New York: Free, 1967).

12. See Durkheim, *The Elementary Forms,* 236–45 and 462–72.

13. Giorgio Agamben, *La comunità che viene* (Torino: Einaudi, 1990), 65.

14. Durkheim, *The Elementary Forms,* 470.

15. Hans Jonas, "Unsterblichkeit und heutige Existenz," in *Zwischen Nichts und Ewigkeit: Zur Lehre des Menschen* (Göttingen: Vandenhoeck und Ruprecht, 1987), p. 61.

16. Peter Dews, "Disenchantment and the Persistence of Evil," paper delivered to the Hannah Arendt Symposium "Evil and Responsibility," New School for Social Research, November 1996, 3. See also Peter Dews, "Secularization and the Persistence of Evil: Habermas, Jonas, Badiou," in Alan Schrift, ed., *Modernity and the Problem of Evil* (Bloomington: Indiana University Press, 2004).

5. Political Republicanism and the Force of the Example

1. See Hannah Arendt, *The Human Condition: A Study of the Central Dilemmas Facing Modern Manx* (Garden City, NY: Doubleday Anchor, 1959); and John G. A.

Pocock, *The Machiavellian Moment: Florentine Political Thought and the Atlantic Republican Tradition* (Princeton: Princeton University Press, 1975).

2. See Michael Sandel, *Liberalism and the Limits of Justice* (Cambridge: Cambridge University Press, 1982) and *Democracy's Discontent: America in Search of a Public Philosophy* (Cambridge: Harvard University Press, 1996). See also Alasdair MacIntyre, *After Virtue: A Study in Moral Theory* (Notre Dame: University of Notre Dame Press, 1981).

3. See Quentin Skinner, *The Foundations of Modern Political Thought*, vol. 1, *The Renaissance* (Cambridge: Cambridge University Press, 1978), *The Foundations of Modern Political Thought*, vol. 1, *The Age of Reformation* (Cambridge: Cambridge University Press, 1978), and *Visions of Politics*, vol. 2, *Renaissance Virtues* (Cambridge: Cambridge University Press, 2002).

4. Niccolò Machiavelli, *The Discourses*, ed., with an introduction, Bernard Crick, with revisions by Brian Richardson (Harmondsworth: Penguin, 1970), 162.

5. See Maurizio Viroli, *From Politics to Reason of State: The Acquisition and Transformation of the Language of Politics, 1250–1600* (Cambridge: Cambridge University Press, 1992), *For Love of Country* (Oxford: Oxford University Press, 1995), and *Machiavelli* (Oxford: Oxford University Press, 1998).

6. Philip Pettit, *Republicanism: A Theory of Freedom and Government* (Oxford: Clarendon, 1997).

7. See Thomas Hobbes, *Leviathan*, ed., with an introduction, C. B. Macpherson (Harmondsworth: Penguin, 1972), 266.

8. See Isaiah Berlin, "Two Concepts of Liberty," in Anthony Quinton, ed., *Political Philosophy* (Oxford: Oxford University Press, 1967), 141–52.

9. Philip Pettit, "Republican Liberty and Contestatory Democratization," in Ian Shapiro and C. Hacker-Cordòn, eds., *Democracy's Value* (Cambridge: Cambridge University Press, 1999), 163–90.

10. See Pettit, *Republicanism*, 186.

11. Ibid, 186–87.

12. Cass R. Sunstein, "Beyond the Republican Revival," *Harvard Law Review* 102(2): 1531. See also Cass R. Sunstein, *Republic.com* (Princeton: Princeton University Press, 2001).

13. See Robert N. Bellah, Richard Madsen, William M. Sullivan, Ann Swidler, and Steven M. Tipton, *Habits of the Heart: Individualism and Commitment in American Life* (Berkeley: University of California Press, 1985) and, by the same authors, *The Good Society* (New York: Random House, 1992).

14. Frank I. Michelman, "Higher Law: On the Legal Theory of Constitutional Democracy" (unpublished manuscript, 1995), 20.

15. Ibid., 22.

16. Ibid., 32.

17. Frank I. Michelman, "Traces of Self-Government," *Harvard Law Review* 100(4): 4–77.

18. Ibid., 74.

19. See Bruce Ackerman and James Fishkin, *Deliberation Day* (New Haven: Yale University Press, 2004).

20. Jürgen Habermas, *The Inclusion of the Other: Studies in Political Theory*, ed. C. Cronin and P. DeGreiff (Cambridge: MIT Press, 1998), chapter 3; and Ronald Dworkin, "Liberal Community," *California Law Review* 77(3): 479–504.

21. Machiavelli, *The Discourses*, 244–45.

22. See Pettit, *Republicanism*, 10.

23. See John Rawls, *A Theory of Justice* (Cambridge: Harvard University Press, 1971), 201–5.

24. John Rawls, *Political Liberalism* (New York: Columbia University Press, 1993), 4.

25. Charles Larmore, "The Moral Basis of Political Liberalism," *Journal of Philosophy* 96(12): 610.

26. Ibid., 608.

27. See Ronald Dworkin, *Sovereign Virtue: The Theory and Practice of Equality* (Cambridge: Harvard University Press, 2002), chapter 1.

28. Dworkin, "Liberal Community," 496.

29. Ibid., 495.

30. Ibid., 501.

31. Ibid.

32. See Ronald Dworkin, *Freedom's Law: The Moral Reading of the American Constitution* (Cambridge: Harvard University Press, 1996), 32–35.

33. See Ronald Dworkin, "What is Equality?" part 2: "Equality of Resources," *Philosophy and Public Affairs* 10(4): 285.

34. John Dewey, *Liberalism and Social Action* (New York: Capricorn, 1963), 26.

35. See John Dewey, *The Public and Its Problems* (Denver: Swallow, 1954), 150.

36. Quoted in Bruce Ackerman, *We the People*, vol. 2, *Transformations* (Cambridge: Harvard University Press, 1998), 309.

37. See John Stuart Mill, "On Liberty," in Jeremy Bentham and John Stuart Mill, *The Utilitarians* (Garden City: Doubleday, 1961), 539–42.

38. On this point see Charles Larmore, "Republicanism: History, Theory and Practice," *Critical Review of International Social and Political Philosophy*, 6, 1 (2003), 109–10.

39. John Locke, *Two Treatises of Government*, ed. Peter Laslett (New York: Mentor, 1965), § 22, p. 324. See also § 57 where Locke adds, "The end of law is not to abolish or restrain, but to preserve and enlarge freedom. . . . Where there is no law, there is no freedom"; 348.

40. See Franklin D. Roosevelt, "Acceptance Speech for the Renomination for the Presidency," Philadelphia, June 27, 1936, in John Woolley and Gerhard Peters, *The American Presidency Project* (Santa Barbara: University of California): http://www.presidency.ucsb.edu/shownomination.php?convid = 37.

41. Ibid. On various aspects of the New Deal and its impact, see William H. Chafe, ed., *The Achievement of American Liberalism: The New Deal and Its Legacies* (New York: Columbia University Press, 2003); Melvyn Dubofsky, ed., *The New Deal: Conflicting Interpretations and Shifting Perspectives* (New York: Garland, 1992); Robert Eden, ed., *New Deal and Its Legacy: Critique and Reappraisal* (Westport: Greenwood, 1989); Steve Fraser and Gary Gerstle, eds., *The Rise and Fall of the New Deal Order* (Princeton, Princeton University Press, 1989); Sidney M. Milkis and Jerome M. Mileur, eds., *The New Deal and the Triumph of Liberalism* (Amherst: University of Massachusetts Press, 2002); Harvard Sitkoff, ed., *Fifty Years Later: The New Deal Evaluated* (New York: McGraw Hill, 1984).

42. See Max Weber, *Economy and Society,* ed. Günther Roth and Claus Wittich (Berkeley: University of California Press, 1978), 1:241.

43. Ibid., 249.

6. Exemplarity and Human Rights

1. See John Rawls, *The Law of Peoples* (Cambridge: Harvard University Press, 1999), 80.

2. Ibid, 80–81.

3. See John Rawls, "Reply to Habermas," *Journal of Philosophy* 92(3): 150–61.

4. Jürgen Habermas, *The Inclusion of the Other: Studies in Political Theory,* 221.

5. Ibid., 222.

6. See ibid., 224.

7. For an interesting reconstruction of the three models into which the various conceptions of international human rights can be grouped—namely, 1. the *statist* model, according to which the positive law of each nation-state is the only locus of legally binding human rights, 2. the *international* model, according to which they can be anchored also in the idea of an "international community," including the states but also significant NGOs, and 3. the *cosmopolitan* model, according to which they can be anchored to the notion of a global political community—see Jack Donnelly, *International Human Rights* (Boulder: Westview, 1998), 28–30. See also Henry J. Steiner and Philip Alston, eds., *International Human Rights in Context: Law, Politics, Morality* (Oxford: Oxford University Press, 1996); and Yael Danieli, Elsa Stamatopoulau, and Clarence J. Dias, eds., *The Universal Declaration of Human Rights: Fifty Years and Beyond* (Amityville, NY: Baywood, 1999).

8. Jürgen Habermas, "Remarks on Legitimation Through Human Rights," *Philosophy and Social Criticism* 24(2/3): 160–61.

9. The same holds for some of the rights protected by the *International Covenant on Civil and Political Rights* (for example, Article 22 provides for right to freedom of association with others, Article 21 for the "right of peaceful assembly," and Article 13 provides that marriage be entered with the free and full consent of the intending parties) and by the *International Covenant of Economic, Social, and Cultural Rights*.

10. That in nearly all nondemocratic regimes there are individuals, groups, and movements struggling for democracy, the effectiveness of whose action would not be enhanced by the indirect legitimation rulers would draw from the country's acceptance—as long as they respect human rights—in the "society of peoples" is a sad, tragic, and undeniable fact. On the other hand, two separate planes are to be distinguished. Just as, on the domestic plane, neutrality is requested only of public institutions and not of individuals, groups, associations, and so on, so when considering a just international order we should feel free to demand that our governments support the democrats and the liberals worldwide, but at the same time we should not be carried away by our own democratic fervor to demanding that international institutions reflect our own intuitions even at the cost of their neutrality. This is the dividing line that separates the liberal view of justice on a global scale from any church's project of acquiring and actively defending as many followers as possible worldwide. Thanks are due to Hauke Brunkhorst for prompting my reflection on this point.

11. See Frank Michelman, "Human Rights and the Limits of Constitutional Theory," *Ratio Juris* 13(1): 66.

12. I am indebted to Christoph Menke for having suggested this formulation and having alerted me to the need to clarify further how moral, political, and legal considerations interact in determining the nature of human rights.

13. See my *Justice and Judgment: The Rise and the Prospect of the Judgment Model in Contemporary Political Philosophy* (London: Sage, 1999), 182–87.

14. For a more detailed presentation of this point, see my *Reflective Authenticity. Rethinking the Project of Modernity* (New York: Routledge, 1998), 70–107, and *Justice and Judgment*, 202–13.

15. This sort of idea was anticipated in certain pioneering considerations of Durkheim on the nexus of cooperation, justice, and the inclusiveness of social collectives. Looking favorably at the incipient formation of a "European society" and underscoring that the impossibility of a unitary *human* society has not yet been proven, Durkheim seems to envisage a hierarchy of normative standpoints of increasingly general scope yet always *situated*—a hierarchy of standpoints on whose basis it becomes possible to normatively regulate the particularism of individual and group interest. In his words: "Just as private conflicts can be regulated only by the action of the society in which the individuals live, so inter-social conflicts can be regulated

only by a society which comprises in its scope all others"; Emile Durkheim, *The Division of Labor in Society* (New York: Free, 1964), 405. In our times similar considerations reappear in different forms and couched in different vocabularies in the work of Charles Taylor, Michael Walzer, and Richard Rorty. See Charles Taylor, "Atomism," in *Philosophy and the Human Sciences,* vol. 2 of *Philosophical Papers* (Cambridge: Cambridge University Press 1985), 187–210; Michael Walzer, *Thick and Thin* (Notre Dame: University of Notre Dame Press, 1994), 2–10; Richard Rorty, "Justice as a Larger Loyalty," in R. Bontekoe and E. M.Stepaniants, eds., *Justice and Democracy. Cross-Cultural Perspectives* (Honolulu: University of Haway Press 1997), 9–22.

16. It is worth emphasizing that the sharing of an artistic project, just as the sharing of a political project, is not comparable to the commonality of comprehensive ends that is distinctive of the "community of saints" contrasted by Rawls with a (modern) community based on the acceptance of pluralism. Such sharing of an artistic or of an identity project resembles much more closely, instead, the limited and reflective sharing of a nontotalizing project, as is the case, for example, with the orchestra mentioned by Dworkin in "Liberal Community" or with Habermas's notion of constitutional patriotism. See Ronald Dworkin, "Liberal Community," *California Law Review* 77(3): 479–504; and Jürgen Habermas, "Struggles for Recognition in Constitutional States," *European Journal of Philosophy* 1(2): 128–55.

17. In fact, evidence for the fact that, in a modern context, the idea of rendering justice to parties in conflict without paying equal respect to all of them is ultimately incoherent comes from the fact that even those authors who, like Hegel and Nietzsche, envisaged the possibility of denying that equal respect is owed to common human beings and world-historical figures, herdmen and exceptional ones, were forced to operate with *two* distinct notions of justice—a "base" or "petty" one for one kind of human beings and a superior and truer kind of justice for the other. Nietzsche does not think of exceptional men as living in a state-of-nature sort of relation to each other, but rather in relations that lead them to recognize each other as *equally self-creating creatures.*

18. For arguments in defense of these theses, see my *Justice and Judgment,* 192–94 and 221–30.

19. See ibid., 196–97.

20. See Rawls, *The Law of Peoples.* 30–35.

21. In one important passage, however, Rawls equates the two terms. See ibid., 90.

22. Similar reflections, in the context of an analysis of the different meanings of the pronoun *we,* can be found in Salvatore Veca, *Dell'incertezza* (Milano: Feltrinelli 1997), 243–44.

23. On this notion of the "human community" as including those who partake of the *humana condicio,* see Jean-Luc Nancy, *The Inoperative Community,* ed. P. Connor (Minneapolis: University of Minnesota Press, 1991).

24. These two distinct planes—designated by the terms *moral* and *political conceptions of justice on a global level*—are reflected in Kant's distinction between the notion of a *Weltrepublik*, on the one hand, which is one of the ideas of moral reason, and what he calls its "negative surrogate," namely, that *Völkerbund* or "league of nations," on the other, which unites all peoples toward the goal of preserving peace and keeping human life worth living. See Immanuel Kant, "Perpetual Peace," in Immanuel Kant, *On History,* ed. L. W. Beck (Indianapolis: Bobbs-Merrill, 1963), 98.

25. I am indebted to Hans Jonas for having drawn my attention to the need to specify the nature of the claim concerning the difficulty of conceiving a future identity of humanity based on the assumption that Auschwitz "doesn't matter."

26. See James Bernauer, "Nazi-Ethik. Über Heinrich Himmler und die Karriere der Neuen Moral," *Babylon* 6 (1989): 54.

27. I avoid using here the Rawlsian term *political conception* in order to avoid generating a confusing assonance with the phrase *political conceptions of justice on a global level* mentioned above, but the meaning of the phrase *noncomprehensive conception* is the same as that of Rawls's *political conception.*

28. For an excellent reconstruction of the internal tensions of Hegel's notion of a modern ethical life, see Lucio Cortella, "L'ethos della modernità," in A. Ferrara, V. Gessa, and S. Maffettone, eds., *Etica individuale e giustizia* (Napoli: Liguori, 2000), 345–57.

29. Ibid., 345.

30. Ibid.

31. Georg Wilhelm Friedrich Hegel, *Elements of the Philosophy of Right.* ed. A. W. Wood, trans. H. Nisbet (Cambridge: Cambridge University Press, 2000), § 142.

32. In Cortella's interpretation, "just as the traditional *ethos* included in the character and habits of its participants a natural disposition to follow certain mores and customs, so a post-traditional *ethos* inclines individuals to orient themselves to rights and duties grounded in freedom. But there is a crucial difference between the two models of the ethical life. The tradition of freedom contains none of the particularities that used to characterize the ancient *ethos.* Because freedom means equal freedom for all, the institutions of modern freedom maintain a *universal* quality [which the institutions of ancient freedom did not possess]," Cortella, "Dialettica dell'eticità moderna," 137.

33. Hegel, *Elements of the Philosophy of Right,* § 183.

34. See Jürgen Habermas, *The Philosophical Discourse of Modernity* (Cambridge: MIT Press, 1987), chapter 1.

35. Lucio Cortella, "L'ethos della modernità," in Alessandro Ferrara, Vanna Gessa, and Sebastiano Maffettone, eds., *Etica individuale e giustizia* (Naples: Liguori, 2000), 351–52.

36. The work of Wallerstein amounts to a reconstruction of the coming into being of a global civil society, understood as a "world-system." See Immanuel

Wallerstein, *The Modern World System,* vol. 1: *Capitalist Agriculture and the Origins of the European World-Economy in the Sixteenth Century* (New York: Academic, 1974); *The Modern World System,* vol. 2: *Mercantilism and the Consolidation of the European World-Economy, 1600–1750* (New York: Academic, 1980); and *The Modern World System,* vol. 3: *The Second Era of Great Expansion of the Capitalist World-Economy* (New York: Academic, 1989).

37. See George Herbert Mead, *Mind, Self, and Society from the Standpoint of a Social Behaviorist* (Chicago; University of Chicago Press, 1974), 154–55, and *The Philosophy of the Act* (Chicago: University of Chicago Press, 1972), 448–49.

7. Enforcing Human Rights Between Westphalia and Cosmopolis

1. Kofi Annan, *In Larger Freedom,* address of the secretary-general of the United Nations, 2005, § 78.

2. Ibid., § 130.

3. Michal Walzer, *Just and Unjust Wars* (Harmondsworth: Penguin, 1980), 107.

4. Niccolò Machiavelli, *Discourses on the First Ten Books by Titus Livius,* vol. 2 of *The Historical, Political and Diplomatic Writings of Niccolò Machiavelli,* trans. Christian E. Detmold, online edition by the Liberty Fund (Boston: Osgood, 1882), 66.

5. Ibid., 62.

6. See Kofi Annan, "Two Concepts of Sovereignty," quoted in Peter Singer, *One World* (New Haven: Yale University Press, 2002), 123.

7. International Commission on Intervention and State Sovereignty, *The Responsibility to Protect: Report of the International Commission on Intervention and State Sovereignty* (Ottawa: International Development Research Centre, 2001), § 4.19, 32.

8. For example, actions mentioned in the 1948 genocide convention: terrorist actions aimed at decreasing the presence of a certain group from an area, the use of ethnic mass rape, crimes of war and crimes against humanity, situations of state collapse that expose the population to mass starvation or to the risk of a civil war, natural or environmental disasters "where the State concerned is either unwilling or unable to cope, or call for assistance, and significant loss of life is occurring or threatened." Ibid., § 4.20, 33.

9. Ibid., § 4.21, 33.

10. For interesting reflections on how the criterion of last resort may prove to be problematic, in that "lastness" is never actually reached, see Michael Walzer, *Arguing About War* (New Haven: Yale University Press, 2004), 88–89.

11. ICISS, *The Responsibility to Protect,* § 4.42, 37.

12. Ibid., § 6.12, 49.

13. Ibid., § 6.14, 49.

14. Article 2 of the Charter of the United Nations assigns the General Assembly a responsibility concerning the maintenance of peace and security, but only insofar as the elaboration of general proposals and not specific and binding decisions are concerned. Article 12 purports to avoid the risk of a possible confrontation between the two organs of the United Nations by establishing that the General Assembly cannot discuss peace and security matters at the same time as the Security Council does.

15. For example, the commission recommends "that the members of the Security Council should consider and seek to reach agreement on a set of guidelines, embracing the 'Principles for Military Intervention' . . . to govern their responses to claims for military intervention for human protection purposes" (ibid., 8.29, 74). It recommends also "that the permanent five members of the Security Council should consider and seek to reach agreement not to apply their veto power, in matters where their vital state interests are not involved, to obstruct the passage of resolutions authorizing military intervention for human protection purposes for which there is otherwise majority support" (ibid., 8.29, 75) and that "the Secretary General give consideration, and consult as appropriate with the President of the Security Council and the President of the General Assembly, as to how the substance and action recommendations of this report can best be advanced in those two bodies, and by his own further action" (ibid., 8.30, 75).

8. Europe as a Special Area for Human Hope

1. The continental nation-state is the solution advocated by Glyn Morgan, *The Idea of a European Superstate: Public Justification and European Integration* (Princeton: Princeton University Press, 2005). For a different view, see Craig Parsons, *A Certain Idea of Europe* (Ithaca: Cornell University Press, 2006). And for a classical intergovernmental view of the European Union, see Andrew Moravcsik, *European Union and World Politics* (London: Routledge, 2006).

2. See Giovanni Reale, *Radici culturali e spirituali dell'Europa* (Milano: Cortina, 2003); V. E. Parsi (a cura di), *Cittadinanza e identità costituzionale europea* (Bologna: Il Mulino, 2001); Luisa Passerini, ed., *Identità culturale europea. Idee, sentimenti, relazioni* (Scandicci: La Nuova Italia, 1998); George Steiner, *Une certain idée de l'Europe* (Arles: Actes Sud, 2006); for a different view see Furio Cerutti's "Introduction," in Furio Cerutti and Sonia Lucarelli, eds., *Political Identity and Legitimacy of the European Union* (New York: Routledge, forthcoming); and also Klaus Eder and Willfried Spohn, eds., *Collective Memory and European Identity: The Effects of Integration and Enlargement* (Aldershot: Ashgate, 2005); Mary Ann

Perkins, *Christendom and European Identity: The Legacy of a Grand Narrative Since 1789* (Berlin: de Gruyter, 2004). In a still different vein see Edgar Morin, *Penser l'Europe* (Paris: Gallimard, 1987); Jacques Attali, *Europe(s)* (Paris: Fayard, 1994); and Peter Sloterdijk, *Falls Europa erwacht* (Frankfurt: Suhrkamp, 1994).

3. At the moment of going to press, it appears that the Constitutional Treaty might be superseded by the Draft Treaty Amending the Treaty on the European Union and the Treaty Establishing the European Union approved during the informal European Council in Lisbon on October 18–19, 2007, and expected to be signed by the member states in December 2007 and subsequently ratified by the twenty-seven member states. The newly introduced amendments, however, do not significantly modify the parts of the Constitutional Treaty on which my reconstruction of a European "political" identity is based and therefore do not affect the argument developed here.

4. "Convinced that thus 'united in diversity' Europe offers them the best chance of pursuing, with due regard for the rigths of each individual and in awareness of their responsibilities towards future generations and the Earth, the great venture which makes of it a special area of human hope," Preamble of the *Constitutional Treaty.*

5. Cf. Samuel D. Warren and Louis D. Brandeis, "The Right to Privacy" (1890), in Ferdinand D. Schoeman, ed., *Philosophical Dimensions of Privacy* (Cambridge: Cambridge University Press, 1984), 75–103.

6. Charles Fried, "Privacy (A Moral Analysis)" (1978), in Schoeman, *Philosophical Dimensions of Privacy,* 203–22; Robert S. Gernstein, "Intimacy and Privacy" (1978), ibid., 265–71.

7. Edward J. Bloustein, "Privacy as an Aspect of Human Dignity: An Answer to Dean Prosser" (1964), ibid., 188.

8. This formal proposal for an amendment, approved by Congress in 1972, has been the last proposal for constitutional reform to be submitted to a formal process of ratification, which came to an unfavorable close in 1982. The proposed amendment runs, "Equality of rights under the law shall not be denied or abridged by the United States or by any State on account of sex" ("United States Statutes at Large," 86: 1523–24).

9. Jürgen Habermas and Jacques Derrida, "February 15, or What Binds Europeans Together. A Plea for a Common Foreign Policy," *Constellations* 10(3): 291–97.

10. On this specific lexical indicator of the persistence of the culture of the frontier in the American public imaginary, see Bruce Ackerman, *Before the Next Attack: Preserving Civil Liberties in an Age of Terrorism* (New Haven: Yale University Press, 2006), 40.

11. Bassam Tibi, *Euro-Islam. L'integrazione mancata* (Venezia: Marsilio, 2003).

12. See Edward Luttwak, *Turbo-Capitalism: Winners and Losers in the Global Economy* (New York: Texere, 2001).

13. See Ralph W. Emerson, *Self-reliance and Other Essays* (New York: Dover, 1993). On Emerson's democratic individualism, see George Kateb, *The Inner Ocean: Individualism and Democratic Culture* (Ithaca: Cornell University Press, 1994) and *Emerson and Self-reliance* (Totowa, NJ: Rowman and Littlefield, 2002).

14. See Richard H. Tawney, *Religion and the Rise of Capitalism* (1922) (Harmondsworth: Penguin, 1980), 229–51.

15. See John Dewey, *The Public and Its Problems* (Denver: Swallow, 1954). See also his *Liberalism and Social Action* (New York: Capricorn, 1962).

16. In fact, recent studies indicate that at least 40 percent of the voters who rejected the Constitutional TreatyTK were motivated by the perception that it embedded a vision of society too much tilted in a neoliberal direction and failed instead to do justice to the solidary vision of a welfare society. See Renaud Dehousse, "The Unmaking of a Constitution: Lessons from the European Referenda," *Constellations* 13(2): 155.

17. The literature on the subject is immense. See among others Joseph H. H. Weiler, "The Transformation of Europe," *Yale Law Review*, vol. 100 (1991) and *The Constitution of Europe* (Cambridge: Cambridge University Press, 1999); AA.VV.,TK *Una Costituzione per l'Europa* (Bologna: il Mulino, 2003); AA.VV.,TK *Diritti e Costituzione nell'Unione Europea* (Bari: Laterza, 2003); Richard Bellamy, "The Constitution of Europe: Rights or Democracy?" in Richard Bellamy, Vittorio Bufacchi, and Dario Castiglione, eds., *Democracy and Constitutional Culture in the Union of Europe* (London: Lothian Foundation, 1995); Jürgen Habermas, *The Postnational Constellation: Political Essays* (Cambridge: MIT Press, 2001) and *The Divided West* (Cambridge: Polity, 2006); Angela Augustin, *Das Volk der Europäischen Union. Zu Inhalt und Kritik eines normativen Begriffs* (Berlin: Duncker and Humblot, 2000).

9. Religion Within the Limits of Reasonableness

1. Peter L. Berger, ed., *The Desecularization of the World: Resurgent Religion and World Politics* (Washington: Ethics and Public Policy Center, 1999); José Casanova, *Public Religions in the Modern World* (Chicago: University of Chicago Press, 1994); Adam B. Seligman, *Modernity's Wager* (Princeton: Princeton University Press, 2000). See also Steve Bruce, ed., *Religion and Modernization. Sociologists and Historians Debate the Secularization Thesis* (Oxford: Clarendon Press, 1992); and Giovanni Filoramo, *Le vie del sacro* (Turin: Einaudi 1994). For a classical statement of the problem, see David Martin, *A General Theory of Secularization* (Oxford: Blackwell, 1978).

2. The thesis according to which within American law, all the way up to Supreme Court jurispridence, a transition has occurred from a customary defense of religious

freedom based only on the principle of equality to a new kind of defense of religious freedom that includes a positive assessment of the value of religion as a practice contributing to social cohesion, as a source of meaning nourishing and strengthening identity, and as a source of motivation for solidarity. See the insightful essay by Steven H. Shiffrin, "The Pluralistic Foundations of the Religion Clauses," *Cornell Law Review* 90(1): 9–96.

3. John Rawls, "The Idea of Public Reason Revisited," in *The Law of Peoples and The Idea of Public Reason Revisited* (Cambridge: Harvard University Press, 1999), 129–80; and Jürgen Habermas, "Religion in the Public Sphere," *European Journal of Philosophy* 14(1): 1–25. See also Jürgen Habermas, "Faith and Knowledge," speech on the occasion of the award of the Peace Prize, in http://socialpolicy.ucc.ie/Habermas_Faith_and_knowledge_ev07-4_en.htm.

4. See Jürgen Habermas, *Between Facts and Norms: Contributions to a Discourse Theory of Law and Democracy,* trans. William Rehg (Cambridge: Polity, 1996), chapter 7, where he adopts a distinction suggested by Nancy Fraser in her "Rethinking the Public Sphere," in Craig Calhoun, ed., *Habermas and the Public Sphere* (Cambridge: MIT Press, 1992).

5. See Rawls, "The Idea of Public Reason Revisited," 152.

6. Ibid. 155–56.

7. See ibid., 143–44.

8. See Habermas, "Religion in the Public Sphere," 8–9.

9. Ibid, 16.

10. Ibid., 9.

11. Charles Taylor, "A Catholic Modernity?" in James L. Heft, *A Catholic Modernity? Charles Taylor's Marianist Award Lecture* (New York: Oxford Univeristy Press, 1999), 13–37. See also Charles Taylor, "Religion Today," *Varieties of Religion Today: William James Revisited* (Cambridge: Harvard University Press, 2002), 63–107.

12. Taylor, "A Catholic Modernity?" 19.

13. Charles Taylor, "Modes of Secularism," in Rajeev Bhargava, ed., *Secularism and Its Critics* (Oxford: Oxford University Press, 1998), 36.

14. Ronald Dworkin, *Is Democracy Possible Here? Principles for a New Political Debate* (Princeton: Princeton University Press, 2006), 56.

15. First Amendment to the Constitution of the United States of America: "Congress shall make no law respecting an establishment of religion, or prohibiting the free exercise thereof; or abridging the freedom of speech, or of the press; or the right of the people peaceably to assemble, and to petition the Government for a redress of grievances."

16. Dworkin, *Is Democracy Possible Here?* 58–60.

17. Ibid., 60–62.

18. Ibid., 64.

19. Ibid., 65.

20. Dworkin coins the distinction between "personally judgmental" and "impersonally judgmental" justifications for legal coercion. Personally judgmental are those instances of legal coercion that rest on (controversial) conceptions of what kind of life is acceptable and thus usurp the person's autonomy to choose her own values. Impersonally judgmental are rather those instances of legal coercion that appeal to the intrinsic value of some good for the flourishing of life. See ibid., 70–71. Only the second are for Dworkin legitimate forms of legal coercion, much in agreement with Rawls's principle of liberal legitimacy.

21. John Locke, "A Letter Concerning Toleration," in Locke, *On Politics and Education* (Roslyn, NY: Black, 1947), 45. For an interesting discussion of toleration in the light of contemporary concerns, see Anna Elisabetta Galeotti, *Toleration as Recognition* (Cambridge: Cambridge University Press, 2002); and Rainer Forst, *Toleranz im Konflikt. Geschichte, gehalt und Gegenwart eines umstrittenen Begriffs* (Frankfurt: Suhrkamp, 2003).

22. Locke, "A Letter Concerning Toleration," 45–6.

23. Ibid., 46.

24. Ibid., 47.

25. For illuminating reflections on the relation of societal acceleration to democracy, see William E. Scheuerman, *Liberal Democracy and the Social Acceleration of Time* (Baltimore: Johns Hopkins University Press, 2004), 187–224. See also Hartmut Rosa, *Beschleunigung. Die Veränderung der Zeitstruktur in der Moderne* (Frankfurt: Suhrkamp, 2005), 161–198 and 396–427, and Matthias Eberling, *Beschleunigung und Politik* (Frankfurt: Peter Lang, 1996). For the groundbreaking idea of exploring the consequences of an accelerated tempo in social life, see Paul Virilio, *Speed and Politics* (New York: Semiotexte, 1986); and Reinhart Koselleck's "Gibt es eine Beschleunigung der Geschichte?" in his *Zeitschichten* (Frankfurt: Suhrkamp, 2000), 150–76.

26. Italian Corte Costituzionale, 12/4/1989, n. 203.

27. Italian Corte Costituzionale, 20/11/2000, n. 508.

28. Civil section 10 of the civil court of Naples, Ordinanza of 26/3/2005.

29. See civil section 1 of the civil court of Bologna, Ordinanza of 24/3/2005.

30. Section 3 of the regional administrative court of law of Veneto, Sentenza of 17/3/2005.

31. 545 U.S. Supreme Court (2005), *McCreary County, Kentucky et al. vs. American Civil Liberties Union of Kentucky et al.*, 12.

32. Ibid., 8.

33. Ibid., 25.

34. See Antonin Scalia (dissenting opinion), 545 U.S. Supreme Court (2005), *McCreary County, Kentucky et al. vs American Civil Liberties Union of Kentucky et*

al. Scalia argues that "those who wrote the Constitution believed that morality was essential to the well-being of society and that encouragement of religion was the best possible way to foster morality" (3), and therefore the Constitution does not mention at any point the "demonstrably false principle that the government cannot favor religion over irreligion" (9).

Index